D0590519

INTERNATIONAL ECONOMICS
OF POLLUTION

International Economics of Pollution

INGO WALTER

*Professor of Economics and Finance, Graduate
School of Business Administration,
New York University*

A HALSTED PRESS BOOK

JOHN WILEY & SONS
New York – Toronto

First published in the United Kingdom 1975 by
The Macmillan Press Ltd

Published in the U.S.A. and Canada by
Halsted Press, a Division of
John Wiley & Sons, Inc.
New York

Printed in Great Britain

Library of Congress Cataloging in Publication Data

Walter, Ingo.
 International economics of pollution.

 (Problems of economic integration)
 Bibliography: p.
 Includes index.
 1. Pollution—Economic aspects. 2. International
economic relations. 3. Environmental policy. I. Title.

HC79. P55W3   301.31   75–28273
ISBN 0 470–91928–0

Contents

List of Tables

List of Figures

General Editor's Preface

Since the Second World War, the economies of Europe, North America, Japan and the developing world have become increasingly interdependent. This has taken place at various levels. On the one hand we have seen the formation and growth of a formal organisation, the European Economic Community, whose aim it is to strengthen existing political and economic ties amongst its members. But interdependence is not solely the result of legal treaties; it is also the outcome of economic innovation and evolution. The growth of the multinational corporation, the development of the Euro-currency system and the rapid growth of international trade are but examples of the trend.

Yet the resulting closer ties among nations have been a mixed blessing. It is no longer possible for governments to formulate national objectives in isolation from activity in the rest of the world. Monetary, fiscal, anti-trust and social policies now have widespread implications beyond national frontiers. How to cope with the complex implications of the current petroleum price developments is but an example of the sort of problem arising in an interdependent world.

Despite its obvious importance most economics textbooks give only cursory attention to international economic interdependence. The purpose of this series is to fill this gap by providing critical surveys and analyses of specific types of economic linkages among nations. It is thus hoped that the volumes will appeal not only to students, researchers and government bodies working in the field of international economics but also to those dealing with the problems of industrial organisation, monetary economics and other aspects of public policy which have traditionally been studied from a narrow, nationalistic viewpoint.

Department of Economics,　　　　　　　　　　GEORGE W. McKENZIE
Southampton University

Preface

When the wave of 'environment-consciousness' struck in the late 1960s, public fervour quickly outpaced sober and reasoned analysis. There was little knowledge and much speculation about the causes and consequences of pollution. Even less was known about the cost of environmental protection. Who would pay the price, and how much? Still, policies had to be devised and battles waged among groups whose environmental interests pointed in different directions. The issues could not wait. Mistakes were made. Some remedies were too little and too late. Some exceeded by far what was required and inevitably set into motion an environmental backlash. But the trend was clearly toward a view of the environment as a social asset, to be treasured and conserved. Environment, in short, is here to stay.

The dimensions of environmental management are truly complex, and very little is certain except that the political, economic and social life of nations is being profoundly affected. This book concerns itself with but one of these dimensions – the relationship between the restoration and maintenance of environmental balance and international economic interdependence. What happens to international trade, investment, payments and related elements as different nations pursue different environmental targets, using different policy instruments, under different environmental conditions, and according to different time-tables? Very little that is definitive can be said at this point of time. But most of the cause-and-effect links can be clearly spelled out even at this early stage, and some directions for public policy can be indicated that seem to make sense.

The discussion in this volume draws heavily on research undertaken with the aid of a grant from The Ford Foundation during 1972 to 1973, and on a number of papers that resulted from that project. D. C. Heath & Co., as well as the editors of *Economic Enquiry* and *Weltwirtschaftliches Archiv*, were kind enough to give permission to reprint selected passages, in revised form, in this book. Much of the discussion of pollution-control instruments is based on work that was initially sponsored by the Environment Directorate of the O.E.C.D., and my interest in these aspects of the problem owes much to Michel Potier. The book was written while I was a Visiting Research Fellow at the International Institute of Management of the Science Center, Berlin, and I am particularly grateful to Walter Goldberg and Fritz Scharpf for the support provided in a setting that proved to be ideal for serious writing.

Financial assistance for the project was provided by The Rockefeller Foundation, and is gratefully acknowledged.

I have discussed and argued many of the points raised in this volume with quite a number of individuals over the years. John Welles, Robert Hawkins, Larry Ruff, David Pearce, Henry Brodie, Charles Pearson, Martin Pfaff and Ralph d'Arge are some of these, but they cannot be held accountable for the results. Mrs Helen Seifert in Berlin and Miss Marion Epps in New York capably and cheerfully typed various drafts of the manuscript.

INGO WALTER

New York City

I

Politics, Economics and Environment

Only a few years ago popular concern with the quality of the environment could be dismissed more or less out of hand by public officials charged with setting social priorities and charting the course of nations. Apart from a few fringe groups, pollution and ecology simply were not particularly important as political issues – certainly not as issues demanding an immediate public policy response and perhaps a fundamental reordering of national goals and priorities. But things have a way of changing – of creeping up on the man in the street and the government official alike – until the realisation suddenly strikes that a real crisis of rather substantial proportions is looming on the immediate horizon, demanding quick and decisive action.

The environmental 'crisis' hit the United States, Canada and Japan in the late 1960s (perhaps 1969 could be singled out more precisely) and most countries in Western Europe a year or two later. The mass media took up the cause, helped along by a few rather dismal exercises in futurology that predicted global disaster in the shockingly near future unless drastic remedial action were undertaken immediately – and even then, things did not look too good.[1] Students took to the streets, 'Earth Day' was established, and environment became the watchword. The dam had burst, although it was not yet time for serious thought about the nature and measurement of environmental deterioration, its alleviation through sensible public policy, and the social and economic trade-offs involved. But at least a political mandate had emerged, and the time for action was clearly at hand.

Some years have passed since the early days of the environmental 'crisis'. The excitement is over, but so is the superficiality. The issue was not, as some feared, a matter of momentary enthusiasm. The issue is a real and a serious one, and work on the substantive dimensions of the problem has begun. Institutions have been established to deal with pollution control where none existed before, and strengthened where they did. Not least important, a significant research effort has focused on the implications of environmental management for virtually all aspects of economic and social life.

As nations increasingly build environmental quality standards into the calculus of social welfare, there will inevitably result pressures on the international economic system and on the degree and character of international economic interdependence. These pressures will be rather important and need to be clearly understood if the public-policy measures intended to deal with them are to make sense, now and in the future. The purpose of this book is to outline what we know, or think we know, about the ways in which environmental management can and does influence – and is influenced by – international economic relations.

ENVIRONMENT OF UNCERTAINTY

Public concern with the quality of the human environment is hardly a new departure in the definition and determination of social welfare.[2] It has traditionally played a subordinate role, however, to the more conventional requisites of improved material levels of living. The marginal social cost of environmental degradation either was not explicitly recognised or was not considered significant in relation to the marginal social benefits of the economic activity which caused that degradation. Over time, the balance has altered in the face of the growth of population, shifts in its distribution, and a rapid rise in the level of economic activity. The biosphere – a complex dynamic physical, chemical, and biological system – began to show its limits. Invisible damage to the environment became visible. Damage that once could be safely ignored in time became consequential.

The problem of environmental despoilation has perhaps grown in general proportion to national and international economic advance over decades and centuries. So why the crisis? Because of slippage between the emergence of environmental problems and their political recognition; because changes in levels of living bring changes in social values and priorities; because the assimilative capacity of the environment – its ability to cleanse itself – is increasingly being attained and surpassed; and because, quite simply, when one begins to look for something what one finds often exceeds expectations.

A fundamental characteristic of environmental despoilation and its alleviation is *uncertainty*, both in an objective and in a subjective context. This makes it virtually impossible to discuss the issue of pollution in unequivocal terms, and forecasting becomes a risky proposition at best. Under such conditions, policy actions can easily take on dimensions quite different from what would have been if everything that needed to be known was indeed known. And since we are principally concerned here with the consequences of such policies for the international economy, it is often impossible to present much more than a series of alternative scenarios of possible outcomes. Uncertainty in problems of environmental management can be traced to a variety of factors.

First, what are the *sources* of environmental despoilation? Generally pollution of the environment may be considered any departure from its 'natural' state caused by: (*a*) gaseous discharges into the atmosphere, whether toxic or not, that alter the composition of a given airshed; (b) liquid and solid discharges into bodies of water affecting their quality, particularly their ability to sustain life and to serve as an economic or social resource; (c) thermal discharges affecting water quality; (d) noise; (e) radiation; (f) disposal of solid waste; (g) degradation of natural scenery and terrain, and the elimination of recreational opportunities; (h) endangering of wildlife species; and (i) congestion. Clearly, there are differences of views on each of these in terms of the need for and desirability of maintaining the 'natural' state.[3]

Secondly, what are some of the principal *consequences* of environmental despoilation? In the case of each of the aforementioned areas – in some more than in others – controversies rage among specialists. How should environmental quality be measured? What are the environmental consequences of an alternative course of action intended to produce the same or similar results? What are the social, economic and environmental consequences of abstaining from certain activities altogether? Particularly in the alteration of water quality through material and thermal discharges, air pollution and protection of wildlife, the experts are often poles apart.* Without consensus or even substantial agreement, and given the time and resources that may be involved in reversing environmental damage once it occurs (if it is reversible at all), confusion may turn into extreme caution. As a result, the economic consequences of environmental management may be greatly magnified in degree, accelerated in time and inflated in real costs, in relation to the net benefits achieved once all the returns are in.

Thirdly, and closely related to the previous issue, what are the environmental limits? We know that the environment can assimilate certain types of pollutants in certain volumes without raising the disharmonies in the ecological system that are associated with environmental degradation. But what kind of pollutants, and in what volumes? Again, uncertainty is paramount, and without knowing the depth of the 'environmental sink' economic development can easily be restrained unduly or, at the other extreme, forced beyond its ecological limits.

Fourthly, even if all sources of environmental despoilation could be identified and their consequences clearly delineated within known assimilative limits, there is still the question : What is an 'acceptable' environment? This issue is a political one, subject to collective decision-making once the relevant trade-offs are known. Will a given river system better serve as a common-property social resource by virtue of its potential as a

---

* There are even differences of view with respect to the basic concept of pollution. For example, one view holds that *ambient* levels of environmental quality are most important, while another emphasises *immissions* of pollutants by human beings, plants and animals to the detriment of their health or well-being. This issue is discussed in detail in Chapter 2.

sewer? A source of potable water? A transportation artery? A recreational resource? A source of power? A decision has to be made. Often the decision is not made – or not soon enough – because of imperfections in the political system, the changing goals of society and other related factors. Again the question of uncertainty arises, and its impact is amplified by the tendency for costs of alleviating past damage to rise exponentially with the degree of environmental restoration required.

There may also be questions with respect to the basic ground-rules under which environmental policy is required. For example, standards may be enforced on a 'case-by-case' basis, with the political collectivity in each instance bearing the burden of proof regarding environmental damage and culpability for apparent pollution. Alternatively, a 'blanket' system of enforcement may be applied to substantially all instances of environmental damage, with adequate proof required of the individual polluter that environmental damage exceeding the agreed standards did not indeed occur. There is a fundamental difference between these two approaches.

Lastly, there is the question of environmental sovereignty. We shall argue throughout our discussion that each political collectivity has the right to determine *for itself*, via accepted political processes, what level of environmental quality it wishes to achieve, and how it wishes to achieve them.[4] This answer need not be consistent internationally, or even inter-regionally within a given national state, as long as any environmental damage that occurs in one political collectivity does not spill over to affect another. When such 'transfrontier pollution' occurs, it may simply represent the least-cost manner in which Collectivity A has chosen to achieve its standards, thereby damaging Collectivity B. Or it may be a question of different standards adopted by A and B. In either instance, a strong case can be made for reconciling the 'right' to pollute with the 'right' not to be polluted – for concerted remedial action through co-operation, establishment of a broader-based environmental authority, harmonisation of standards or, in the extreme, political and economic sanctions between the affected groups. The transboundary issue of concern may be bilateral, multilateral or even global in nature.

Because of uncertainties in all of the aforementioned areas, and because the problem of environmental management is at base a political issue, policy measures are frequently inconsistent over time. Imperceptible environmental damage may become serious as measurement techniques are refined. Environmental quality that may be acceptable today may not be acceptable tomorrow. Measures adopted under the present state of knowledge may turn out to have side-effects that are sufficiently serious to mandate a fundamentally new departure a few years hence. Economic adjustment and readjustment to environmental constraints is a costly and socially painful process. This redoubles the disruptive consequences of

environmental uncertainty and marks the process of environmental adjustment with a degree of unevenness, error, hesitation and acrimony seldom
encountered in other fields of public-policy formation.

THE ECONOMIC DIMENSION

Economists like to view the question of environmental management as
basically a matter of 'externalities', the impact of economic activities –
consumption or production – by one economic entity on the welfare of
others. In standard 'general equilibrium' systems, such interdependence
always exists via the indirect linkage of relative prices and returns to
productive factors. But externalities produce a *direct* link via production
and utility functions. Externalities are generally recognised as a major
reason for the apparent difference between 'net private product' and 'net
social product', and in a policy context for the rejection of perfect competition as a universal norm in the search for maximum social welfare. If
the market mechanism is left alone, externalities are not reflected in
relative prices, and a wedge is driven between private and social costs
and benefits. The resultant price signals to producers and consumers lead
to supply and demand patterns that diverge from the corresponding social
optima. The market fails because common-property resources, including
environmental quality, generally have not been and often cannot be
priced. But externalities can be internalised via the market mechanism,
either wholly or partially, if a price is placed on the damaging spillover.
A new market created for current waste-products, for example, will succeed in partial internalisation, and so will a charge levied on 'bad' spillovers if the common-property resources involved were previously un-
priced. The problem is that the market functions only imperfectly, and
that public-policy measures must be applied on behalf of the political
collectivity itself in order to push the system closer to some kind of societal
optimum.[5]

Environmental externalities appear to develop rapidly as an economy
grows, with a substantial impact on society at large, as a problem 'not so
much as between firms or industries, but as between, on the one hand,
the producers and/or the users of spillover-creating goods and, on the
other, the public at large'.[6] As a result, any collective measures to deal
with environmental spillovers embody serious implications for both the
distribution of welfare and for the applicable welfare criterion itself. This
is because movement toward whatever welfare criterion has been selected
to incorporate (for example) quality of the environment involves costs
which do not fall equally on members of the collectivity. These so-called
'transaction costs' include the cost of reaching an agreement among the
affected parties and identifying who they are, the cost of maintaining and

revising the agreed-upon standards, and the capital and continuing costs of implementing those standards.[7]

Specific social hypotheses that have arisen out of the issue of environmental spillovers include the following. (a) Environmental 'bads' are inherently regressive in that environmental damage is associated with economic activities of higher-income groups in society and impacts disproportionately on lower-income groups. (b) Environment-control policies may cause enterprises to intensify the environmental spillovers in order to reap greater rewards from whatever remedial actions may be undertaken by government. (c) There is a difference between 'welfare' and 'ethical' aspects of environmental spillovers and their control. Pollution benefits one group and harms another, but so does abstinence from pollution; and yet ethical guidelines can be devised which may indeed be used to justify environmental controls and pollution abatement. (d) Much depends on the marginal social utility of additional real income relative to the marginal social disutility of accompanying environmental despoilation. Unless the preference functions can be shifted, this determines the extent to which per capita real-income growth may need to be constrained or even revised.[8] (e) The fact that certain kinds of environmental spillovers may have intergenerational consequences redefines the collectivity whose welfare needs to be maximised – with one group not having any voice in the relevant decisions. Consequently, the trade-off built into current policy may not reflect losses inflicted on posterity, and hence does not represent the internalisation of environmental externalities in the time dimension. (f) The time element in the development of new products, productive facilities, and processes does not necessarily coincide with the time element in assessment of their long-term environmental consequences. This raises the probability of ecological catastrophe and calls for extreme caution.[9]

In short, economic activity tends to cause environmental deterioration, which serves to offset the resultant economic gains and may alter their distribution quite drastically. Conversely, improvement of environmental quality may require substantial modification of the scope and pattern of economic activity, and in the distribution of income. Society is thus faced with a set of trade-offs, encompassing very serious questions of equity, which can only be resolved through collective decision processes. Indeed, the application of conventional social discount rates virtually guarantees that the environmental interests of future generations will be ignored – and thus requires an entirely new way of thinking.

While internalisation of environmental externalities – and narrowing the gap between private and social costs and benefits – perhaps cannot be left to the market, the market mechanism may be used to achieve maximum efficiency in the internalisation process once policies have been adopted on behalf of the political collectivity to prohibit 'bad' spillovers, levy a charge on the use of common-property resources previously un-priced or create new uses for environmentally-damaging waste pro-ducts.[10] The task of public policy is to use the available tools – including taxation, direct controls and subsidies – to move toward a solution that reflects both environmental assimilative capacities and social preferences regarding environmental quality.

A SIMPLE MODEL

Leaving aside the uncertainties noted earlier, we may assume the existence of something called a 'pristine' environment (zero pollution) which might exist in nature without pollution by man. Clearly, with reference to society's collectively-determined welfare this *maximum* level of environ-mental quality is not only impossible but also undesirable.* The relevant target should be, instead, the socially *optimum* level of environmental quality. In economic terminology, this optimum is reached when the ratio of the marginal social benefit to the marginal resource cost of an *improve-ment* in environmental quality equals the corresponding ratios for incre-ments in the consumption of all other available goods and services. As such, the real resource cost of environmental control can be said to influence the social demand for environmental quality in the conventional manner (the higher the cost, the lower the amount demanded), except that the rele-vant decisions are made by a political collectivity of some sort – with the decision mechanism operating at the subnational, national or supranational level.

Desired environmental quality (DEQ)

If the collectively-expressed social demand for environmental quality is negatively related to price, it is likely also to be positively related to income. As income rises, all else equal, so will the demand for environmental quality. The curve *DEQ* in Figure 1.1 represents the demand for en-vironmental quality (*EQ*) as a function of gross product, or income. Its income elasticity remains open to question on an *a priori* basis. The func-tion materialises at some 'threshold' income level Q_2 below which environ-mental quality fails to make itself felt at all in the collective decision process.

Environmental assimilative capacity (EAC)

The extent to which environmental spillovers arise from productive ac-tivity depends in large measure, as noted earlier, on the ability of the environment to assimilate pollutants without perceptibly deteriorating in quality. To cite two examples: (*a*) characteristics such as the size,

* This discussion is based on my 'International Trade and Resource Division: The Case of Environmental Management', *Weltwirtschaftliches Archiv* (September 1974).

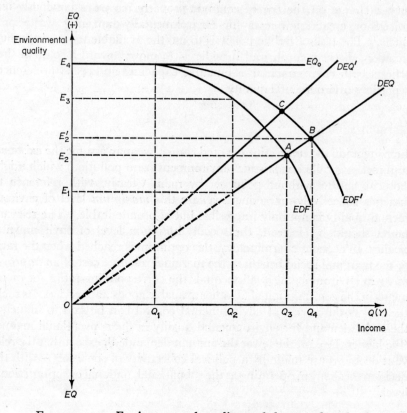

FIGURE I.I   Environmental quality and damage functions

depth and temperature of a body of water determine its ability to assimilate nutrients contained in industrial, residential and agricultural effluents; and (b) temperature, currents and precipitation influence the
ambient quality of a given airshed subject to pollution. Environmental
assimilative capacity determines the response of environmental quality to
incremental doses of effluents and, hence, to increments in output.

If we assume a linear relationship between output and effluents, a
non-linear relationship between effluents and environmental quality, we
can draw an 'environmental damage function' such as EDF in Figure I.I.
Over a range of output such as OQ_1, little or no deterioration in environmental quality (EQ_0) may be perceived. But beyond this threshold, the
latter presumably declines at an increasing rate as assimilative limits are
attained and surpassed in successive environmental sectors, and as the
problem of non-reversibility of environmental damage is increasingly

encountered. *EAC* determines the *shape* of the environmental damage function, so long as the output-effluent ratio remains constant.*

Given functions *EDF* and *DEQ* in Figure 1.1, the maximum quantity of output that can be supported is OQ_3 at environmental quality level E_2. A higher level of output can be supported only at a lower *EQ* level, which is precluded by *DEQ*. It can be supported only if environmental-control measures are undertaken (increasing the output–effluent ratio), shifting *EDF* to the right (e.g. *EDF'*), and permitting Q_4 to be achieved at E'_2. This shift absorbs productive resources, and thus involves an opportunity cost to society in the form of output (real income) forgone. The implications of induced or autonomous shifts in *DEQ* (e.g. to *DEQ'*) should also be clear and need not be further elaborated. The point is that the desired environmental-quality and environmental-damage functions are joint determinants of the achievable level of output and environmental quality.† Environmental assimilative capacity itself represents a productive *resource* that determines the economic cost of attaining whatever composite environmental-quality level is set as a social goal.

THE COST OF ENVIRONMENTAL CONTROL

While the internalisation of environmental externalities benefits society at large, the real costs of internalisation also fall on society at large. They are passed forward on to the prices of goods and services, as well as backward on to factor returns and fiscal levies. There are two kinds of cost involved. *Transitional costs* involve the adaptation of existing plant and equipment, management practices, technology, labour and consumption patterns in ways that reduce damage to the environment. They may also involve the cost of environment-induced shifts in the location of production. Transitional costs normally have to be met only once, unless changes in environmental policies mandate a further shift later on. *Recurring costs* involve using more resource inputs per unit of output or consumption, or using these resources less efficiently, in order to avoid environmental spillovers – costs are internalised that previously were borne by society at large in the form of environmental degradation.

That environmental management involves costs is generally accepted. The question is, who pays? Regardless of how these costs are met, society pays. Productive resources are diverted from other purposes to environmental control, and with given technology fewer resources can go toward the production of other goods and services. Society as a whole may well

---

* The shape of the *EDF* and *DEQ* functions presented are purely hypothetical, with very little empirical evidence regarding either available to date.

† Changes in the output *mix* among products with differing environmental characteristics in production, in normal use, or as residuals will also influence the character of *EDF*. See National Academy of Sciences, *Man, Materials and Environment* (Cambridge: M.I.T. Press, 1973).

be better off, all things considered – and presumably is if the right collective decisions have been made – but *not* in terms of the conventional definition of economic welfare. Pollution control may involve application of the so-called 'polluter pays' principle, with the costs of compliance with environmental-quality standards being passed forward to consumer and user in the form of higher prices (see Chapter 5). Or punitive taxation may be used, with assessments based on the amount of environmental damage induced, but with the same end-result. Or direct and indirect subsidies may be used to defray part or all of the environment-control costs impacting on the polluter, using national fiscal mechanisms. Or some combination of such techniques may be applied. In any event, society ultimately bears the burden, no matter how the environmental goals are achieved.

The aggregate cost of environmental control can be measured in various ways. One could be the gap between Gross National Product (G.N.P.) with pollution control and what it might otherwise have been. One symptom might be a decline in the rate of capital formation. Another could be unemployment induced by environmental safeguards imposed on firms and industries – in this case involving a transitional cost only. Still another might be an acceleration in the rate of inflation induced by pollution control, again a transistional phenomenon. It makes little sense to quote figures purported to represent *the* cost of pollution control without relating them to basic economic indicators associated with generally accepted domestic-policy goals of minimum unemployment, price-level stability and economic growth.

One of the more systematic assessments of the aggregate cost of pollution control in the recent past was done for the United States. It involved applying the anticipated cost of environmental management to an aggregate econometric model of the U.S. economy, with projections up to 1980. There are three estimates for each variable : (*a*) a 'baseline average' that might be expected *in the absence of* pollution control ; (*b*) the impact on the baseline average of pollution control; and (*c*) the impact on the baseline estimates if, in addition, any undesirable macroeconomic effects of pollution control are offset by government monetary ana fiscal policies.[11]

For the period from 1972 to 1980, as noted in Table 1.1, pollution control and compensatory macroeconomic policy measures are expected to reduce the U.S. G.N.P. by 6 billion dollars, raise the unemployment rate by 0.3 per cent, raise the average annual rate of inflation by 0.26 per cent, and reduce fixed investment not related to pollution control by an average of 2.3 billion dollars annually. If, on the other hand, pollution-control costs are 50 per cent higher than current estimates, or standards are raised correspondingly, the cost estimates in this event are raised commensurately.

Table 1.1 Estimated effects of the cost of pollution control on the U.S. economy (1972–1980)

	Units	Input of best estimate of pollution-control costs			Input 150 per cent of best estimate of pollution-control costs		
		1972–6	1977–80	1972–80	1972–6	1977–80	1972–80
G.N.P. – baseline average	billions of 1958 dollars	872·2	1062·8	956·9	872·2	1062·8	956·9
With pollution-control costs (P.C.)		−4·7	−7·6	−6·0	−7·0	−13·1	−9·7
With P.C. and monetary/fiscal policy offsets*		0·0	0·0	0·0	0·4	1·6	0·9
Annual growth of constant dollar G.N.P. – baseline average	per cent	5·17	4·35	4·80	5·17	4·35	4·80
With P.C.		−0·29	0·16	−0·09	−0·46	0·37	−0·09
With P.C. and offsets*		0·0	0·0	0·0	0·01	−0·01	0·0
Unemployment rate – baseline average	per cent	4·82	4·43	4·64	4·82	4·43	4·64
With P.C.		0·1	0·15	0·12	0·18	0·28	0·22
With P.C. and offsets*		0·06	0·0	0·03	0·04	−0·02	0·01
Annual rate of inflation (C.P.I.) – baseline average	per cent	4·0	3·73	3·87	4·0	3·73	3·87
With P.C.		0·23	−0·30	0·0	0·34	−0·78	−0·15
With P.C. and offsets*		0·29	0·23	0·26	0·49	0·36	0·43
Fixed investment less P.C. investment – baseline average	billions of 1958 dollars	124·8	153·6	137·6	124·8	153·6	137·6
With P.C.		−2·3	−2·5	−2·3	−3·5	−2·7	−3·1
With P.C. and offsets*		−1·9	−2·8	−2·3	−2·9	−4·3	−3·4

* The contractor experimented with monetary fiscal policy adjustments to force the economy back to baseline values of G.N.P. and unemployment. In the case in which costs were increased by 50 per cent, the policy offsets do not quite achieve resumption of baseline product and employment paths only because the contractor lacked the time to refine the policy effects.

Source: Adapted from Chase Econometric Associates, Inc., 'The General Economy' in The Economic Impact of Pollution Control, Council on Environmental Quality, Department of Commerce and Environmental Protection Agency (Washington, D.C.: Government Printing Office, 1972) p 14.

General sensitivity to pollution control in other countries may, of course, be higher or lower than in the United States, depending on the availability of substitute fuels, comparative efficiency in applying environmental-control techniques and differences in economic structure. Another set of estimates – for air pollution only – has been developed using survey methodology in the Federal Republic of Germany. Covering some 18,000 firms with more than 100 employees, the study found that the aggregate outlays for pollution control excluding capital costs came to 3.3 billion Deutschmarks annually during the period from 1969 to 1971.[12]

Such examples seem to indicate that over-all pollution-control costs indeed tend to be substantial, but not in relation to aggregate economic activity. As one authoritative report states : 'the present consideration of the macroeconomic effects of pollution control does not indicate any *considerable* risk of substantial adverse effects on economic growth, balance of payments, employment, price stability or other objectives of general economic policy'.[13]

Apart from their aggregate cost of society, environmental-management problems, when viewed in the light of economic structure, turn out to be highly industry-specific and product-specific. Some goods and services tend to be rather pollution-intensive. Others do not. Hence the impact of pollution control will tend not to fall evenly upon individual products, industries, economic sectors, population groups, geographic regions or national states. Moreover, the problem is highly localised in the case of most pollutants, with the deleterious social impact diminishing with geographic distance from the source. On both counts, in the light of the evident costs, there is a built-in bias to delay action for competitive reasons at the industry and firm levels – a fact reinforced by rapidly-evolving technology and the prospect of future improvements in pollution-control efficiency.

A number of studies have attempted to focus on the cost of pollution control at the industry level. Most have concentrated on *tangible capital investment* required for environmental protection, relative to total expenditures on plant and equipment. In U.S. durable-goods industries, for example, 9.8 per cent of new investment during the late 1960s was earmarked for pollution control, but in the machinery industry it was only 1.5 per cent. For non-durables, the proportion was 9.1 per cent in the pulp and paper industry, but only 0.1 per cent in the rubber industry.[14]

Most comprehensive interindustry studies have added to this in-place capital cost such items as depreciation, operating costs, and research and development expenditures in order to arrive at defensible estimates of annual pollution-control outlays and their probable impact on product prices given prevailing competitive conditions. Again using the United

States as an example, a number of detailed industry studies of pollution-control costs have yielded the results summarised in Table 1.2. Note the wide variations between industries in terms of the estimated annual cost of environmental management for 1976 and its expected impact on price and demand levels. Also noted are the prospective effects on employment levels and plant closings, as well as possible international competitive implications.

Most estimates of this type, whether aggregative or at the industry level, are subject to a great many limitations. Some of these limitations are related to the uncertainties mentioned earlier. Environmental standards and the policy instruments used in their application do change over time, and costs of compliance shift accordingly. Sometimes the disruptive impact of a particular policy measure is so severe that regulatory authorities are forced to back off and to postpone. Sometimes the costs encountered are so high and the anticipated consequences so great that government assistance, in the form of subsidies or other aids, is granted and effectively lowers the internalisation cost to the affected industry itself. Sometimes, too, the environmental side-effects of the measures applied are such that further, unforeseen controls are called for. Such factors call for extreme caution in evaluating *any* estimates of the anticipated cost of pollution control.

No less important are measurement problems encountered in assessments of pollution-control costs. Estimates of current levels of investment in pollution-control facilities may not be worth very much as indicators of things to come, at least in the case of the 1960s and the 1970s, because these are highly biased by 'catch-up' investment. Firms build their stock of environmental hardware from zero or very low levels to whatever is required by current regulations in a relatively short period of time. More appropriate would be estimates of what the total in-place capital stock for environmental purposes *may be* in future years, so that the composite cost of capital and depreciation charges associated with pollution-control plant and equipment can be derived. Also included must be estimates of research and development expenditures, whereby care must be taken in some industries to exclude such costs resulting from the manufacture of pollution-control equipment and supplies intended for sale to other firms. An assessment of the operating costs of pollution-control facilities must also be made, involving careful separation of labour and other variable charges allocated to environmental and non-environmental purposes. The latter is frequently impossible or subject to wide margins of error. Lastly, estimates of the *net* cost of pollution control to firms and industries require that the market value of recovered secondary materials, whether sold or re-used within the firm, be deducted. It should be clear that estimation problems in each of these areas, together with the survey methodology

Table 1.2 Estimated effects of 1976 air and water pollution-control standards on selected industries in the United States

Industry	Capital Investment 1972–6 (million dollars)	Annual cost 1976 (million dollars)	Expected unit-price increase – 1976	Expected impact on Firms and Employment in industry	Expected impact on demand level	Expected impact on trade
Baking	11·8–21·3	2	0·011–0·02c/lb (bread) 0·05–0·09c/lb (other)	nil	nil	nil
Cement	122	43	4–5 per cent ($0·08–0·10 per barrel)	25 plant closings, large replace small plants, minimum employment losses	nil	small, indeterminate increase in imports
Electric power	17,800	2500	2·8 per cent West/South/Central 10·7 per cent Tennessee Valley 7·0 per cent over-all U.S.	nil	minimal	minimal*
Fruit and vegetable packing	120	21·3	5·5–9·6 per cent maximum 1·4–2·3 per cent minimum	400 plant closings (33 per cent) 28,000 job losses large replace small plants	0·5–1·0 per cent (decrease)	minimal
Iron foundries	348	125	1·7–5·0 per cent (per ton of castings)	indeterminate small plant closings	not estimated	minimal
Leather tanning	89	10·7	1·2–2·0 per cent	600 job losses	minimal	minimal
Aluminium smelting and refining	935	290	5–8 per cent (short run) 10 per cent (long run)	nil	4–6 per cent (short run) 13 per cent (long run)	100–200 million dollars export decrease 50–100 million dollars import increase
Copper smelting and refining	300–690	95	0–8 per cent depending on import-competition	2 smelter-closings 2800–10,000 job losses (3·6–14·0 per cent)	3·5–14·0 per cent (output) 0–9 per cent (demand)	significant but not estimated (negative)

Industry						
Lead smelting and refining	70	20	5 per cent (per lb)	minimal, replacement by efficient producers of high-cost producers will continue	minimal	minimal
Zinc smelting and refining	62	27	1·23–2·67c/lb	3000 job losses, replacement of inefficient by efficient manufacturers	minimal	increased imports 74–124 million dollars
Petroleum refining	634–1155	129	1·4 per cent per bbl.	12 refinery closings 1000 job losses	nil	40 million dollars increased imports (desulphurisation)
Pulp and paper	3300	198	3·5–10·0 per cent	329 mill closings (15 per cent) 16,000 job losses	minimal	nil
Steel	2400–3500	760–1100	$6·60–9·60/ton (0·7–1·5 per cent)	nil	nil	nil
Automobiles (motor-vehicle emission control standards only)	—	—	$294–343 per automobile (84·98 per cent of estimated unit-cost)	18,000 job losses in automobile industry (1·8 per cent) 35,000 job losses including linked industries (0·35 per cent)	insignificant; major substitution of small for large cars	700 million dollars in increased imports

* Important secondary effects on atomic energy, primary aluminium, electro-metallurgical products, alkalis and chlorine, industrial gases, hydraulics, cement and fossil fuels not considered in the direct impact.

Source: *The Economic Impact of Pollution Control, A Summary of Recent Studies by the Council on Environmental Quality, the Department of Commerce, and the Environmental Protection Agency* (Washington, D.C.: Government Printing Office, March 1972).

that is often relied upon at the industry level or above, provide ample opportunity for error and reason for caution in using such estimates for analytical and policy-making purposes.

THE POLITICAL DIMENSION

We have said a good deal about the economics of environmental management, both in conceptual and empirical terms, and yet emphasised very early that environmental decisions are fundamentally *political* in nature. It seems therefore appropriate to offer a few concluding comments in this opening chapter about the political dimensions of the problem.

Pollution originates basically from four sources in the economic process. The first might be called *materials-source pollution*, and involves environmental damage caused by extracting and transporting virgin renewable and non-renewable raw materials, and recycling used materials, required for production. Examples include the environmental consequences of strip mining, accidental oil spillage, pipeline construction, timbering, use of pesticides and herbicides in agriculture as well as fertiliser run-offs, and so forth. A second category can be called *process pollution*, and originates in the production process itself. Some examples of this category include sludge from pulp and paper production, various emissions from stationary power plants, construction wastes, aromatic emissions from chemical and pharmaceutical plants, and so on.

A third category may be termed *product pollution*, and concerns damage done to the environment by products in their everyday use. Probably the most striking example is automotive emissions, but other transport-related pollution such as aircraft noise as well as such consumer goods as television sets may be considered deleterious to the environment. A final type of environmental damage may be termed *residual pollution*, involving the disposal of products once they have lived out their useful lives. Each product has a particular residuals profile, and items such as detergents, non-biodegradeable packaging materials, as well as automobiles and other consumer durables have been considered particularly damaging to the environment in the form of residuals.

The four types of pollution are associated with their respective sources in Figure 1.2, with all having a bearing on the quality of the environment. Individuals impacted by pollution are at the same time owners of productive factors and consumers. As a group, they carry both the costs and benefits of pollution – benefits via (a) reduced cost of raw material inputs; (b) reduced production costs; (c) simpler and cheaper products; and (d) reduced waste-disposal costs – all tending to raise the earnings of productive factors and reduce prices relative to what would exist if pollution were controlled. Of course, as we have noted, the benefits and costs do not fall symetrically on consumers and suppliers of productive factors, and the

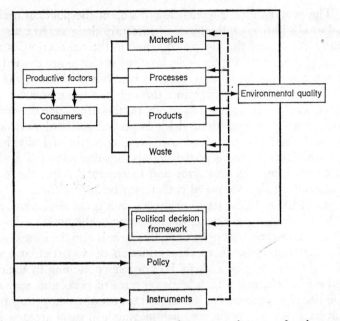

FIGURE 1.2 Interdependence of consumption, production and pollution control

two groups unified as a body politic divides into essentially pro- and anti-pollution forces, according to individual and group self-interest.

The division is hardly 'clean', with individuals and groups variously torn between the dual objectives, and taking positions all along the spectrum from hard-line environmentalists to environment-be-damned *laissez-faire* advocates. In the early stages of environmental awareness, many refused to acknowledge that a trade-off existed at all – believing that a cleaner environment could be achieved at essentially zero cost to themselves. This was followed by a widespread view that the 'other fellow', particularly business firms seen most directly as the polluting agents, would be made to pay. Eventually the notion that virtually all costs would be passed through via taxes or product prices became generally accepted and all illusions disappeared, and this sharpened the inherent conflicts of interest within the collective decision unit.

The welfare interests of individuals and groups are translated into political interests, and are reconciled via the existing political process. The conversion of substantive into political pressures involves a great deal of slippage as well as substantial neutrality and apathy, so that the political debate may or may not accurately reflect the underlying interest configurations. Once resolutions on individual or general aspects of environmental control are developed, these are translated into public policy, which in turn is implemented by means of a variety of available instruments. The protagonists' interests do not stop at the political decision, of course, but also influence the kinds of measures designed to carry out the political mandate and the instruments used in their execution. It makes a great deal of difference, for example, how fast decisions are carried out and how much government subsidy (if any) is involved. Hence, the various interest groups continue their effort through executive agencies and via the courts. The policy action that finally results affects one or more of the four basic sources of pollution, yields improved levels of environmental quality, and alters the perceived cost–benefit matrix of individuals and groups – which then serve as further inputs for subsequent political action. In this manner, by trial and error and incremental steps, the 'optimum environmental quality' we noted earlier may be approached.

Of course, the political decision process is a great deal more complex than this. There is, for example, the influence of the mass media and the skill of various interest groups in using it. There is also the issue of environmental catastrophe – such as the extinction of a particular species of animal or the discovery of a 'dead' lake or mass poisoning by toxic materials in the food chain – which lends an aura of crisis and may severely alter the decision process. No less important are the competing priorities that may exist, such as reducing unemployment in rural areas or improving health care for the aged. Environmental management must be inserted into this list of social priorities, and its position often hinges on the urgency of more or less unrelated competing goals.

There is also the problem of uncertainty with which we began this chapter. We simply do not know what some of the environmental consequences of economic activity are, and this – together with the substantial irreversibility of certain types of environmental damage – may bias the decision system toward caution. Finally, there is a 'ratchet effect' in the formation and execution of environmental policy, which may make it difficult to overturn bad policy or to revise or slow down environmental programmes considered excessively disruptive from an economic or social standpoint.

The economics and politics of environmental management, in summary, is a complex business fraught with risk and uncertainty. It becomes even more complex, as we shall see, when the discussion is expanded to the international context.

FURTHER READING

R. U. Ayres and A. V. Kneese, 'Production, Consumption, and Externality', *American Economic Review* (June 1969).

P. Bohm, 'Pollution, Purification and the Theory of External Effects', *Swedish Journal of Economics*, vol. 72 (1970).

Ronald H. Coase, 'The Problem of Social Cost', *Journal of Law and Economics* (October 1971).

Boyd Collier, *Measurement and Environmental Deterioration* (Austin: University of Texas, 1971).

Ralph C. d'Arge, 'Essay on Economic Growth and Environmental Quality', *Swedish Journal of Economics*, vol. 73 (1971).

A. C. Fisher *et al.*, 'The Economics of Environmental Preservation: A Theoretical and Empirical Analysis', *American Economic Review* (September 1972).

A. M. Freeman, *The Economics of Pollution Control and Environmental Quality* (New York: Random House, 1971).

E. J. Mishan, 'The Postwar Literature on Externalities: An Interpretive Essay', *Journal of Economic Literature* (March 1971).

Organization for Economic Cooperation and Development, *Problems of Environmental Economics* (Paris: O.E.C.D., 1972).

S. H. Schorr, *Energy, Economic Growth, and the Environment* (Washington, D.C.: Resources for the Future, 1972).

2

Environmental Management and Economic Interdependence

The question of environmental management has been characterised in the previous chapter as primarily a problem of public policy. No matter what the organisation of production, whether market-orientated or centrally-planned, there is no inherent mechanism that tends automatically to curb environmental damage resulting from production and consumption, and to bring about the internalisation of the attendant social costs. The necessary decisions have to be taken in a public-policy context – under existing environmental conditions and employing policy instruments considered most appropriate – with full knowledge of the relevant costs and benefits to society.

It seems logical that the implicit weighing of social and economic costs and benefits underlying public-policy decisions on environmental quality should differ internationally. Nations with different historical backgrounds, different cultures, different political systems and different levels of economic development cannot reasonably be expected to apply uniform environmental priorities, or to adopt identical ways of implementing policy decisions concerning the environment.

Nations have certain collective goals. Besides the standard macroeconomic objectives of full employment, price stability, economic growth and balance in international payments, these may include improved health and medical care, improved educational delivery systems, equality of opportunity among minority groups, urbanisation and regional balance, improved transport systems, better care for the aged, a stronger national defence, and so on. Policy-makers recognise that there are economic trade-offs involved and that these goals often conflict with one another, and implicit or explicit priority rankings are invariably established at the national level. Environmental protection assumes a unique position in each nation's ranking of economic and social objectives, and this will in large measure determine the kinds of material and intellectual resources devoted to it – and the time-table for environmental action.

Similarly, nations have unique ways of doing things. Public policy may be carried out via government directives, which may or may not be subject to test in the courts. Punitive taxation may be a standard policy tool, or subsidies and other kinds of fiscal incentives may be used routinely to guide the actions of individuals and enterprises. In some countries, moral suasion may be an effective device for use under a wide variety of circumstances. Again, the implication is that the implementation of whatever environmental policies are decided upon at the national level will tend to differ between nations.

And finally, nations are endowed with unique environmental characteristics. There are wide international variations in size, population density, industrial development, temperature, rainfall, topology, land-use patterns, species of wildlife, river systems, lakes, seas, coastal zones, and so forth. Such factors in part condition the environmental priorities set at the national level and the way they are carried out. But, more importantly, they determine the capacity of the national environment to assimilate pollutants – to absorb emissions from homes, farms and factories without deteriorating perceptibly in quality. As noted earlier, environmental assimilative capacity in large measure determines the real economic cost of achieving whatever national environmental goals are set.

It may thus be reasonable to conclude that international variations in collectively determined environmental priorities, systems of public administration and environmental assimilative capacity can be expected to produce significant differences in the economic impact of environmental management on national economies and, in turn, on economic relations between nations. Nor are the interconnections between environment and the international economy purely one way. International trade can have a distinct impact on domesic environmental affairs. If, for example, a country cannot produce enough of a particular product under given environmental constraints – or can do so only at excessive cost – it can always *import* this product from another country where its manufacture is economically consistent with prevailing environmental conditions and priorities. Hence, international economic relations may influence the quality of the environment at the national level, just as the latter influences international economic relations.

ECONOMIC INTERDEPENDENCE OF NATIONS

It is not necessary at this point to restate the basic principles that serve to shape international economic relations. It may, however, be useful to make a few simple points to provide a setting for the subsequent analysis of the implications of environmental management.

First, there is profit in international trade, not just for the firms and individuals most directly involved, but also for society at large. Producers sell where the effective price is highest, and thereby maximise their returns on invested resources. Consumers and users buy where the effective price is lowest, and thereby maximise the purchasing power that is at their disposal. In the process, production is allocated internationally in accordance with the relative cost of productive factors and the efficiency with which those factors are used in the productive process. As a result, real income and material welfare at the global level far exceed what would

B

be possible without international commerce.[1] At the same time, it is possible via international trade to satisfy differences between countries in tastes and preferences which might otherwise remain unrequited, thereby strengthening further its impact on world welfare.

Whereas trade, as a dominant feature of international economic interdependence, is generally regarded as both necessary and desirable, it is hardly free of controversy. In any given nation, trade harms the interests of some groups in society and benefits others. To be sure, production that is uncompetitive in international markets should logically be displaced by imports and the labour, capital and other resources thus released for reabsorption in productive activities elsewhere in the economy that are internationally viable. Indeed this 'scavenging' effect of import competition as part of the process of economic growth, continually promoting resource reallocation from less productive to more productive employments, is one of the most useful contributions of international trade. But resource displacement and reallocation may be economically costly and socially traumatic, so that the impacted interest groups continually press for protection from imports – given that a 'fair' shifting of the resultant adjustment burden to the economy as a whole is not forthcoming. Those who gain from freer trade compete with those who lose in the national political arena, and the result – tempered by due consideration of the 'national interest' – takes the form either of more liberal trade or increased protectionism.[2]

International trade in goods and services thus has broad implications for real income, output and employment, economic adjustment, income distribution and economic growth, and a change in trade policy will influence all of these. Furthermore, a change in one country's trade policy will influence these same variables in other nations, dependent on penetration of foreign markets for their exports and reliable access to foreign supplies for their imports. A change in trade policy can also shift the gains from international specialisation in favour of one country and against another via the terms of trade. Hence questions of access to international markets and access of international sources of supply tend to be matters of inter-government negotiation and bargaining. Once the internal forces have been resolved via the political process and a national trade-policy position has been established, this serves as the basis for negotiation and perhaps reciprocal concessions at the international level.

The implications of all this would seem to be that, at least from a national and global perspective, freer trade tends to be 'good' and trade barriers tend to be 'bad'. Not at all! Freer trade may be good or bad, depending on its net effect on the national and international economy – its 'impact profile'. It may, for example, cause greater inequality in the distribution of incomes, or a greater degree of military vulnerability, or increased monopolisation of industry, or increased pollution. Or it may have precisely the opposite effects. The point is that it is very difficult to determine, on an *a priori* basis. whether freer or more restrictive trade will tend to benefit (or harm) over-all national social welfare, given the complex of values and priorities that underlie this concept. Freer trade is good only if, after all of the relevant elements have been taken into account, it leads to a convergence (at the margin) of social benefits and social costs.[3]

It is also true, of course, that international commercial policy is an integral part of a nation's foreign policiy, and that some of the afore-mentioned costs and benefits are political in nature. Economic inter-dependence may well be one of the principal guarantors of peace, not only because it makes war more costly but also because it draws people together in many ways and opens up channels of the peaceful resolution of conflict. Certainly one of the primary motivations behind the creation of the European Communities, as well as the on-going expansion of East–West trade, was the dividend promised in terms of reduced political friction. From the standpoint of world peace, therefore, trade liberal-isation and economic interdependence may make a great deal of sense.

Of course, international trade is only one way in which international economic interdependence may be achieved. International flows of pro-ductive factors and technology is another. If a nation is lacking a certain resource – be it land, labour, capital or raw materials – it can either import the resource itself or it can import goods embodying that resource. Hence trade and flows of productive factors can and do substitute for one another, and both may contribute the same kinds of allocational and dynamic gains for the participating national economies. Sometimes it makes more sense to rely on trade, and sometimes factor transfers are more efficient. International factor transfers include, primarily, migration (international movement of labour) and international capital flows. In both sectors, public policy plays an important role in discouraging or facilitating flows of productive factors, and is based on the same kinds of social and economic considerations that underlie trade policy. And again, international economic interdependence through factor movements may generate important political dividends as well as create certain politi-cal frictions.

No less important is international transfer of useful knowledge – tech-nology. Technology may be bought and sold internationally, like products and services, by means of licences, consulting contracts, management fees, know-how agreements, and the like. It may also be embodied in human beings who migrate (e.g. the 'brain drain') as well as in capital equip-ment. Perhaps most importantly, technology may be part of a 'package' of services that comprise direct foreign investment by multinational enter-prises. Such investment brings with it not only the physical plant itself, but also access to foreign markets and sources of import supply, new technical knowledge as well as direct and continuing access to new developments abroad, and managerial know-how. Perhaps more than any other factor, multinational corporations serve as a catalyst in promoting international economic interdependence by *acting as if* there were no political frontiers and transferring goods, productive factors and knowledge on a global basis. Such activities are certainly not without consequences for income distribution or adjustment costs, but over all the multinational enterprise probably is developing into the most powerful available tool for extracting maximum returns from economic relations among nations.

The symptoms of international economic and financial interdependence, then, are trade, movements of productive factors, technology including management and entrepreneurship and business planning that transcends national political frontiers. This may occur on a regional basis – as within the European Communities, the Andean Pact or the Association of South-east Asian Nations (A.S.E.A.N.) – or it may be truly global in nature. It certainly encompasses nations with widely differing political, economic and social systems. During the past several decades international economic interdependence has developed substantially more rapidly than the economic growth of the participating economies, indicating the increasing internationalisation of economic activity as a central phenomenon of the evolving world order.

One of the consequences of growing economic interdependence has been a commensurate increase in the importance of international payments flows and the world monetary system. Rapid expansion in the volume of international financial transactions and international payments imbalances have resulted in increased pressure on the institutions and instruments that comprise international monetary relations. The system was subject to increasing shocks in the late 1960s, so that by 1971 a fundamental change was required away from fixed exchange rates, and its emphasis on *financing* international payments imbalances, toward increased flexibility and resiliency based on flexible exchange rates and an emphasis on the *adjustment* of payments imbalances. International monetary reform, involving floating currencies, the creation of a new international reserve asset (Special Drawing Rights) and new borrowing facilities for countries in payments difficulty thus occurred during the early 1970s.

A test of a good monetary mechanism is efficiency in lubricating the kinds of flows identified above as promoting economic interdependence among nations. The mechanism should be efficient and permit the financing of international trade and payments at minimum cost and with minimum uncertainty. It should be *neutral* and not cause disruptions or adverse policy reactions in the real sector, implying among other things resistance to financial crises. It should not force countries to sacrifice major alternative economic goals for the sake of the balance of payments, nor should it breed instability by forcing sequential structural readjustments in response to shifting exchange rates. And it should absorb the inevitable international economic shocks that are part of economic interdependence without triggering significant and potentially damaging countershocks of its own. It seems clear that such a monetary system is now in place, even if the formal rules according to which the system functions have yet to be finally worked out.

Environmental management as a social priority, subject to public policy and potentially absorbing significant amounts of real resources, will influence each of the aspects of international economic interdependence mentioned here. Historically, environmental damage has not greatly influenced international economic relations, simply because the associated costs were not internalised. This has changed, and will continue to change, and it is important to determine how each of the aforementioned components of international economic interdependence will be affected as a result. Environmental management can be considered a *shock* to the system, and aside from the more immediate issues involved it is important to know how, in general, the system tends to react to such shocks.

INTERNATIONAL ECONOMIC ADAPTATION

One of the important aspects of international economic interdependence is its impact on the adaptation of nations to economic disturbances and on the way in which this adaptation takes place. If freer trade, factor mobility and technology transfers convey economic benefits, so they also carry with them potential costs in the form of general and specific disturbances that originate outside the national economy, as well as the imposition of a set of implicit constraints on the conduct of domestic macroeconomic and structural policy. Policy interdependence thus follows from economic interdependence and takes a number of forms.

First, in the monetary sector it is clear that national policy independence no longer exists. Restrictive financial policies pursued by one country to combat inflation, for example, reverberate throughout the international monetary system. Capital flows respond and influence the attainment of policy objectives both in the home country and in other nations. Such flows, in turn, affect exchange rates, promoting in this case an appreciation of the home country's currency relative to others. This has an impact on the relative prices of goods and services in the international market-place, to the disadvantage of the home country's exports, but stimulates its imports – with the reverse trade implications for principal competitor nations. From the home country's perspective the international repercussions make its policy target harder to achieve, while at the same time complicating any structural side-effects that may occur. From the perspective of other countries, they are subjected to shocks on both the monetary and trade sides which may not coincide with their own domestic policy goals.

In the real sector as well, international interdependence complicates the problems of maintaining economic balance. Economic expansion abroad tends to stimulate the size of export markets for the home country, but increased exports may or may not be consistent with the prevailing direction of domestic macroeconomic policy. Conversely, recession abroad invariably spills over national political frontiers by depressing export production and employment. On the supply side as well, economic expansion abroad may create shortages of imported raw materials, capital equipment and other traded products, with the result that bottlenecks develop in the domestic economy. Conversely, recession abroad may bring about significant increases in the competitive pressure of imports and result in adjustment problems in the import-competing industrial sector.

Macroeconomic and monetary disturbances and adjustment are only two facets of the problem, of course, and the structural implications of international economic shifts require even more serious and continuing efforts to adapt national economies to changing conditions. There are several dimensions to this issue. First, a technological breakthrough in a particular industry abroad may abruptly improve the competitiveness of imports to the detriment of the domestic import-competing industry. Unless the impacted industry can itself adapt rapidly, either by bringing in technology from abroad or by generating it internally, structural adaptation will be required involving displacement of productive factors and their reabsorption in other sectors. This is hardly a costless process, and the burden will have to be borne by the factors of production immediately involved unless publicy financed adjustment assistance can be secured.

Structural adaptation in response to stiffened international competition may, of course, come from a wide variety of sources. Domestic labour or capital costs may diverge from those prevailing abroad, to the detriment of domestic export- or import-competing suppliers; or the availability of raw materials and fuels may alter drastically; or international investment activity may generate a supply capability abroad, where none existed before. In particular the activities of multinational corporations – by transferring the aforementioned package of technology, management, entrepreneurship and capital quickly and efficiently – may cause a significant acceleration in this adjustment, and with it raise the social cost of structural adaptation.

In general, the larger the international sector relative to the over-all size of the national economy, the greater will be the need for continued adaptation to aggregate and structural shocks emanating abroad, and the greater the need to gear public policy to the conditions created by these shocks. And while economic interdependence increases conflicts and demands on public policy, it also narrows the degrees of freedom available to policy-makers. A commitment to freer trade under the rules of the General Agreement on Tariffs and Trade (GATT), for example, at least in principle preclude reliance on increased tariffs as a way of alleviating domestic adjustment burdens. Other trade barriers, including import quotas, are similarly subject to internationally-agreed rules of the game which can only be violated at the risk of retaliation from abroad. Discriminatory treatment in favour of domestic suppliers of goods and services, as well as government subsidisation, for example, are highly suspect. In extreme cases, as under a commitment to regional free trade within a customs union, freedom of action *vis-à-vis* partner countries in the trade-policy sphere is essentially precluded, at least in theory.

International economic interdependence narrows policy alternatives on a broader scale as well. Regional or social policy measures may have an impact on international competition, and constitute grounds for concern abroad. Changes in tax structures may do likewise. Efforts to achieve the domestic goals of full employment and price-level stability may impact adversely on other countries, or they may be deemed inadequate as seen from a foreign persepective. It is perhaps not far wrong to assert that total economic policy independence is a thing of the past (if it ever really existed) and that policy co-ordination and harmonisation among governments will be a permanent and growing feature of the international economy in the years to come. Certainly if such co-operation is not achieved to the extent required, the limits to international economic integration will make themselves rather readily apparent.

How does all of this relate to the problem of environmental management? Environment will absorb a significant share of economic resources in the years to come. As we shall see, it will tend to enhance the degree of economic interdependence and at the same time trigger some of the 'shocks' that require adaptation to changing conditions in the international economy. It will influence the flow of international trade – its volume, direction and product-composition – as well as the international flows of productive resources. It will influence international payments and it will affect the forward planning of multinational enterprises. Occasionally it will influence relations between nations directly, especially in the case of transfrontier pollution. And it will influence policy. The fact of economic interdependence will affect the way countries go about the business of environmental control and the pace of progress in this endeavour. Not least important, it will influence the developing countries in terms of their prospects for economic advance and their approaches to their own environmental problems.

THE LARGER ISSUE : POPULATION AND GROWTH

If recent projections of the environmental consequences of continued historical growth trends (including resource depletion) are anywhere near the mark, the kinds of environmental problems discussed in this volume, instead of being major issues of concern, simply become minor symptoms of a problem that calls into question the very prospect of human survival. Demands on the life-support capabilities of the globe, caused by more people using more resources without adequately reintroducing those resources into the system, will eventually force severe limits on growth – and the only question is at what level of living will that essentially stationary state occur.[4]

Projections along these lines, based on dynamic growth models with essentially static constraints, inevitably conclude that growth must stop – that we can only get more out of whatever limited capacity for growth remains by drastically rearranging our priorities in virtually all areas of human activity. It is easy to dismiss such projections on the basis of serious flaws in the assumptions, and point to the dismal failure of such forecasts in the past. But this would be imprudent. Such studies do point out that bottlenecks will in fact develop, some earlier than others and some more serious and abrupt than others. They also indicate that if ultimate doom is to be prevented (or at least delayed) then the restoration of balance in the use and re-use of natural and common-property resources must be given top priority. If governments take this seriously, as they should, then some of the implications of environmental control for the international economy discussed here become very much more pronounced.[5] Lastly, they indicate that there are limits to everything within a given time-frame, and as those limits are approached the real cost of further expansion becomes successively higher.

It is rather doubtful that economic growth will be purposely and seriously throttled for the sake of the global environment. After all, economic growth may be viewed both as a cause of and a cure for environmental despoilation. The political feasibility of enforced growth limits is another question entirely.[6] But the limits will indeed make themselves felt as environmental damage becomes increasingly apparent, and as resources are directed to its restoration and control, so that growth in conventional terms will be slower than it would be otherwise.

There is one direct link between the normative policy prescriptions of growth/environment models of population control already being applied or considered in a majority of nations. Whereas global population planning seems well beyond reach at present, population control at the national level seems to be growing steadily – stimulated periodically by threats of international displacement of people, migration and localised overcrowding in urban areas. This will affect growth, and it will also affect the international economy, since both demand for, and supply of, traded goods and services are in part dependent on population.

DIRECTIONS OF ENVIRONMENTAL POLICY : A SCENARIO

We have identified the demand for environmental quality as a principal determinant of the international economic repercussions of pollution control. If we accept the proposition that social preferences can and do differ, both over time and among nations, the important question concerns the nature of these differences and how they will evolve in the future. The greater the divergences that develop, the greater will be the significance of environmental management for international economic relations.

The evidence available thus far is sketchy. Certain countries, such as Sweden, Japan and the United States, have begun to articulate national environmental policies which indicate serious public concern with the issue and provide reasonable grounds for projecting what kinds of standards may exist in 1980 or 1985. In the case of the United States, for example, much of the enabling legislation was passed in the late 1960s, calling for far-reaching environmental reforms during the last third of the century. The establishment of an appropriate executive body, which has taken its mandate seriously, together with vigorous use of the judicial system, have indicated quite clearly that an implicit – and often explicit – time-table indeed exists and will generally be adhered to. Environment in the United States today is a matter of national priority, backed by meaningful political support, that has been thoroughly debated and will be actively pursued in the coming decades.

Other countries – some with long-standing and rigorous environmental norms at the regional and local level – are only beginning to adopt the issue as a matter of high national priority. Many have not yet reached the point where environmental management has become a serious domestic political issue, a condition that probably is a prerequisite to national planning for environmental restoration and maintenance. Indeed, few coherent national environmental plans have been articulated at all, much less their scheduled phasing-in. In some cases, environmental management will be advanced in an *ad hoc* manner dealing with individual crises as they arise – often vigorously and expeditiously – but without the sense of purpose that would permit defensible projections of what conditions will be like five or ten years hence.

It is perhaps useful to sketch out a scenario that seems likely to depict the time-path of international environmental policy during the coming decades. Several hypotheses seem likely to be borne out by the facts as they emerge : *

* For an earlier version of this scenario, see Ingo Walter, 'Environmental Management and the International Economic Order', in *The Future of the International Economic Order*, ed. C. Fred Bergsten (Lexington, Mass.: D. C. Heath, 1973).

(a) There are at present very considerable differences between nations concerning the idea of what constitutes an 'acceptable' level of environmental quality. These differences are the product of an extremely complex set of national social priorities. The level of *per capita* income appears to be one important determinant. However, it is one of many and differences in demand for environmental quality among countries at similar levels of income sometimes exceed those among countries at quite different income levels.

(b) The 1970s will witness a 'catch-up' phase, during the course of which the gap between the *desired* level of environmental quality and the *realised* level will narrow, both within and between nations. This means that resources devoted to pollution control in the years immediately ahead will vary rather widely internationally, and that the international economic disturbances that result may be rather sharp. It also means, however, that the intermediate effects may overstate those likely to prevail over the longer term.

(c) As incomes rise and as knowledge about the environment and its management gets diffused internationally, the concept of what is an 'acceptable' state of the environment will gradually converge, and may ultimately become relatively uniform among the industrial countries of the world. Such convergence will tend to be gradual, however, and may be several decades in duration.

(d) The convergence process will not be a smooth one. Rather, there will be significant leads and lags – periods where one country may move very rapidly toward a serious effort to manage the environment, followed by periods of stagnation and even backsliding. As noted in the previous chapter, the political dynamics of environmental management are highly complex, which makes this sort of unevenness virtually inevitable.

(e) Closely related to the previous point is the problem of environmental 'backlash'. The trade-offs involved in environmental management are not always apparent from the outset, and public awareness is often created by specific events – such as the oil crises of 1973 and 1974, the Alaska pipeline controversy, dramatic legal action initiated by environmentalists, environment-induced cost increases or quality reductions in such highly visible consumer goods as automobiles, and so forth. Once the trade-offs are apparent, public support for environmental programmes may wane at least temporarily – frequently helped along by over-zealous environmentalists espousing obviously extreme positions or refusing to work incrementally within the confines of what is politically possible.

(f) Whereas international differences in the commitment to environmental management – in terms of the definition of acceptable pollution levels – may be a transitional issue among the industrial countries, it will tend to be rather durable so far as the developing countries are concerned. In many cases the priorities are so different and the resources so limited that a major environmental management effort by the poor countries may be unrealistic in the foreseeable future. This does not mean, however, that environmental safeguards will be entirely absent in many of the developing nations, or that rather significant differences will not emerge between them.

(g) There will be considerable inter-country variations in environmental-control trends as they relate to various types of pollution problems – for example water quality versus noise versus visual despoilation – both as to the degree of rigour applied and the timing of policy measures.

(h) Different countries will continue to approach environmental problems using different instruments. Some will force the polluter to pay the cost of avoiding and repairing environmental damage, while others will finance pollution control in part from public revenues. Despite international agreements to the contrary (see Chapter 5) international variations in pollution-control techniques are inevitable, given the diversity in national ways of doing things, and this will tend to influence international economic relations.

(i) Lastly, prospects for international administration of environmental management are not bright. Apart from the questions concerning the appropriateness of international harmonisation of environmental standards, the problem of national sovereignty will make it exceedingly difficult to establish supranational environmental organisations with a meaningful mandate. Even when such harmonisation has appeared to be clearly justified policy developments have been limited in the past. Some progress has been achieved in negotiations among countries in cases where two-way transfrontier pollution (see Chapter 7) tangibly affected national interests. On the other hand, very little progress has been made in the multilateral and global context, in part because the required mutuality of economic and social interests at the national level – and the required degree of supranational concern – have not developed to a sufficient degree. A beginning was made in 1972 at the Stockholm Conference on the Human Environment, where nations agreed in principle to accept responsibility for environmental damage to others. But the creation of inter-government or supranational machinery to give substance to this pledge – in the form of environmental co-ordination and enforcement – remains for the future. Although limited successes in environmental co-ordination and harmonisation may be achieved within regional or problem-orientated institutions, it is relatively safe to conclude at this point that international environmental variations will persist, perhaps increasingly, in influencing international economic relations.

Whether or not the above points are borne out in detail by the events, it seems clear that national priorities in the environmental field will continue to differ and that they will generate corresponding variations internationally, both in the economic resources devoted to the problem and in the manner in which environmental problems are handled.

DIRECTIONS OF ENVIRONMENTAL POLICY : AN OVERVIEW

At present, the kind of comprehensive analysis of international differences in pollution-control measures required for definitive analysis of their international economic implications does not exist. Nevertheless, the existence of considerable international variations in approach and timing, as proposed above, was confirmed in a recent survey carried out by the U.S. Department of Commerce.[7] The survey covered nine industrial countries and reviewed each nation's pollution problems, the environmental awareness of the people, pollution-abatement policies and programmes, pollution costs, governmental assistance and the direction of environmental policy in the future. The principal findings may be summarised as follows :

Belgium

Programmes for air and water pollution control are of relatively recent vintage. New water pollution regulations were issued in 1973. Air pollution standards for industrial plants and electric power generation are still under development (1973). Sulphur content of domestic heating oil was limited to 1 per cent beginning in 1973.

Canada

Comprehensive water resource management legislation is in place, which when fully implemented will enable regional agencies to control all aspects of water use including pollution standards. Strict effluent limits have been set for the pulp and paper industry, with similar standards for other industries presently under development. Federal government sets national air quality objectives for specific pollutants, but provincial governments set actual air quality standards. As of 1973, only the province of Ontario had strict air pollution regulations.

France

Relatively loose control of air pollution has been applied. National authorities may impose conditions regarding the quality and content of gaseous emissions into the air prior to the construction of industrial facilities. Standards are rigorously enforced in nationalised industries and utilities, generally less so with respect to private firms. France also has established laws for surveying and controlling river pollution and the power of water-management agencies is being strengthened.

Germany

There appears to be increasing concern with environmental programmes and priorities. The *Länder* have constitutional authority to regulate air and water pollution. While the federal government may recommend emission and discharge standards, it must rely on the *Länder* to adopt and to enforce them. As such, standards and enforcement vary widely. Amendments to the German constitution to centralise environmental control authority were promulgated, as were ambitious federal legislative proposals to control air and water quality. A new federal office for environmental protection was established in Berlin in 1974.

Italy

No water pollution legislation exists as yet, but Italy does have a 1972 air pollution law which provides for the establishment of emission standards regulating heating installations, industrial plants and motor vehicles. The development and enforcement of standards vary regionally, but on the whole there is only minimal control at present.

Japan

Major progress in pollution control was achieved through the recent provision, *inter alia*, of comprehensive controls of air and water pollution. Whether and to what extent these new efforts will be effective in abating Japan's serious pollution problems must await their implementation and enforcement. A serious setback due to the oil crisis of 1973 and 1974 seems likely.

The Netherlands

A comprehensive water pollution programme is in force, which includes the prohibition of discharging effluents into surface water without a permit. The permits specify what water quality or discharge standards must be met. Air pollution is controlled through the imposition of emission standards for manufacturing and service plants. To assist in the enforcement of these standards, a national network of 250 monitoring stations and ten regional measuring centres has been created.

Sweden

Industrial air and water pollution is regulated through a licence procedure required of firms using specified production processes. Emission limits, which follow national recommended standards, and other operating conditions for the protection of the environment, are set forth in the operating licence of each firm and are legally enforceable. The terms of each licence are negotiated with the government, taking into consideration the ability of the firm to meet the recommended national standards, with the burden of proof residing with the firm itself to show that compliance is not possible.

United Kingdom

Local and regional authorities establish and enforce emission standards on a case-by-case basis, applying a 'best practicable means' approach in determining the extent to which a firm is technically or economically capable of compliance. Significant progress has been made in reducing particular emission from industrial plants, residential heating and electric power generation. All water discharges are subject to the approval of river authorities, whose mandate includes conservation, restitution and augmentation of water resources, in addition to setting effluent standards for new and existing sources of pollution.

The United States

Water pollution control legislation was enacted in 1972, while the Federal Clean Air Act of 1967 sets national standards for air quality. Phased implementation of air and water pollution controls is being undertaken, with administration and monitoring at the national level by the Environmental Protection Agency and the Council on Environmental Quality. State, local and regional authorities may set standards exceeding federal regulations.

Assessment of differences, such as the foregoing in pollution control, measures early stages and remains entirely qualitative in nature. But the existence and sharpening of the kinds of international variations proposed in the previous section clearly seem to be emerging.

ENVIRONMENTAL ASSIMILATIVE VARIATIONS

Whatever the pattern of environmental policy that develops over time, its impact on the international economy will be determined largely by the economic cost of meeting whatever environmental standards are set at the national level. This, in turn, depends on the nature of the environmental resources that characterise each country – its environmental assimilative capacity. That these resources differ internationally is clear. Each nation has a unique climatological, geographical and topological profile which determines the amount of pollutants the environment can be expected to absorb without perceptible deterioration in quality – that defines the position and shape of its 'environmental damage function' as discussed in Chapter 1 (Fig. 1.1). The greater environmental assimilative capacity the lower will be the real resource cost of meeting a given set of environmental preferences.

An important issue in attempting to determine environmental assimilative capacity is the measurement of environmental quality. Ambient measurement is the most common, and attempts to determine the technical level of pollutants in a given environmental resource, such as the presence of nitrogen oxides, particulates, carbon monoxide and sulphur dioxide in a given airshed. Ambient environmental standards are then set by the political collectivity affected, but always with reference to its impact on individuals and groups of individuals. For this reason environmental quality is sometimes measured by human 'immissions', that is the amount of pollution absorbed by the individual in the course of his or her normal activity multiplied by the number of people exposed to the pollution.

In many cases, of course, the two measures amount to the same thing, but often they do not. For example, the ambient level of air quality can only be improved through reduced pollution, but the level of immissions can be improved through better air conditioning and filtration systems in homes, offices and public buildings. Moreover, for certain types of pollution (such as noise) ambient measures are irrelevant, and only immissions are important. The difference is rather significant in the determination of environmental assimilative capacity because of population density. Whereas the ability of the airshed to disperse pollutants may be the same in the Netherlands as in New Zealand, for example, the number of people exposed to a given pollutant will be quite different. And while an ambient definition of environmental quality would permit similar pollutive activities in both, an immissions definition might not. Under the latter concept, population density is thus a principal determinant of environmental assimilative capacity, with considerably wider scope existing for international variations.

It is difficult to go much beyond the conceptual level in defining international differences in environmental assimilative capacity because its principal indicator, the cost of pollution control, is determined jointly by supply *and* demand factors. However, since the cost of pollution control is the most important variable in determining the international economic implications, empirical separation of the two issues may not be crucial in the last analysis. Even so, comparable measures of pollution-control costs between countries are notoriously difficult to develop. Table 2.1 gives some recent estimates of pollution-control investments and operating costs from 1971 to 1975 for six industrial countries, as a percentage of G.N.P. (at constant market prices). The table also compares these values with the percentage of G.N.P. devoted to such competing priorities as defence, residential construction, education and health. The data indicate rather wide variations in relative outlays for pollution control, variations that are reflected in the other sectors as well. It also appears that environmental management absorbs considerably fewer resources than most of the social priorities listed.

Corresponding estimates for other countries seem to show similar

Table 2.1 Pollution-control expenditures relative to G.N.P. and competing priorities

Country	Pollution-control investment[a]	Pollution-control operating costs[a]	Total: pollution control[a]	Defence[b]	Residential Construction[c]	Health[d]	Education[e]
United States	0·5	1·1	1·6	8·2	3·5	7·0	7·5
Federal Republic Germany	0·9	0·9	1·8	2·9	5·4	3·9	7·8
Italy	0·4	0·2	0·6	3·6	6·6	5·2	5·5
Japan	2·2	N.A.*	N.A.	N.A.	6·9	2·0	5·9
Netherlands	N.A.	N.A.	0·5	3·5	5·5	4·6	5·5
Sweden	0·7	N.A.	N.A.	3·8	6·1	6·3	5·2

[a] Average for 1971–5 except United States (1970–5) and Netherlands (1975 only).
[b] 1970 except Sweden (1969).
[c] Average 1967–9.
[d] 1970 except the Federal Republic of Germany and Sweden (1969). Japan – government sector only. Netherlands – private sector only.
[e] 1970 except Sweden (1969), Japan (1965) and the Federal Republic of Germany (1968).
* Data not available.

Source: O.E.C.D. Environment Committee, Collection and Analysis of Pollution Control Cost Data (Paris: O.E.C.D. Document AEU/ENV/72.4, 24 March 1972).

variations: France 0.25 per cent of G.N.P. in 1969; the United Kingdom 1.0 per cent in 1968–9 covering mostly public expenditures; Switzerland 0.75 per cent in 1969, again mostly public expenditures; and Austria 0.5 per cent in 1971 for water pollution alone. Expenditures vary over time as well. U.S. industries' *costs* for pollution control are estimated to increase from 0.9 per cent of G.N.P. in 1970 to 1.4 per cent in 1974. Japanese outlays in the period from 1971 to 1975 are due to rise from 1.2 to 2.1 per cent of G.N.P. for mining, manufacturing and public utilities alone, while the share increase from 1970 to 1975 for the Federal Republic of Germany is estimated at 0.7 percentage points.[8]

Of course, it is not so much aggregate differences in pollution-control expenditures that are important in assessing the international economic implications, but rather differences at the industry level – to be discussed in detail in Chapter 3. Here the differences seem to be somewhat greater. For example, Japanese data show that 14–18 per cent of total investment in the thermal electric power, mining, petroleum-refining, and the pulp and paper industries is earmarked for pollution control, while a roughly comparable figure for the United States is only 8–10 per cent.[9]

Perhaps the most comprehensive study of international pollution-control cost differences to date has focused on the pulp and paper industry.[10] It confirmed the existence of variations in cost levels among the major producers and in addition noted wide differences at the level of individual products. Figure 2.1 illustrates this in the case of sulphite pulp. The vertical axis is an index of the pollution level, measured in kilograms of residual pollution* per metric ton (1000 kg) of production. The horizontal axis indicates pollution-control costs in U.S. dollars per ton of production. Points on the diagram depict estimates for 1970 and projections for 1975 and 1980. Note the differences in the position and shape of the curves for the seven countries included. These differences are repeated for other major products of the industry (such as semi-chemical pulp, integrated sulphite pulp and paper, newsprint, other paper and paperboard), although not for non-integrated sulphate pulp production.

INTERNATIONAL ECONOMIC DIMENSIONS

We have tried to show that collective environmental preferences and environmental assimilative capacity will tend to differ among nations, as will the application of policy instruments, and that these differences will shift in various ways over time. We also outlined rather briefly the various dimensions of economic interdependence among nations, and the

* Measured in terms of suspended solids (S.S.), and 'basic oxygen demand' (B.O.D.) contained in the effluent, with B.O.D. weighted twice the S.S. value.

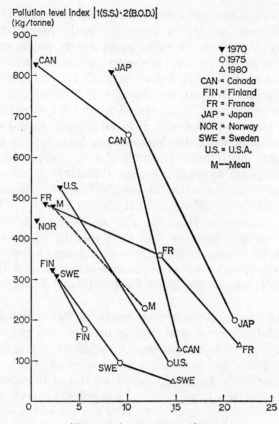

Pollution level index |1(S.S.)·2(B.O.D.)|
(Kg/tonne)

▼ 1970
○ 1975
△ 1980
CAN = Canada
FIN = Finland
FR = France
JAP = Japan
NOR = Norway
SWE = Sweden
U.S. = U.S.A.
M—Mean

Water pollution control costs ($/tonne)

FIGURE 2.1   Actual and projected pollution-control costs: sulphite pulp

Source: O.E.C.D., *Pollution by the Pulp and Paper Industry* (Paris: O.E.C.D., 1973) p. 103.

costs and benefits that go along with it – both in terms of policy constraints and in terms of the necessity to adapt to a variety of external disturbances. Environmental management was identified as a 'shock' to international economic relations, one which may in the end prove to be relatively minor in terms of its aggregate impact but which may have significant implications in specific sectors and industries. The following chapters are concerned with the identification of these implications and assessment of their importance. The principal links between environment and economic interdependence are as follows.

Short-term competitive effects

Environmental control raises production costs and this affects the competitiveness of domestic export- and import-competing industries. Dependding on the relative impact of such cost increases, firms may suffer sales declines or even go out of business, with productive factors released to be reabsorbed elsewhere in the economy – or the reverse may happen. Either way, there will be structural readjustments required of the national economy which may involve substantial costs.

Balance-of-trade effects

By altering the terms of trade (the price of exports relative to the price of imports), environmental control costs can influence the balance of trade. If export- and import-competing goods become more expensive, then the balance of trade can be expected to worsen if imports and/or exports are relatively sensitive to the price changes induced by pollution control.

Comparative advantage effects

By influencing the cost of producing different products in different ways, environmental management will also have an impact on the structure of trade, that is on its direction and commodity composition. A previously unpriced, immobile resource becomes priced, and this price will be reflected in international competitive advantage. Resources are diverted away from the production of tradeable goods and services and toward the avoidance and alleviation of environmental damage. The pattern of this resource transfer will influence the basic structure of international competitive advantage and trade. At the same time, by internalising environmental externalities, it will reduce the misallocation of resources implicit in pollution and promote maximum efficiency in the use of existing environmental assimilative capacity.

Factor-movement effects

If an industry or firm is threatened with competitive disadvantages due to environmental policies, it may choose to shift the location of its production facilities – or at least incremental productive capacity – to sites characterised by greater environmental assimilative capacity or more modest environmental preferences, or both. To the extent that this occurs *within* nations, it will help to forestall some of the international competitive effects just noted – changes in industrial structure may be avoided, but not shifts in the geographic distribution of industry. But alternative plant sites also include other countries, and the locational response will tend to result in international flows of capital and other productive factors, as well as reinforced shifts in trade flows.

Environmental-policy repercussions

International economic interdependence makes the achievement of environmental targets more difficult. It increases the degree of effective competition and hence reduces the willingness of firms to go along with environmental programmes that serve to raise capital and operating costs. This may lead to delays and heightened conflict in policy implementation, and may add to the sensitivity of adjustment problems in response to environmental controls. At the same time, the possible international economic repercussions of environmental policy tend to bias decisions in the direction of instruments that will have the least possible deleterious impact on international competitiveness – subsidies for example.

International economic policy effects

Increases in production costs and losses in international competitive position (real or imagined) attributable to environmental measures may trigger charges of 'unfair' competition from firms subject to lower standards of pollution control and demands for compensatory protection from imports in the form of tariffs and non-tariff trade-policy measures. International differences in the *instruments* of pollution control will tend to raise the probability of commercial policy reactions. Similar pressures may develop to prevent capital outflows on the grounds that they are in search of 'pollution havens' and designed to exploit the environment of other countries. It is difficult to justify such policy reactions on economic grounds except in so far as they serve to ease the economic cost of adaptation to environmental control, but this hardly means that pollution control will not be used as a pretext for protectionism. Lastly, the degree of international interdependence – including the level of tariffs and other barriers to trade and factor movements – will determine the relative importance of environmental policy for international economic relations, so that its impact within a customs union or other regional arrangement involving free trade may well exceed its impact in the international economy at large.

Transfrontier pollution

All of the foregoing international economic repercussions of environmental management involve politically sovereign countries independently pursuing environmental objectives within their own national borders. There may, of course, be *direct* international transmission of pollution as well, wherein economic activity in one country causes environmental damage to another. Transfrontier pollution also has numerous implications for such critical components of the international economy as ocean transport, and raises a host of substantive and policy-related questions that are quite different from those noted above and which may be extremely complex.

Institutions

Differences in environmental preferences and assimilative capacities among political collectivities is, of course, a national issue as well as an international one – and the aforementioned effects are basically similar whether the frame of reference is interregional or international. The difference is the existence of a policy mandate at the national level to co-ordinate environmental policy and facilitate economic adjustment, which does not exist at the international level. The fact of national sovereignty will thus ensure the durability of international economic repercussions of environmental management and render a co-ordinated approach to the problem exceedingly difficult.

Pollution and international development

Finally, there are a variety of implications for the economic development of nations. Pollution control will cause a general shift of demand away from products that are environmentally damaging toward those found to be less pollutive. New products and new industries are emerging, involving firms in the production of pollution-control equipment and know-how, much of which is internationally traded. Conservation policies, whether or not justified on environmental grounds, may lead to periodic supply shortages. Developing nations, to the extent that they are less able to cope with international environmental policy measures, may be relatively more severely affected than other nations.

There are a host of links between environmental management and international economic interdependence. On the side of international trade and factor movements this applies to the goals of optimum common-property use-patterns and social-welfare maximisation *within* the political collectivities that are the relevant decision units in this respect. It is these collectivities which also possess the capability of implementing the required public policies for environmental control – whether or not such policies are, or should be, applied uniformly at the national, regional or local level. International and interregional trade flows and production patterns will reflect any differences that emerge. Shifts in these patterns will be greater : (a) the greater are the relevant differences in environmental assimilative capacity for the specific effluents involved; (b) the greater are inter-country variations in social preferences for environmental quality; (c) the wider are inter-country divergences in approaches to environmental restoration and maintenance; (d) the fewer barriers are applied to trade and capital flows; and (e) the higher the substitution and price sensitivity of the traded products affected, and the greater the sensitivity of capital-investment decisions to present and prospective future environmental considerations.

FURTHER READING

C. Fred Bergsten (ed.), *The Future of the International Economic Order* (Lexington, Mass: D. C. Heath, 1973).

Michael B. Connolly and Alexander K. Swoboda (eds), *International Trade and Money* (London: George Allen & Unwin, 1973).

Richard N. Cooper, *Economics of Interdependence* (New York: McGraw-Hill, 1968).

Robert G. Hawkins and Ingo Walter (eds), *The United States and International Markets* (Lexington, Mass.: D. C. Heath, 1972).

Allen V. Kneese *et al.* (ed.), *Managing the Environment: International Economic Cooperation for Pollution Control* (New York: Frederick A. Praeger, 1971).

O.E.C.D., *Problems of Environmental Economics* (Paris: O.E.C.D., 1972).

Charles Pearson and Wendy Takacz, 'International Economic Implications of Environmental Control and Pollution Abatement Programs', in *United States International Economic Policy in an Interdependent World*, Compendium of Papers (Washington, D.C.: Government Printing Office, 1971).

3

Environmental Control and International Trade: Competitive Effects

In this and the following chapter, we shall endeavour to trace through the impact of environmental management on international trade. We will be concerned with the more immediate impact of environmental policies on costs of production, product prices, international competiveness, the terms of trade, and the balance of trade. Chapter 4 will deal with the implications of pollution control for more fundamental and long-range questions of economic structure and international comparative advantage.

Throughout we shall make the assumption that the 'polluter pays' principle (PPP) is universally adopted – that is the cost of internalising environmental externalities is ultimately borne by the final purchaser of the goods and services whose production caused the pollution in the first place. What happens when this assumption is relaxed – when the costs are borne by governments or by the productive factors themselves – will be discussed in Chapter 5. In this chapter we shall concern ourselves initially with the international competitive effects of *process pollution* and subsequently turn our attention to the control of product and *residuals pollution*.

AGGREGATE COMPETITIVE IMPACT

A general presumption seems to be that vigorous environmental control is 'bad' for the international economic relations of a country, in that it is disadvantageous for the competitive position of domestic goods in export markets and simultaneously erodes the competitive position of domestic producers who have to compete with imports for the home market. As pollution control pushes up domestic prices relative to foreign prices, so the argument goes, the volume of exports is bound to drop even as the volume of imports is bound to rise, and this will represent an adverse influence on the nation's balance of trade and balance of payments.

This reasoning can be formalised as follows. Suppose we let M represent the physical quantity of imports, Yd domestic real income, PM the price of imports, PMC the price of domestic goods that compete with imports and PR the price of domestic goods that do not compete with imports.[1] Then we can write

$$M = f(Yd, PM, PMC, PR)$$

In other words, the volume of imports would seem to be (a) positively related to income, (b) negatively related to the price of imports, (c) positively related to the price of import-competing goods, and (d) negatively related to the price of non-competing goods produced domestically. Specifying this import demand function in logarithmic form, we have

$$M = a_1 + a_2 \log Yd + a_3 \log PM + a_4 \log PMC + a_5 \log PR$$

with all of the coefficients being elasticities: a_2 is the income elasticity of demand for imports, a_3 the own-price elasticity of demand for imports, a_4 and a_5 the cross-price elasticity of import demand with respect to domestic-competing and non-competing goods respectively. As noted, we would expect a_2 and a_4 to be positive, and a_3 and a_5 to be negative.

If we assume for the moment that supply is infinitely elastic (or that the home country is too small to influence the price of what it buys from abroad), then domestic pollution-control measures which serve to increase price levels at home – assuming real income is unaffected and foreign prices remain constant – will tend to raise PMC and PR. Depending on the size of a_4 and a_5, this will tend to increase the volume of imports. In other words, imports will partially displace import-competing goods in satisfying domestic demand, which will be to the disadvantage of the import-competing industry and to the productive factors employed by them. The import expansion will be diminished, of course, if the price of imports themselves rise in response to the induced rise in import-competing prices, in which case the increase in import volumes and the import-competing production displacement will be correspondingly less. In both cases, the effect on the balance of trade will be adverse: expenditures for imports will rise either because the volume of imports increases, or because the prices of imports rise, or both.

These simple relationships can be developed on the export side as well. If we let Yf represent the level of income abroad, PX the price of domestic exports, PXC the price of import-competing products abroad and PT the price of non-competitive products abroad, we have the logarithmic export function

$$X = b_1 + b_2 \log Yf + b_3 \log PX + b_4 \log PXC + b_5 \log PT$$

With the coefficient again representing elasticities, we would expect b_2 and b_4 to be negative and b_2 and b_5 to be positive. In other words, exports will tend to grow when increases in prices of products competing with the home country's export rise abroad; however, they will tend to fall when the prices of the home country's exports themselves rise or when the price increases of non-competing goods and services abroad – assumed to be gross complements for imports – cause a reduction in purchasing power that otherwise would have gone into their imports. Under the same assumption of environment-induced cost increases at home which are not reflected abroad, exports would weaken as PX increases while all of the remaining variables stay the same.

The competitive position of the home country thus tends to weaken on both the import *and* export sides. Outlays for imports rise while export receipts decline (if b_3 exceeds unity). The *balance* of trade under these conditions is almost certain to worsen although the *terms* of trade may improve – depending on what happens to foreign export prices.

In more general terms, what we are principally interested in is how unilateral action on the part of a given country to impose (or not to impose) environmental controls affects the price of import-competing goods PMC, the price of non-competing domestic goods PR, and the price of export goods PX, and how these in turn will influence the volume of exports and imports via the relevant elasticities. If other countries are engaging in environmental-management programmes as well, the induced price changes have to be examined in relation to one another. Assuming all countries abide by the 'polluter pays' principle, the aggregate balance of trade impact depends on the relative degree of rigour employed – whether by effluent taxation or via the enforcement of standards – as well as the efficiency employed in pollution-control activities on the part of industry.

There is as yet very little empirical evidence as to the expected aggregate competitive effects of pollution control on trade flows. One study for the United States anticipated that the adverse effect of anti-pollution measures on the balance of payments – due to relative price changes only – would be 1.5 billion dollars during 1972–6 and 2.5 billion dollars during 1977–80 (in constant dollars). It would, however, rise to 2.3 and 4.3 billion dollars respectively if U.S. pollution-control costs turn out to be half again as high as the best available estimates.[2]

Estimates such as these focus entirely on the price variables and ignore the effect of pollution control on incomes. Suppose environmental management in a particular country had the effect of reducing G.N.P. below what it would have been otherwise. In terms of the above notation, Yd would decline and, depending on the income elasticity of the demand for imports a_2, so would the volume of purchase from abroad. Hence the positive income effect of pollution-control expenditures on the trade balance would tend to offset the negative price effect and perhaps override it entirely. The income effect could come from several sources. One would be supply bottlenecks created by environmental controls which constrain the ability of the economy as a whole or specific sectors to produce. Another might be the income repercussions of the trade-balance shift itself : exports decline and imports rise, thereby reducing aggregate demand and depressing the level of income via the Keynesian multiplier and reducing imports via the income elasticity of demand.

With offsetting income effects, the negative annual impact of unilateral environmental controls on the U.S. balance of trade is expected to be 1.2 billion dollars during 1972–5 and 0.15 billion dollars during 1977– 80. These values are 0.3 and 2.35 billion dollars better than the corresponding estimates which assume that any possible income effects will be offset by countervailing macroeconomic policy.[3] Another study calculates that the combined price and income effects of a 3.6 per cent pollution-control-induced price increase for the United States would cause an adverse balance-of-trade change of the order of 2.7 per cent of 1968 exports. The corresponding values for a 4 per cent cost increase in the United Kingdom, the Federal Republic of Germany, and Japan are 1.1, 3.1 and 10.7 per cent of 1968 exports respectively.[4] Such estimates, of course, are highly tentative in nature and should not be taken too seriously. But they do point out the importance of weighing all possible factors that may influence the balance-of-trade impact of environmental management.

The development of defensible estimates of the over-all short-term trade effects of pollution control is a hazardous proposition at best. What is needed at the outset is a reliable assessment of comparative aggregate pollution-control costs in the principal countries that compete for international markets. These values depend on what kinds of pollution-control policies will be implemented, how they will be implemented and how efficiently industry is able to cope with them. Once costs have been estimated, their impact on international trade depends on the relevant import-demand, export-supply and cross-price elasticities, which are themselves notoriously difficult to measure, even in the absence of possible income effects.

BALANCE-OF-PAYMENTS IMPLICATIONS

The aggregate competitive effects of pollution control will, as we have tried to show, tend to have an impact on national balance of trade and payments. Even given the relatively small percentage of cost increases attributable to pollution control in most cases, the impact on over-all imports and exports may not be negligible. One study has shown, for example, that for certain U.S. industrial sectors a 1 per cent production-cost increase attributable to environmental controls is roughly the equivalent of a 5 per cent increase in the wage rate.[5] Judging by the response of policy-makers to differential shifts in real wages equivalent to the anticipated aggregate pollution-control costs, from a balance-of-payments standpoint it is difficult to ignore environmental management costs entirely.

As noted in Chapter 2, these may vary from rather negligible amounts to 2 per cent or more of G.N.P. for the principal industrial countries. This can be considered a 'shock' to the balance of payments of countries at the upper end of this range, in that the trade effect alone will tend to induce payments deficits, while at the same time promoting payments surpluses for their trading partners. Absorption of this shock –

which is very much less serious than that induced by the abrupt oil price increases in 1973–4 for example – depends on the mechanisms and policy instruments that are available for balance-of-payments adjustment.

Considerable attention might be focused on the balance-of-payment effects of differential pollution-control costs if exchange rates were pegged. They would necessitate the financing of the resultant payments imbalances, and their alleviation by means of balance-of-payments policies designed to induce net capital inflows, reduce expenditures on imports, stimulate export receipts, or some combination of these, by means of direct intervention in international trade and payments or through macro-economic policy instruments. Such measures either reduce the gains from international trade and factor movements or require that the economy be constrained to output levels below what could alternatively have been achieved. Either way, the balance-of-payments policy implications of environmental management would involve additional social costs, and these would serve to augment the direct costs associated with pollution-control programmes.

This would have been sufficient reason for concern with this issue prior to 1971. Since then, of course, the degree of fixity in exchange rates has been modified substantially and a system of 'managed floating' prevails. Increases in costs and prices attributable to pollution control, reflected in competitive shifts in international markets, simply cause corresponding shifts in relative currency values which in turn result in equilibriating trade flows. For example, suppose U.S. costs and prices moved up faster due to pollution control than those of its main industrial competitors, all else being equal. The dollar would depreciate in foreign exchange markets, imports would become more expensive and exports cheaper and payments balance would be restored. There would be no need for compensatory policy measures and the associated costs would be largely avoided. The industries primarily impacted would still lose in international competitiveness, however, and the displaced productive factors would be reabsorbed in relatively less-pollutive export- and import-competing industries. Adaptation of this type is certainly not costless, but it is something that accompanies environmental control in any case. Hence the international monetary implications, *given exchange-rate flexibility*, tend to reinforce the structural adjustment required by environmental management and may well serve to accelerate it.

All of this seems to indicate that the balance-of-payments implications of environmental management are not particularly serious since the advent of effective exchange-rate flexibility. Hence arguments to delay environmental policies or to soften their international competitive impact via export aids or import restraints for balance-of-payments reasons carry very little weight. Arguments that balance-of-payments aspects of the issue mandate efforts to co-ordinate and harmonise environmental policy internationally also lose some (but not all) of their force. A significant exception may be regional arrangements for tying together national currencies, and a great deal more attention may have to be paid to the balance-of-payments implications of pollution control among the participants of the joint European currency float, for example, than is generally the case. Indeed, this may eventually require the harmonisation of environmental policies and/or offsetting balance-of-payments policy reactions within the European Community.

INTERNATIONAL COMPETITIVE EFFECTS AT THE INDUSTRY LEVEL

Perhaps of more immediate concern than the aggregate competitive implications of environmental management is its impact on the international competitive position of individual industries. There are, first of all, wide variations in the pollutive characteristics of industrial production. Some, such as the assembly of electronic equipment, are relatively free of environmental externalities, while others such as steel-making are highly pollutive. This means that compliance with environmental standards will be more costly for some industries than for others, and that even wider variance may be found in industry pollution-control costs *relative* to the value of final sales.

An inter-industry breakdown of the principal pollution-control outlays for the United States, based on survey data, is given in Table 3.1. It indicates that the capital expenditures needed to bring U.S. business up to 1973 pollution standards was roughly 22.3 billion dollars at the beginning of that year. Among industries involved in international trade, this 'catch-up' investment varies from 2.74 billion dollars for petroleum and 2.25 billion dollars for chemicals, to 110 million dollars for rubber and 140 million dollars for textiles. A similar variation is found in current and planned levels of capital spending for pollution control, both in absolute terms and in relation to over-all investment in plant and equipment. The latter is highest in the case of the paper, petroleum-refining and metal industries, and lowest for textiles, aerospace and electrical machinery.

Table 3.1 also shows that there are substantial inter-industry differences in the allocation of investment as between air and water pollution control, with air pollution being relatively most important for the electric utility, petroleum and non-ferrous metal industries, and water pollution in the food and beverage, chemical and paper industries. Lastly, Table 3.1 compares expenditures in research and development among industries. Again wide variations are evident: from 1976 planned levels of 297 million dollars in non-ferrous metals and 95 million dollars in electrical machinery, to 58 million dollars in the textile industry.

Such inter-industry variations in pollution-control outlays are apparent in other countries as well. In the Federal Republic of Germany, for exam-

Table 3.1 Pollution-control expenditures by U.S. industrial sectors

Industry	'Catch-up' investment[a] (billion dollars)	Pollution-control investment as percentage of total capital spending 1972 (%)	Planned 1976 (%)	Capital spending for pollution control 1972 (million dollars)	Planned 1976 (million dollars)	Allocation of 1972 pollution-control investment Air (million dollars)	Water (million dollars)	Expenditures on research and development for pollution control 1972 (million dollars)	Planned 1976 (million dollars)
Iron and steel	1·74	12·3	18·8	193	517	104	89	26	19
Non-ferrous metals	1·47	15·3	15·9	181	297	151	30	18	22
Electrical machinery	0·32	2·8	3·1	67	95	31	36	145	238
Machinery	0·51	3·8	6·6	111	262	58	53	119	204
Autos, trucks and parts	0·80	6·6	5·9	122	158	72	50	109	142
Aerospace	0·19	6·2	3·5	26	23	15	11	77	87
Other transportation equipment	0·12	2·0	3·6	5	13	4	1	b	b
Fabricated metals	0·77	7·3	8·3	110	166	68	42	15	21
Instruments	0·24	3·2	9·2	23	94	8	15	51	72
Stone, clay and glass	1·32	9·6	10·6	115	211	72	43	7	20
Other durables	1·04	4·8	3·5	79	91	58	21	2	4
Total durables	8·52	6·6	8·4	1032	1927	641	391	569	829
Chemicals	2·25	10·9	13·8	376	652	162	214	112	120
Paper	1·62	23·3	19·5	321	335	172	149	16	27
Rubber	0·11	5·8	6·7	62	104	31	31	4	7
Petroleum	2·74	10·7	17·6	562	1315	373	189	74	122
Food and beverages	0·63	5·2	9·5	132	289	64	68	9	15
Textiles	0·14	2·6	7·6	19	58	9	10	6	5
Other non-durables	0·08	5·0	4·5	63	50	33	30	c	c
Total non-durables	7·57	9·8	13·8	1535	2803	844	691	221	296

Table 3.1 (cont.) Pollution-control expenditures by U.S. industrial sectors

Industry	'Catch-up' investment[a] (billion dollars)	Pollution-control investment as percentage of total capital spending 1972 (%)	Planned 1976 (%)	Capital spending for pollution control 1972 (million dollars)	Planned 1976 (million dollars)	Allocation of 1972 pollution-control investment Air (million dollars)	Water (million dollars)	Expenditures on research and development for pollution control 1972 (million dollars)	Planned 1976 (million dollars)
All manufacturing	16·09	8·2	10·9	2567	4730	1485	1082	792	1125
Mining	0·45	5·1	3·4	124	104	82	42		
Railroads	0·84	1·6	3·0	29	63	9	20		
Airlines	0·11	2·4	4·8	59	64	54	5		
Other transportation	0·19	0·8	2·6	12	52	5	7	678	518
Communications	0·16	2·4	1·2	285	219	95	190		
Electric utilities	3·88	7·9	5·9	1144	1249	912	232		
Gas utilities	0·12	1·6	1·9	41	73	23	18		
Commercial (1)	0·50	1·2	2·4	240	593	140	100		
All business	22·34	5·1	5·9	4501	7147	2805	1696	1470	1643

a. Total cost of bringing industries' existing facilities up to present pollution-control standards, as of 1 January 1973.
b. Included in autos, trucks and parts.
c. Included in other durables.

Source: McGraw-Hill Economics Department, *6th Annual McGraw-Hill Survey of Pollution Control Expenditures (mimeo.)* (18 May 1973).

ple, industry outlays during 1969–71 are estimated at about 1.1 billion dollars, of which 4.3 per cent involved mining, 22.7 per cent electric utilities; and 34.4 per cent the metal industries, 22.6 per cent petroleum and chemicals; and 16 per cent other industries.[6] A survey by the Japanese Ministry of International Trade and Industry in 1974 likewise showed that industries devoting a relatively high percentage of new capital spending to pollution control included electric power (17.7), mining (15.7), petroleum refining (14.1), pulp and paper (14.1), while those on the lower end included machinery (3.0), construction materials (5.6), ceramics (5.8), and petro-chemicals (5.1).[7] Swedish data indicate that the estimated share of pollution-control investment in total capital outlays for 1971–5 range from 12.1 per cent in the pulp and paper industry to 7.4 per cent for food, 6.0 per cent for chemicals, 5.5 per cent for iron and steel, 3.3 per cent for non-metallic minerals and 2.2 per cent for mining.[8]

While data on pollution-control investments serve as an important indicator of inter-industry differences in prospective costs, they represent only imperfectly the differential competitive impact of pollution control on industries. What is relevant from a cost standpoint is not current or prospective investment rates, but the annual cost of in-place pollution-control equipment allocated on a per-unit basis to output. The capital costs are composed of (a) the firm's internal rate of return on the capital stock in question and (b) the depreciation of that stock. To these must be added (c) research and development expenditures and (d) recurring operating expenses associated with pollution control. The sum of these costs represent the *direct* burden of environmental control that ultimately may impact on product prices. A recent U.S. study of twelve industries showed the cost of pollution control per unit ouput as depicted in Table 3.2. For example, existing pollution-control programmes are estimated to

Table 3.2 Estimated direct pollution-control costs for selected U.S. industries

Industry	Pollution-Control costs per unit of output (allocated)
Automobiles	210–425 dollars per vehicle
Baking	0·011–0·02 cents per pound for bread and related products
	0·05–0·09 cents per pound for biscuits and crackers
Cement manufacture	0·08–0·10 dollars per barrel of cement
Electric power generation	0·22 dollars–1·52 mills per kilowatt hour
Iron foundries	2–14 dollars per ton of castings
Aluminium smelting and refining	0·020–0·032 dollars per pound of aluminium
Copper smelting and refining	0·025–0·05 dollars per pound of copper
Lead smelting and refining	0·012–0·017 dollars per pound of lead
Zinc smelting and refining	0·0123–0·0267 dollars per pound of zinc
Petroleum refining	0·06 dollars per pound barrel of petroleum
Pulp and paper mills	5·50–12·50 dollars per ton of paper products
Steel-making	0·47–0·73 dollars per ton of steel products in 1972
	6·60–9·60 dollars per ton of steel products in 1976

Source: Council on Environmental Quality *et al., The Economic Impact of Pollution Control* (Washington, D.C.: Government Printing Office, 1972).

raise production costs in the pulp and paper industry from 5.50 to 12.50 dollars per ton of paper products, probably sufficient to have an international competitive impact, while unit-cost increases in other sectors appear to be considerably less.

Unfortunately, comparable estimates are still unavailable for competitive industries in other countries. Even if they were, they still would not represent an indication of the over-all cost impact of pollution control because they exclude the *indirect* pollution-control costs. In effect, the measurement of direct pollution-control costs, as above, attempts to ascertain for each internationally traded commodity what the value of that product *would be* if it and its production process fully conformed to accepted environmental norms without absorbing any economic resources to achieve this conformity.* The hypothetical value of a given internationally traded product P_H can then be compared with its actual market price P_A in order to determine its 'direct environment-control loading' (*DECL*). Thus

$$DECL = (P_A - P_H)/P_A$$

Since each of the raw material and intermediate inputs in the traded product is also subject to pollution-control costs, the 'over-all environmental control loading' (*OECL*) of a given tradeable product is its own *DECL* plus that of each input weighted by the contribution of that input to final export or import value. This approach requires the use of a national input–output table, which indicates the money value of how much of its outputs (inputs) each industry sold to (brought from) every other industry in a given year. These inter-industry transactions in money terms can then be converted into proportions, called 'flow coefficients', which in turn can be applied to the calculated *DECL* values to determine pollution-control costs embodied in an industry's inputs. When added to that industry's own *DECL* value, this gives an indication of the relative direct and indirect costs of pollution control embodied in its output. If we thus let j represent the traded product, i a given input and a_{ij} the contribution of i to the unit trade value of j, then

$$OECL_j = \frac{(P_A - P_H)_j + \sum_{i=1}^{n} a_{ij}(P_a - P_H)_i}{P_{Aj}}$$

While it is impossible to generate observable values for P_H direct and indirect costs attributable to environmental management can be estimated. These may be assumed to approximate $(P_A - P_H)_j$ for tradeable products and $(P_A - P_H)_i$ for inputs† and estimates for the over-all

* This discussion is based on Ingo Walter, 'The Pollution Content of American Trade', *Western Economic Journal* (March 1973).
† Constant costs are assumed. The price response to pollution-control costs will clearly differ for increasing-cost and decreasing-cost industries.

environment-control loadings can be developed. Pollution-control costs are again broken down into (a) current research and development expenditures, (b) depreciation charges on in-place pollution-control equipment, (c) the capital cost of in-place pollution-control equipment, and (d) current operating costs associated with environmental management. The sum of the above charges for each of eighteen U.S. manufacturing industries, and for aggregate mining, transportation utilities, commercial services, communications, and agriculture was divided in each case by gross sales or billings in 1971 to obtain for each sector estimated pollution-control costs per dollar of sales. The results are presented in Table 3.3.

Table 3.3 Estimated environmental-control costs per dollar of final sales, various U.S. industries, 1971

Industry	Direct pollution-control costs, cents per dollar of final sales
Iron and steel	1·47
Non-ferrous metals	1·76
Electrical machinery	0·49
Machinery	1·03
Autos, trucks and parts	1·19
Aerospace	0·57
Other transportation equipment	0·72
Fabricated metals	0·52
Instruments	3·37
Stone, clay and glass	1·75
Other durables	0·60
Chemicals	2·19
Paper	1·63
Rubber	0·63
Petroleum	3·73
Food and beverages	0·36
Textiles	0·38
Other non-durables	0·10
Mining	0·82
Railroads	0·46
Airlines	0·27
Other transportation	0·63
Communications	0·08
Electric utilities	7·00
Gas utilities	0·12
Commercial	0·32
Agriculture and fisheries	0·11
Total durables	1·18
Total non-durables	1·15
All business	1·16

Source: Ingo Walter, 'The Pollution Content of American Trade', *Western Economic Journal* (March 1973).

C

It is important to remember that the values presented incorporate three factors : (a) internalisation of environmental externalities attributable to the production *process*; (b) expenditure required to render *products* environmentally acceptable; and (c) costs attributable to the production of pollution-control *hardware* and technology – which are responsible for the high loading indicated for the 'instruments' sector for example. Separation of the latter pollution-control-cost element is impossible. Hence, while high environment-control charges per dollar of sales generally bear a negative international competitive connotation, this is not uniformly true of all industries.

To disaggregate the industry-based estimates of environmental costs into product-based *OECL* estimates useful for application in an international trade context, 83 goods and service categories contained in the U.S. input–output table were employed.* The relevant values shown in the first column of Table 3.4, together with U.S. input–output (I/O) co-efficients in 1966, were used to derive the *OECL* values presented in the second column of that table.

These estimates of over-all environmental-control loadings by the product groups yield a pollution-loading profile of U.S. trade. On the export side, the *OECL* values in Table 3.4 are simply multiplied by the value of average sales abroad during 1968–70 for each product or service group. The product mix within each group for exports is assumed identical to the product mix for total sales, and average prices charged on exports are assumed to be the same as on domestic sales. The result is column 4 of Table 3.4, indicating that the average annual *OECL* of U.S. exports during the period from 1968 to 1970 was about 751 billion dollars, or about 1.75 per cent of total exports.

Since there is no way of knowing the *OECL* values of foreign suppliers, we assume them to be the same as for domestic import-competing firms and estimate what the over-all pollution-control loading of U.S. imports *would have been* if the imported goods had been produced at home. We again assume that the product-mix of imports within each group is identical to the mix of total sales of the import-competing industry, and that imported and import-competing product prices are the same. The results, given in column 5 of Table 3.4 indicate that in 1968–70 the U.S. average annual *OECL* on imports was about 609 million dollars, or 1.52 per cent of total imports.

Over the entire range of traded goods and services, it appears that 1.75 per cent of the value of U.S. exports consisted of pollution-related costs, which is about 15 per cent higher than the 1.52 per cent estimated for U.S. imports. This difference does not appear very significant, and

---

* For the methodology, see Ingo Walter, 'The Pollution Content of American Trade', *Western Economic Journal* (March 1973).

suggests that pollution-control measures bearing on the respective suppliers of U.S. exports and imports will in general be trade-neutral, or at worst only marginally biased against the United States. In short, the product profile of U.S. exports does not seem to be systematically more or less pollution-intensive than the product profile of U.S. imports.[9]

This does not mean, of course, that U.S. trade in individual industries may not be vulnerable to increased environmental costs in terms of their international competitiveness. This vulnerability of a given industry will be larger (a) the more competitive its products are in the international market-place, and (b) the higher its over-all environmental-control loading.

A proxy for international competitiveness is the export/import ratio given in column 3 of Table 3.4. When this is multiplied by the $OECL$ values given in column 2, of that table, the 'relative impact index' given in column 6 is the result. These values show that, all else being equal, the international competitive position of the United States may be affected in industries such as ordnance and accessories, construction and mining equipment, and plastics, relative to such industries as apparel, fishery and forest products, and footwear, which are already characterised by a substantial competitivie disadvantage (or alternatively pollution-control costs may not be very important).

It follows that U.S. trade with individual foreign countries may be affected differently in terms of the trade impact of pollution-control regulation. For example, the average annual pollution-control loading of U.S. exports to Canada during the period from 1968 to 1970 was 157 million dollars, compared with 174 million dollars for imports – representing $OECL$ percentage values of 1.70 for exports and 1.70 for imports. During the same period, the pollution-control loading of U.S. exports to Japan was 68 million dollars compared with 88 million dollars for imports, but with percentage $OECL$ values of 1.70 for exports and 1.50 for imports. Relative to imports from Japan, therefore, U.S. exports to Japan appear to be relatively pollution-intensive, which is much less true of trade between the United States and Canada.

Empirical analysis of the cost effects of pollution control on internationally traded products are, of course, somewhat suspect because of high margins for error in the underlying data as well as methodological problems with the input–output approach. Conceptually, however, the methodology seems sound. What is required for a definitive analysis of competitive effects of pollution control are comparable $DECL$ estimates for each of the supplier countries, then used to derive corresponding $OECL$ values employing national input–output tables. Sources of variance in the latter could then be traced to differences in (a) pollution-control standards, (b) efficiency, (c) enforcement techniques and instruments, and (d)

Table 3.4 Pollution content of U.S. exports and imports: estimated direct (*DECL*) and over-all (*OECL*) environmental-control loadings entering U.S. international trade flows, 1968–70

I/O product or service group	(1) DECL[a]	(2) OECL[a]	(3) Export/import ratio U.S.–rest of world	(4) OECL exports[b] ($)	(5) OECL imports[b] ($)	(6) Relative impact index[c]
1. Livestock and products	1·28	1·98	0·61	10·06	16·49	1·10
2. Other agricultural products	1·92	2·46	1·84	117·93	64·12	4·52
3. Forestry and fishery products	0·64	1·05	0·11	0·83	7·40	0·12
5. Iron and ferroalloy ores mining	0·82	1·16	0·15	0·77	5·14	0·18
6. Non-ferrous metal ores mining	0·82	1·29	0·36	2·41	6·66	0·47
7. Coal mining	1·76	2·21	42·02	16·22	0·39	92·86
8. Crude petroleum and natural gas	0·41	0·64	0·08	0·86	10·54	0·05
9. Stone and clay mining and quarrying	0·41	0·95	0·73	1·62	2·23	0·69
10. Chemical and fertiliser mining	0·82	1·31	2·42	1·51	0·81	3·17
13. Ordnance and accessories	0·53	2·36	12·72	15·81	1·24	30·02
14. Food and kindred products	0·36	1·01	0·28	5·47	19·33	0·29
15. Tobacco manufactures	0·18	0·51	4·93	3·50	0·71	2·51
16. Broad and narrow fabrics, yarn, thread	0·38	1·02	0·47	3·87	8·19	0·48
17. Miscellaneous fabricated textile products	0·38	1·10	0·93	1·08	1·15	1·02
18. Apparel	0·19	0·50	0·20	0·49	5·38	0·10
19. Miscellaneous textile goods and floor covering	0·19	0·55	0·70	0·70	0·70	0·38
20. Lumber and wood productions except containers	0·10	0·45	0·60	2·80	4·68	0·27
21. Wooden containers	0·05	0·56	0·66	0·01	0·02	0·30
22–23. Furniture and fixtures	0·05	0·59	0·29	0·57	1·97	0·17
24. Paper and allied products except containers	1·63	2·33	0·60	21·35	35·48	1·40
25. Paperboard containers and boxes	1·63	2·50	9·42	0·73	0·08	23·56
26. Printing and publishing	0·08	0·56	2·32	1·73	0·75	3·25
27. Chemicals and selected chemical products	2·19	3·25	2·01	55·71	27·71	6·53
28. Plastics and synthetic materials	2·19	3·34	4·40	23·17	5·26	14·71
29. Drugs, cleaning, toilet preparations	1·10	1·78	3·34	9·44	2·83	5·94
30. Paints and allied products	3·29	4·27	1·60	5·44	3·34	6·84
31. Petroleum refining and related products	3·73	4·58	0·39	20·55	53·04	1·77
32. Rubber and miscellaneous plastic products	0·63	1·38	0·82	5·00	6·12	1·13
33. Leather tanning and industrial leather	0·95	1·38	0·21	1·04	4·89	0·29
34. Footwear and other leather products	0·32	0·57	0·02	0·05	2·86	0·10
35. Glass and glass products	0·86	1·55	0·93	2·57	2·80	1·44
36. Stone and clay products	1·72	2·40	0·35	6·57	18·68	0·84
37. Primary iron and steel	1·47	2·16	0·44	20·55	42·41	0·94

No.	Item						
38.	Primary non-ferrous metals	1·76	3·09	0·49	25·67	52·73	1·50
39.	Metal containers	0·53	1·35	2·29	0·44	0·20	3·09
40.	Heating, plumbing, structural metal	0·53	1·28	5·06	1·71	1·87	6·47
41.	Stamping, screw machine products	0·53	1·21	0·42	0·79	2·67	0·51
42.	Other fabricated metal products	0·53	1·23	0·28	0·74		0·34
43.	Engines and turbines	1·03	1·66	2·01	21·16	10·57	3·33
44.	Farm machinery and equipment	1·03	1·66	2·48	10·48	4·23	4·11
45.	Construction, mining, oil field equipment	1·03	1·94	14·83	12·45	0·84	28·77
46.	Metals handling machinery and equipment	1·03	1·75	6·48	1·94	0·30	11·35
47.	Metalworking machinery and equipment	1·03	1·53	1·95	5·47	2·81	2·98
48.	Special industrial machinery and equipment	1·03	1·61	0·94	5·88	6·24	1·52
49.	General industrial machinery and equipment	1·03	1·63	4·32	43·63	10·11	7·04
50.	Machine shop products	1·03	1·58	1·23	5·81	4·55	2·02
51.	Office computing and accounting machines	0·49	0·89	2·95	9·92	3·36	2·63
52.	Service industry machines	1·03	1·63	1·88	2·05	1·09	3·06
53.	Electric industrial equipment	0·49	1·07	2·79	6·12	2·20	2·98
54.	Household appliances	0·49	1·22	1·09	1·51	1·38	1·33
55.	Electric lighting and wiring equipment	0·49	1·14	0·65	1·15	1·75	0·75
56.	Radio, TV, communication equipment	0·49	0·84	0·64	5·07	7·97	0·54
57.	Electronic components and accessories	0·49	1·04	2·33	4·33	1·85	2·42
58.	Miscellaneous electrical machinery and supplies		1·11	2·42	9·60	3·96	2·69
59.	Motor vehicles and equipment	1·19	2·04	0·75	75·78	97·03	1·53
60.	Aircraft and parts	0·57	1·06	8·66	26·02	3·01	9·18
61.	Other transportation equipment	0·72	1·31	2·41	3·47	1·44	3·15
62.	Scientioc and controlling instruments	3·37	4·03	5·66	22·07	3·90	22·82
63.	Oprical, ophthalmic, photographic equipment	3·37	3·96	0·98	8·80	9·03	3·86
64.	Miscellaneous manufacturing	1·17	1·67	0·53	16·36	30·66	0·89
65.	Transportation and warehousing	0·53	0·85	0·80	25·90	29·20	0·75
70.	Finance and insurance	0·16	0·38	0·13	0·08	0·61	0·05
77.	Medical, educational, non-profit	0·01	0·29	0·42	6·42	15·30	0·12
RR.	Miscellaneous services	0·69	1·16	4·97	29·29	5·90	5·76
	Total			0·99	$751·40	$608·50	

a Cents per dollar of final sales.
b Millions of dollars.
c Export/import ratio multiplied by *OECL* value.
d Includes I/O nos. 4, 11, 12, 66, 67, 68, 69, 71, 72, 73, 75 and 76.

Source: Ingo Walter, 'The Pollution Content of American Trade', *Western Economic Journal* (March 1973).

national input–output relationships.* The *OECL* differentials could then be used, together with appropriate input and substitution elasticities developed from empirical studies of the responsiveness of trade flows to international prices, to evaluate the impact of pollution-control costs on the volume, direction and product composition of international trade.

What is clear even at this stage, however, is that inter-industry differences in the impact of pollution-control costs are substantial, and that these will be reflected in international competitive conditions and trade flows. They will also be reflected in the need for individual industries to adapt and, for some, the need for substantial structural readjustment.

INTERNATIONAL TRADE AND COMPETITION IN POLLUTIVE PRODUCTS

The foregoing discussion of the short-term international competitive implications of environmental management has dealt almost entirely with *process* pollution. Pollution by products in their normal use or as residuals have been considered only peripherally – in terms of the increases in production costs required to render them acceptable in the various countries that comprise the international market-place – to the extent that they could not be separated from process costs.

Specifically with respect to pollutive products, the added cost of meeting increasingly stringent environmental standards should clearly be reflected in final costs, the rationale being that these incremental charges fall significantly short of the added benefits of a cleaner environment. In the short run, such costs can be wholly or partially absorbed by the firm, for competitive reasons or by government dictate, but over the long term they will indeed be passed forward to the ultimate consumer, user or taxpayer. A probable result is the restriction of final demand for certain goods and services, raw materials and intermediate inputs, with market forces fostering a substitution of products that have lower pollution-control costs for those more heavily subject to cost-increasing environmental norms. Hence, while the market normally fails at internalising environmental externalities attributable to pollutive products, the market may represent the means by which coherent public policy can overcome this inherent flaw in the system.

In international trade the costs associated with removing the environmentally-damaging aspects of pollutive products may be relatively less distortive than process-related costs. This is because all products sold in

* Input–output coefficients are evidently quite important. One study that superimposed U.S. *OECL* values on the Federal Republic of Germany's input–output structure, for example, showed the input-mix of Germany's industry to be significantly more pollution-intensive than for the United States. See Sezai Demiral, 'Pollution Control Costs and International Trade: A Bilateral Impact Analysis', unpublished Ph.D. dissertation, New York University (1976).

a given national market must meet the same environmental standards – and thus bear equally on domestic suppliers of import-competing goods and on foreign suppliers of imports. Hence, the environmental preferences and assimilative capacity in a particular country are essentially *neutral* with respect to international competitiveness, although trade may be affected as higher prices reduce the demand for affected home-produced goods *and* imports. This does not mean, of course, that the costs of environmental product adaptation will be the same for suppliers in all countries, but differences in this respect can be traced solely to efficiency in product adaptation.

However, the product-adaptation cost aspects of environmental management is but one dimension of international trade in pollutive products.* Another concerns the term 'unforeseen side-effects', which will become increasingly important in this field with respect to the socially risky products. Particularly affected will be the chemical and pharmaceutical industries. To cite an example, the Toxic Substance Control Act, passed by the U.S. Senate in May 1972, is a possible harbinger of the future. In essence, no material may be introduced into the environment in the United States unless it has first been convincingly demonstrated that no ecological or human damage will occur, either in the short or the long run, directly or indirectly. The legislation reflects the public's preoccupation with environmental uncertainties and its nagging suspicion that past mistakes and on-going heavy promotion of products with questionable ecological attributes may well indicate competition's failure to encourage socially responsible behaviour on the part of producers – to be remedied only by stricter public controls.[10]

Nobody knows what the ultimate consequences of a new product will be for the ecosystem. But the trend clearly is toward extreme caution, a trend that has reinforced 'negative proof' as the coming, generally accepted code of conduct in the introduction of new materials and the reassessment of existing ones. In practice, this means that rigorous test protocols must be followed in the case of any new product considered environmentally 'sensitive', under the control of a public agency, with the same procedure applied to any existing product that becomes suspect.

The implications for the international economy are several. Costs of compliance with negative proof requirements will be high, and will vary according to the standards and procedures applied. Marketing and distribution will be impaired, both in terms of logistics and time requirements.[11] Innovation may be dampened to some degree by shifting the cost/payoff balance, with increasing concentration in large firms with sufficient human and capital resources to operate under the new conditions. The sensitivity of supply and trade flows to shifts in individual and collective demand

* This discussion is based on Ingo Walter, 'Environmental Management and the International Economic Order', in *The Future of the International Economic Order*.

patterns may be hindered or stretched out in time. Some shifts in industrial structure may result as and when increasing interfirm co-operation and co-ordination in environmental affairs is made necessary, with parallel implications for national and international rules governing anti-competitive business behaviour.

The principal issue confronting international trade in the field of polluting products concerns the *compatibility* of national and regional standards. Even within nations standards differ. For certain products perhaps they should differ. For others perhaps not. In regulating the environmental characteristics of products, where the issue of transboundary pollution does not exist, the political collectivity concerned should be able to define standards in accordance with its assessment of the various alternatives' respective social and economic costs and benefits. Indeed, to the extent that it has political sovereignty, it will insist on that right.

Within nations, due to the economic cost of interregional variations in environmental product standards, a considerable degree of uniformity can be expected. Transition periods may be employed, but national norms will eventually emerge. Between nations, this conclusion does not necessarily hold (a) because the cost of differing product standards to the world economy are not easily identified and measured; (b) because such costs may be less pronounced, given large national or regional markets within which compatibility exists; and (c) because differences in norms may be upheld by virtue of national political sovereignty and in the absence of supranational authority.

International harmonisation of product standards thus may not be a legitimate goal if it leads to a divergence rather than a convergence of marginal social benefits and costs among countries demonstrating different preferences. But even in that case standardisation will be a drawn-out process most likely subject to inter-government agreement on a product-by-product level. For certain products substantive agreement already exists or can be expected in the intermediate term.[12] For others it is not unreasonable to expect ultimate convergence of standards, particularly among the major trading nations or blocs – as their perceptions of the relevant environmental cost–benefit configurations evolve – with other countries subscribing to the product norms that emerge. For still others, there is little prospect of compatible product standards in the foreseeable future. Much will depend on what happens in other aspects of international economic relations. The liberalisation of trade and payments and growing economic interdependence discussed in Chapter 2 will tend to enhance the importance and the apparent costs of variations in environmental product standards and build pressure for unified norms – while the maintenance or growth of international commercial and financial distortions will obscure them.

In the meantime, nations will continue to translate their particular social values and environmental conditions into product standards which, they will (and should) insist, must be met by all goods and services sold in the national market – whether produced at home or abroad. Imports which do not meet these standards will be barred from entry. Whereas the range of products encountering this difficulty is limited at present, it will widen substantially in the intermediate term to include – besides automobiles and other, less important, traded products already subject to environmental controls – a widening array of manufactures such as aircraft, engines, construction equipment, containers, detergents, synthetic fabrics, pesticides, fungicides, fertilisers, food additives and food products themselves, pharmaceutical products, petroleum products, instruments, and so forth. This raises four sets of problems.

The first is the trade-restrictive impact of product-standard variations themselves. Meeting such standards raises costs even under a unified environmental-policy system. Producing for a global market characterised by incompatibilities in standards compounds supply difficulties and multiplies costs. The extent of the problem is highly industry-specific, however, and dependent on the particular microeconomic conditions encountered. Some product lines may be produced efficiently for different markets in different configurations, just as they are supplied to order for individual buyers, and incompatibilities in environment-related product standards will be of little importance. Others may be geared to the strictest norms imposed in any major market and produced in volume according to those standards, with little or no competitive disadvantages in national markets characterised by more lenient or non-existent standards, again with minimal disruption. For still others all output can only be produced one way or the other (for example in agriculture), and if the incremental costs or the efficiency losses encountered in supplying a given market having strict environmental norms are sufficiently high, then that market may have to be sacrificed altogether, entailing potentially serious economic dislocations.

Between these extremes are product lines that can be adapted to different standards with varying degrees of difficulty – including inadequate production runs, product redesign involving additional research and development expenditures, and so on – with disruptive effects likely but perhaps not prohibitive. It has yet to be determined, considering the emerging matrix of international trade flows during the coming decades, to what extent each of these supply characteristics is relevant in the real world, and what this implies for the over-all impact of international incompatibilities in product standards related to the environment.

The second is the problem of discrimination in the treatment of domestically-produced and imported products with respect to their environmental characteristics. While inconsistencies in standards may be disruptive of trade they do not – as noted earlier (pp. 49–51) – distort

the relative cost and price advantages upon which international trade
is based. Indeed, they may reinforce them. However, when the standards, or their administration, are applied to imports in a manner different from import-competing goods, they may take on the role of a protectionist commercial-policy device – a non-tariff barrier (NTB) that is
applied for reasons not related primarily to protection of domestic industry, but that may easily be employed as a trade-distortive device. This
kind of discrimination has proven to be an important source of NTBs in
such closely related questions as packaging and labelling regulations,
health and safety requirements, industrial standards, and so forth. This
is discussed in some detail in Chapter 5.

Thirdly, on the demand side it is clear that the cost and quality
changes brought about by product-related pollution-control standards
will cause a shift in purchasing patterns. Consumers and industrial
buyers will be induced to adopt less-pollutive products in place of those
that are inherently more damaging to the environment, and hence more
costly to bring up to standard. Substitution between different kinds of
fuels, food products, fertilisers and other products is already under way,
and this trend will intensify and spread, with potentially important implications for patterns of international trade. Then too, desirable characteristics of certain products may deteriorate as a result of compliance with
environmental norms – examples of deterioriation in automotive performance and the quality of paints and pigments may be cited – forcing
consumption shifts within the affected product groups or between them.

Fourthly, there is a possible income effect, with reduced consumption
of affected and unaffected products as a result of significant environment-induced increases in product costs as discussed in Chapter 4.

In the capital-goods sector, certain types of equipment may become
obsolete due to their environmental characteristics. Shifts in the generation of electric power from fossil fuels to nuclear energy will have this
effect, as will new 'clean' ways of generating electricity which dispense
with the heat cycle altogether. If public policy fosters the increased use
of mass transit to replace the private automobile, we can expect demand
and trade patterns to shift to other types of vehicles and transport equipment : a shift in trade flows from consumer durables into substitute
capital goods.

Similar developments can be expected in the consumer non-durables
sector. Demand alterations have already affected the detergent industry
and, although international trade in the final product is fairly limited
relative to total demand, trade in intermediate inputs is substantial. The
packaging-materials industry will also be affected as minimum biodegradeability or other standards are applied to products that are deemed
damaging to the environment in the form of solid wastes. More specula-
tive are prospective shifts in demand for food products in response to

concern with agricultural pollution and toxic residues in the food chain. Trade in fisheries products is the most notable example thus far, with certain types of meat and vegetable potential candidates for the future.

It is difficult to gauge the extent to which individuals will shift their product preferences in response to environmental damage entailed in the manufacture of consumer goods. A good deal depends on the coverage by the media and emotionalism, and to a certain extent the effects may be short-term in character; they will diminish as the environmental damage is alleviated or slips from the public consciousness.[13] Trade flows in certain products will be severely affected, but this phenomenon will tend to be intermittent and without a consistent pattern. The one area where a permanent demand shift has affected trade involves furs, skins and other products from animals in danger of extinction (for example crocodile leather, seal skins, ivory, leopard skins, whale meat) as well as certain types of woods (for example redwood) subject to an extremely long growth cycle or otherwise environmentally sensitive. These products have traditionally occupied an important role in international trade, and can be expected to decline to insignificance in the intermediate term – with possible subsequent resurgence in specific products amenable to conservation and 'controlled harvesting' practices.

Perhaps the most important sectors in international trade potentially affected by demand substitution are raw materials and fuels. The sulphur content of fuels has already produced dramatic trade shifts and these can be expected to intensify. The sulphur content of coal and crude oil is important in determining trade flows because it varies significantly by source, rendering certain sources preferable to others. Where it is too high, desulphurisation must be performed before it is acceptable for use as a fuel in stationary heat and power applications, and this influences competitiveness. Trade in natural gas, an inherently clean fuel, can be expected to grow rapidly, particularly in Europe. And where pipelines are not a feasible mode of transport between origin and destination, trade in liquefied natural gas (L.N.G.) can be expected to develop rapidly. For the same reason, trade in nuclear fuels may also grow substantially in the longer run. Although the global increase in fuel costs and problems of supply logistics will tend to overshadow some of the environmental effects, they will nevertheless influence trade patterns in the intermediate term.

There is also likely to be some shift in demand for raw material inputs from synthetics to natural products, particularly where they are close substitutes and where the production of synthetics involves substantial environmental-control costs, as discussed in Chapter 8. Some examples are substitution of natural rubber for synthetic rubber, and wood and leather for plastics. This may succeed in raising prices of certain raw materials and export receipts of countries producing them. It may also increase the elasticity of demand for the products in question and thereby reduce their price volatility, although the problem of supply capabilities remains.

To summarise, we have tried to outline in this chapter the probable impact of environmental control on international competitive relationships – both in terms of conceptual cause-and-effect analysis and, where possible, employing some empirical assessments. The interconnection between environmental management and international competitiveness involve both differential movements in production costs and changes in product standards. The impact of the latter is principally a matter of access to markets, while the former focuses on basic supply capabilities. Whereas the aggregate competitive effects were not considered of critical importance, particularly from a balance-of-payments standpoint, the prospective impact at the industry and firm level may indeed be significant.

FURTHER READING

J. Brashares, 'Cost Estimates for Environment Improvement Programs', in *Managing the Environment: International Cooperation for Pollution Control*, ed. A. V. Kneese *et al.* (New York: Frederick A. Praeger, 1971).

Council on Environmental Quality, Department of Commerce, and Environmental Protection Agency, *The Economic Impact of Pollution Control* (Washington, D.C.: Government Printing Office, 1972).

Ralph C. d'Arge, 'International Trade and Domestic Environmental Control: Some Empirical Estimates', in *Managing the Environment: International Cooperation for Pollution Control*, ed. A. V. Kneese *et al.* (New York: Frederick A. Praeger, 1971).

Ralph C. d'Arge and Allen V. Kneese, 'Environmental Quality and International Trade', *International Organization* (Spring 1972).

General Agreement on Tariffs and Trade, *Industrial Pollution and Industrial Trade* (Geneva: GATT, 1971).

B. P. Klotz, 'The Trade Effects of Unilateral Pollution Standards,' in *Problems of Environmental Economics* (Paris: O.E.C.D., 1972).

S. P. Magee and W. F. Ford, 'Environmental Pollution, the Terms of Trade and the Balance of Payments of the United States', *Kyklos*, Fasc. 1 (1972).

Ingo Walter, 'The Pollution Content of American Trade', *Western Economic Journal* (March 1973).

Ingo Walter, 'Environmental Management and the International Economic Order', in *The Future of the International Economic Order*, ed. C. Fred Bergsten (Lexington, Mass.: D. C. Heath, 1973).

Ingo Walter, *Environmental Control and Consumer Protection: Emerging Forces in Multinational Corporate Operations* (Washington, D.C.: Center for Multinational Studies, 1972).

4

Trade, Environment and Comparative Advantage

Our discussion of the international aspects of environmental management has thus far focused exclusively on short-run competitive considerations, both in the aggregate and in terms of their differential impact on individual firms and industries. The emphasis was on pollution control as a disturbance to international competitive relationships, which tends to generate certain adjustment costs for the various economies involved and which promotes a reallocation of productive factors, both nationally and internationally.

In this chapter we are more concerned with the longer view. After all of the requisite adjustments have been made, how will the underlying structure of the international economy look as a result of pollution control? How, in other words, does environmental management alter long-term comparative advantage in trade and production among the world's economies? The 'surface' competitive effects, which can and will differ by industry and by products, have already been discussed. Beneath this surface lies the question of how the induced structural changes will affect a nation's comparative advantage in the world economy, and how this in turn will influence what it trades, with whom, in what volume, and what its net gains from international commerce will be.

POLLUTION CONTROL AND COMPARATIVE ADVANTAGE

Clearly, when a country makes a commitment to the maintenance and restoration of environmental quality it must devote substantial economic resources to this task. Environmental control absorbs productive factors by using capital and technology to reduce the negative external effects of existing patterns of economic activity. Or it acts by changing ways of doing things from those most efficient in meeting primary economic wants – but which are environmentally damaging – to those less efficient but less damaging as well. In the latter case, if the same degree of want-satisfaction is to be maintained, more resources must be used in the productive process. Alternatively, consumption patterns can be changed, either as a natural result of changing relative prices or by political and administrative means. Even if pollution control raises aggregate social welfare (as it presumably will) it will tend to reduce overall welfare measured in any way that ignores environmental quality. Environmental management is not a free good. It must be paid for, either by fiscal diversion of purchasing power or by monetary diversion through altered prices and factor earnings.

As we have seen in previous chapters, the amounts involved are not small. Current pollution-control spending in the United States comes to around 9.5 billion dollars, about 7.5 billion dollars of which is by federal and state–local governments. Estimates of future environmental spending for the United States point to a doubling over the inter-mediate term (5 years) to 1–2 per cent of G.N.P., and to a further rise to 2–3 per cent of G.N.P. over the long run. Long-range estimates vary widely between nations, presumably due to differences in perceived en-vironmental assimilative capacity and differences in views of what is needed, ranging from 1.4–1.6 per cent of G.N.P. for Sweden to 4–5 per cent for the Netherlands. Such variances are in part attributable to the uncertainties that exist with respect to pollution-control costs under existing environmental conditions, and a narrower range of around 1.5–2 per cent of G.N.P. is likely to emerge for most industrial countries – depending on what yardstick is used for measurement and what stan-dards are applied.[1]

Comparative advantage in international trade is based on a variety of factors, including availability of natural resources, labour, investment in physical capital, investment in human capital, investment in techno-logy, and so forth, all employed in the production of tradeable goods and services. The precise configuration of a nation's capabilities in the supply of tradeable products and services, relative to its demand for them, determines the pattern of trade among nations.

Environmental assimilative capacity enters into the determination of comparative advantage like any other factor of production. Suppose all nations decide to set the *same* ambient levels of environmental quality as a social goal, and that this level has been attained. Countries with greater environmental assimilative capacity will find that they will need to devote relatively fewer resources to pollution control than countries that are less fortunate, given that pollution-control technology is every-where the same. Hence, environmental assimilative capacity can be con-sidered a productive resource, just like labour, capital, land and raw materials. It is an *immobile* resource – in that it cannot itself be transferred internationally – and it governs the amount of resources that must jointly be used to achieve a given volume of production and level of environmental quality.

The modern theory of international trade attributes the volume, direction and product composition of commerce among nations to a variety of factors, of which the following are the most important. (*a*) International differences in the availability of productive factors which determine relative factor prices and which in turn establish the relative cost of internationally-traded products and services via technical input–

output relationships. (b) International differences in factor productivity, that is in the degree of efficiency with which available factors are employed in the productive process. This is in part a result of technology 'gaps' among countries, which may be of varying duration. (c) International differences in the *quality* of productive factors, especially with respect to human skills. (d) International differences in economies of scale and hence in the average size of production units. (e) The nature of the 'product cycle' of traded commodities, which tends to alter the optimum location of production as a product moves through various stages of invention, development, maturity and obsolescence. (f) International differences in demand patterns, and similarities or dissimilarities of relative preferences.[2] All affect international trade through relative costs and prices – taking due account of product quality – the first five (a)–(e) influencing primarily supply relationships and the last focusing on the role of demand.

Perhaps the simplest way to integrate environmental questions into the theory of comparative advantage is through the supply side – to consider environmental assimilative capacity as being simply another factor or production, whose relative abundance will enter into production costs in the conventional manner. The conclusion is that countries with relatively abundant environmental resources (in terms of high levels of environmental assimilative capacity) will tend to have an international competitive advantage in the production and supply of goods and services whose production is relatively pollutive in nature. If each country moves to force the internalisation of environmental externalities, therefore, comparative advantage will inevitably shift, and so will the flow of trade and the economic structures of the countries involved.

TRADE AND ENVIRONMENT IN PARTIAL EQUILIBRIUM

What has been said above can be made clear by means of standard techniques of trade analysis. The simplest is 'partial equilibrium' analysis of trade in a single product between one country and the rest of the world.

In terms of Figure 4.1, standard supply and demand functions for a particular product are drawn for the home (Sh, Dh) and foreign (Sf, Df) country (for the rest of the world) respectively. Without trade the price of the product in the home country would be Pa with quantity Ql produced and sold, while the corresponding price and quantity equilibria abroad are Pc and Qm. Since $Pa > Pc$, if trade is permitted between the two countries Pa will fall as import supplies become available, while Pb will rise as supplies are withdrawn from the domestic market for export. Equilibrium is attained when the price in the two countries is equalised (assuming no transport costs) at Pb, in which case the production excess abroad ($QcQd$) is exported to the home country, where it exactly equals the production shortfall ($QaQb$) at that price. With trade, in the home country Qa is produced domestically, Qb is consumed and $QaQb$ is imported, while abroad Qd is produced, Qc is consumed and $QcQd$ is exported.

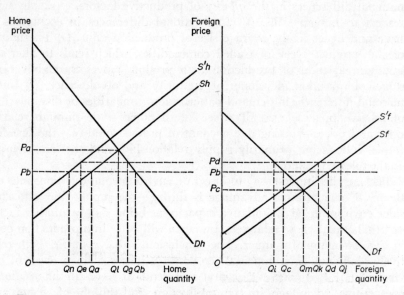

FIGURE 4.1   Pollution control and international trade in partial equilibrium

Now suppose pollution control is imposed on suppliers in the home country. If the 'polluter pays' principle is applied, this may be represented as a leftward shift in the home country's supply function from Sh to $S'h$, indicating that each quantity can only be supplied at a higher price. If the price of imports were to remain constant at Pb, the result would be no change in domestic price or quantity consumed, but an increase in imports from $QaQb$ to $QnQb$, with $QaQn$ of increased imports displacing a like amount of domestic production. Supply conditions abroad, however, will not permit the price to remain constant. Instead, the additional export demand will tend to raise prices abroad, and a new equilibrium price Pd will emerge at which import demand $QeQg$ exactly equals export supply $QiQj$. Output has increased abroad by $QdQj$, while consumption has declined by $QcQi$, both in response to the price rise due to increased export demand. In the home country, price has also risen and demand fallen by $QbQg$, while domestic supply has declined by $QaQe$ – but not by as much as it would have fallen if import supply had been perfectly elastic.

In short, domestic pollution control will tend to increase the volume of imports and the share of imports in satisfying domestic demand, probably at a higher price. At the same time, the supplier countries will find exports rising and some upward pressure on prices, which will tend to discourage domestic consumption and encourage increased production for export.

Suppose, on the other hand, the pollution-control costs impacted on the exporting country, causing a leftward shift in the supply function from Sf to $S'f$. The higher price that results will tend to depress domestic consumption and, via increased export prices (Pd) reduce consumption as well in the home country $(QbQg)$. It will also increase domestic production in the home country from Qn to Qe, partly replacing the reduced volume of imports $(QeQg)$.

Hence, international trade invariably reacts to shifts in pollution-control costs. How great this reaction will be depends on the relevant elasticities of supply and demand. In any case, some of the production displaced by environmental policy will be taken up abroad, thus reallocating pollution as well as production and consumption through international trade.

GENERAL EQUILIBRIUM: RESOURCE DIVERSION AND TRADE

The points raised in the discussion above can be reinforced and made more general by considering a simple two-product model of international trade and economic structure under the assumption that a country eliminates environmental externalities by devoting appropriate economic resources to this task. It thus shifts productive capabilities from things that can be traded internationally to something that cannot – from the production of tradeable goods and services in demand in the international economy to the achievement of environmental balance. As a result, each country's ability to produce tradeable goods and services is lower than it would otherwise have been. In economic terminology, the transformation function as between importables and exportables, in the presence of resource diversion induced by pollution control, falls below where it would be in the absence of environmental protection.

The question is whether or not the reduced potential output is *symmetrical* between those goods and services that a country tends to import and those it tends to export. If it is, the impact of pollution control is relatively neutral: a country's comparative advantage is unchanged, although the volume of, and gains from, international trade decline. Its terms of trade (export prices relative to import prices) also will tend to remain the same, with price of both export- and import-competing goods increasing.

But suppose environmental control does *not* impact on the trade sector symmetrically. Suppose, for example, the kinds of economic activities required for environmental management happen to absorb larger amounts of capital than labour or other productive factors, both in terms of tangible (plant and equipment) and research and development investments required, to achieve a given quantum of environmental protection, however measured. As a result, pollution-control activities will employ relatively greater amounts of capital than joint factors of production. In terms of conventional trade theory, if a country happens to be capital-abundant relative to other productive factors – and exports capital-intensive products and services while importing those using intensively other productive factors – the impact of environmental control on trade cannot be symmetrical.

Potential output of importables (non-capital-intensive goods and services) will decline relatively *less* than potential output of exportables, and this erodes the basis for the nation's comparative advantage in the international economy. Both its comparative advantage in exportables and its comparative disadvantage in importables are reduced, and its production mix of tradeable goods and services becomes less specialised in the export sector. Assuming balanced trade, the volume of trade declines significantly *more* than in the case of equivalent neutral-incidence environmental control, as does the country's gains from international commerce and its corresponding loss in real income.

At the other extreme, suppose the country specialises in the production of *labour-intensive* goods and services, and pollution-control techniques again happen to be fundamentally capital-intensive. The result now is quite different. Potential output in the import-competing sector is reduced substantially *more* than that of labour-intensive exportables. The volume of (balanced) trade may again decline, but less than in the earlier case, and the erosion of gains from international commerce may also be less serious. Indeed, in terms of economic structure the country actually may specialise to a greater degree in the production of exportables than it did before the pollution-control measures were imposed.

In diagrammatic terms, suppose we categorise goods and services produced by an economy into exportables X, importables M and environmental damage avoidance E.* Using a three-dimensional space, we can thus draw an XME transformation surface presented in Figure 4.2, with the standard transformation function for tradeable goods and services lying in the XM plane. Suppose, further, that social preferences can be expressed in the form of a convex XME community indifference surface (not drawn). If no resources are currently being devoted to environmental management, the indifference and transformation surfaces will be tangent at some point in the XM plane and so will the common

* This discussion follows Ingo Walter, 'Resource Diversion and International Trade: The Case of Environmental Management', *Weltwirtschaftliches Archiv* (December 1974).

tangent representing relative product prices, with environmental damage avoidance given a zero price.

Assume that the international terms of trade are given by the slope TT (the 'edge' of the XME relative-price plane) in Figure 4.2, and that

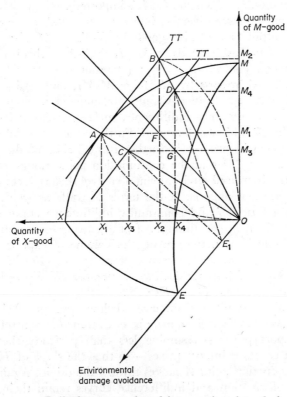

FIGURE 4.2   Pollution control and international trade in general equilibrium

the XM price ratio is equal to the marginal rate of transformation at A and marginal rate of substitution in consumption at B – again in the XM plane. This production mix is OX_1 (of which X_1X_2 is exported) and OM_1, while the consumption mix is OM_2 (of which M_1M_2 is imported) and OX_2. Now suppose that consumers' preferences shift away from conventional goods and services, here represented by X and M goods, and toward avoidance of environmental damage – the value they attach to the latter (and the price they are willing to pay for pollution control) rises relative to X and M. If everything else remains the same the respective tangencies of the price-indifference and price-transformation surfaces will move along vectors BO and AO, and the relative-price plane will 'tilt' – it becomes steeper in the ME and XE planes – as the price attached by society to environmental damage avoidance rises. A new production equilibrium such as C would produce positive environmental damage avoidance E_1, but the tradeable production mix is now OX_3 (of which X_3X_4 is exported) and OM_3, and the consumption mix is now OX_4 and OM_4 (of which M_3M_4 is imported).

We note that resource diversion into environmental management has: (a) reduced output to tradeable goods by $X_1X_3 + M_1M_3$; (b) reduced consumption of tradeable goods by $M_2M_4 + X_2X_4$ – this is the real cost of environmental control to society; (c) reduced exports by $X_1X_2 - X_3X_4$; (d) reduced imports by $M_1M_2 - M_3M_4$; and (e) increased production and consumption of environmental damage avoidance by OE_1. Given the new community indifference surface, social welfare at consumption point D is higher than at B. Further shifts in social preferences in this direction will produce a further inward shift of the production point along vector AO and the consumption point along vector BO in the XM plane. Increased environmental control thus reduces the volume of both imports and exports. If the terms of trade as well as the XM transformation function and community indifference curve remain the same as successively larger amounts of productive resources are siphoned off into environmental management, the volume of exports declines as per the horizontal distance between vectors AO and FO in Figure 4.2, while the volume of imports declines as per the corresponding vertical distance between vectors FO and DO.

A more likely result (as discussed below, pp. 90–3) is that the country's terms of trade will improve as environmental-control costs force a rise in export prices – assuming less than perfectly elastic foreign demand and constant import prices – so that the slope of TT becomes steeper as production point A moves toward the origin. Again assuming that the transformation and indifference curves retain their shape. the path of the production point falls below AO and is asymptotic to the X-axis, while the consumption path falls to the right of BO and is asymptotic to the M-axis. In short, the pollution-control-induced improvement in the terms of trade tends to bias the output mix toward the X-good and increases the degree of national economic specialisation. At the same time, it biases the consumption mix toward the M-good, and permits the maintenance of a level of welfare *above* that possible without positive terms of trade effects.

The traditional factor-endowments theory of international trade, in order to determine the direction and product composition of trade flows, assumes biased production functions – engineering characteristics of products so that X is 'naturally' K-intensive, M is L-intensive, and so on.[3]

We have already noted that environmental assimilative capacity can be added as simply another productive factor, in terms of the E-intensity of tradeable goods and services. Suppose environmental control, representing production of non-tradeables, is itself K-intensive – the literature seems to suggest that this is possible, indeed likely.[4] Referring again to Figure 4.2, this means that the environment-control-induced shift of the transformation function toward the origin in the XM plane occurs asymmetrically.*

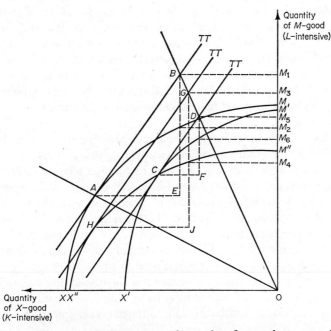

FIGURE 4.3 Asymmetrical resource absorption for environmental control

The result can be seen in Figure 4.3, which reproduces the XM plane of the previous diagram except that the export- and import-competing goods are specified as capital and labour-intensive, respectively. Proportional diversion of resources into environmental management would, as indicated earlier, cause the production and consumption points to recede along vectors AO and BO. If environmental control is capital-intensive, on the other hand, the new transformation function might be $X'M'$. If it is labour-intensive, $X'M''$ might apply. Given proportionate shifts in consumption levels, the first case can be seen to undermine the country's comparative advantage, leading to reduced specialisation in production and a major reduction in the volume of trade. The second strengthens the basis of a country's comparative advantage and may even increase the volume of trade. As a result, the initial gains from trade (measured in

* That is, if X is K-intensive and M is L-intensive, then
for every ΔE $(-\Delta X/X)/(-\Delta M/M) > 1$.

terms of M-goods) of $M_1 M_2$ decline to $M M$ if EC is K-intensive but $M_3 M_4$ if it is L-intensive. In short, resource diversion in the first case can be seen to undermine the country's comparative advantage, leading to reduced specialisation in production and a major reduction in the volume of trade. The second strengthens the basis of a country's comparative advantage and may even increase the volume of trade. As a result, the initial gains from trade (measured in terms of M-goods) of $M_1 M_2$ decline to $M_5 M_6$ if pollution control is K-intensive but $M_3 M_4$ if it is L-intensive. In short, resource diversion into environmental management influences the relative gains from trade – negatively if environmental control uses intensively those productive resources on which a country's comparative advantage is based, and positively if the reverse is true – which in turn will either increase or offset its net cost to society, in terms of conventional goods and services.

From the standpoint of international comparative advantage, therefore, factor intensity of environment-control techniques will affect a nation's gains from trade, both in absolute and in relative terms as international prices respond to pollution-control-induced import and export price changes. One is tempted to speculate, therefore, that even if environmental-control standards are identical between nations, and enforced identically, using the same mix of factor inputs, the trade effects of environmental management will still not fall evenly upon the nations of the world. Those countries whose international competitive advantage is based on the same factor/resource/efficiency matrix underlying environmental control will be affected differently from those countries whose trade position relies on a fundamentally different configuration of supply factors.

If the foregoing is correct, than an assessment of the long-term impact of environmental management on the economic structure and international trade of individual countries depends upon reliable empirical estimates of the pollution intensity of international trade. Such estimates have already been discussed briefly in the previous chapter and substantial inter-industry variations were noted. They were based on the estimated cost of pollution abatement in export- and import-replacement production, and it was determined that for the United States exports were slightly more pollution-intensive than imports.

Another way to approach this problem, again using input–output techniques, is to ascertain the physical volume of pollutants associated with export- and import-replacing production. The assumption is that physical volumes of emissions are indicative of the economic cost of removing them. A recent study – again of U.S. trade and limited to air pollution only – seems to show that U.S. exports are more pollution-intensive than imports with respect to emissions of sulphur oxides (2342.28 versus 2329.32 thousand tons), carbon monoxide (1887.76 versus 1511.84 thousand tons), but the U.S. imports are more pollution-intensive when it comes to particulates (1194.4 versus 800.91 thousand tons), hydrocarbons (216.93 versus 136.57 thousand tons) and nitrogen oxides (220.85 versus 208.21 thousand tons), using 1963 trade data.[5] Data such as the latter seem to indicate that the specific type of pollution to be dealt with is of major importance in determining its implications for international trade and comparative advantage.

THE DEMAND SIDE : ENVIRONMENTAL PREFERENCES AND TRADE

The foregoing discussion has considered only the traditional determinants of international trade as they affect comparative costs and supply capabilities. The second half of the problem involves an assessment of the demand for environmental quality and its bearing on trade and economic structure. As noted, demand for environmental quality will determine the extent to which resources must be devoted to pollution control, and supply-related factors will determine the impact of this shift on trade flows.

We have already made the case, in Chapter 2, that the desired level of environmental quality (DEQ) will vary internationally at any given point in time. If DEQ is indeed sensitive to income, this alone introduces an element of international variation. There may also be shifts in the DEQ functions themselves as 'environmental consciousness' is diffused, with leads and lags arising in the process. Population density may play a dual role as a factor affecting the level of DEQ on the demand side, but also representing a determinant of environmental assimilative capacity (EAC) on the supply side, for example via the environmental impact of crowding and human waste. The latter also applies, as we have noted, if EAC is measured in terms of *human absorption* of pollutants rather than ambient levels of environmental quality.

Referring back to Figure 1.1 (p. 20), two otherwise identical countries are characterised by identical environmental-damage functions (EDF). One (X) operates at a level of output such as Q_2 and would be able to expand output substantially without diverting resources into environmental equilibrium at A, and would have to divert resources into pollution control, in order to grow, by shifting its EDF to the right.[6] Costs of all tradeable goods in Y would rise relative to those in X, but some would rise more than others depending on their respective pollution-intensities and efficiency in the required diversion of resources. Moreover, suppose DEQ is characteristic of country XX and DEQ' applies in country Y. At levels of output above its own equilibrium, country Y would be similarly disadvantaged in trade with X – and even over output-range Q_3–Q_4, increments in output would still disadvantage Y in trade because DEQ is more elastic with respect to Q than DEQ'.

But quite apart from the relevance of the demand for environmental quality in determining the necessity of shifting resources into environmental management, demand factors will have a direct bearing on international trade and resource allocation in at least three ways.

First, a systematic effort to improve the environment may depress real income spendable on conventional goods and services below what would otherwise be attained. And since trade is in part a function of income, international trade flows may also fall somewhat below alternative levels. Different products and services will respond differently to the income effect of environmental management, depending on the income elasticity of demand. Hence, apart from a reduction in the over-all volume of trade, a shift in the direction and product composition of trade may also be expected to arise out of the income effect.

Secondly, we have already seen that each internationally traded product or service has a unique environmental 'profile', that is the environmental costs associated with its manufacture, use and ultimate disposal at the end of its useful life. If environmental externalities are fully internalised in accordance with the 'polluter pays' principle, these profiles will be reflected in incremental pollution-control costs, the relative size of which will be highly product-specific. 'Pollution-intensive' products will rise in price relative to those less sensitive to environmental costs, and this will tend to induce substitution both in consumption and in production inputs. This substitution is bound to be reflected in international trade in the products concerned, and hence in international patterns of production.

Thirdly, environmental control may give rise to the development of a wide variety of goods and services (particularly those that are technological in characteristic) that are internationally traded. Products considered pollutants is their normal use will have to be altered in character to conform to new requirements. In the process, entirely new substitutes will evolve or existing products will be modified using new components. For example, trade may take the form of rights to new automotive anti-pollution equipment, or platinum and other metals for catalystic converters, which can be traced to tightened environmental regulations in the automobile industry, as can aircraft-engine modifications to alleviate particulate emissions. Similarly, trade in new products and services will arise out of requirements to minimise the pollutive attributes of residuals, including a variety of chemicals, biodegradeable and recyclable containers, and other products.

But there is even more potential for the development of trade in hardware and software for use in pollution control. If we are correct that variations in environmental management among at least the industrialised nation states are largely manifestations of lead–lag relationships rather than long-term, enduring absolute differences, then the need for environmental control will eventually influence all national economies. This follows even if its incidence at any point in time may be quite different among individual countries – depending on its specific seriousness at the national and subnational level and on the accompanying political perceptions and public-policy reactions.

Leader-countries and affected firms will tend to be in the forefront in the development of pollution technology which, in turn, becomes highly exportable – through consulting services, licensing and other channels – to countries less advanced in this respect. Furthermore, certain types of pollution-control hardware embodying this technology will evolve into competitive products on world markets. Examples include filters, wet scrubbers, electrostatic precipitators, waste-recycling equipment, cooling towers, sewage-treatment plants and components, measuring devices and instrumentation, materials-handling equipment, and so forth.

Assuming that this proposition is correct, countries leading in the pollution-control effort will then tend on balance to emerge with a competitive advantage in international markets for the relevant product and services. The U.S. market for air-pollution equipment alone is expected to grow from 150 million dollars in 1970 to 600 million dollars in 1980. Preliminary estimates gauge the size of the combined U.S.–European market in the mid-1970s at over 1 billion dollars and growing at the rate of about 20 per cent annually through the early 1980s. If such projections are accurate then the global market including Japan and the other industrial countries, as well as (eventually) the developing nations, could be very substantial indeed.[7]

Moreover, a demonstration effect may develop whereby new and more efficient ways of coping with environmental problems emerge under pressure in the leading countries, causing lagging countries to adopt more vigorous standards and enforcement, and forcing their industries to conform using the technology and hardware developed abroad. A principal factor in this process may be the multinational enterprise, which has the advantage of almost instantaneous intra-firm transfers of the appropriate technology (see Chapter 6). It simply applies capital and technology in the lagging countries to meet environmental requirements that it has already met elsewhere, adapting the most advanced methods and most efficient hardware available globally to the situation in question.

Much depends, however, on what the 'product cycle' for environmental-control hardware looks like.[8] It is clear that required research and development efforts will be massive, and that much of the resultant manufacturing activity will be highly specialised and tailored to the relatively narrow requirements of specific jobs, both in terms of separate items and as components of major production facilities such as steel mills and petrochemical plants. But how rapidly can the built-in technology be transferred? And to what extent will 'standard' products such as pumps, compressors, tanks, fine-mesh stainless steel and fabric filters, and so on, be involved? There is considerable evidence available that points in one direction or the other, but no coherent pattern has emerged as yet. Consequently, it is premature to speculate on what the over-all impact of this phenomenon on trade flows will be.

THE TERMS OF TRADE

If environmental management influences international trade and specialisation through resource diversion on the supply side, and patterns of conventional and pollution-control goods and services transactions on the demand side, its influence will make itself felt in large measure through international price shifts. This means that export and import prices of individual countries will change and so may their terms of trade – defined, once again, as the ratio of export prices to import prices. And since the terms of trade in part determine a country's gains from international specialisation, or more precisely its share of the gains, the influence of environmental policy on the terms of trade may be of considerable importance.

On the supply side, we have determined that, all else being equal, a country that moves ahead of others is likely to have to face rising production costs of internationally traded goods and services. In other words, the prices of goods that it exports as well as goods that compete with its imports will tend to rise. If the country is too small to influence the prices of goods that it buys from the rest of the world, actual import prices will be unaffected and the induced rise in export prices will tend to improve its terms of trade. A country thus receives more imports per unit of exports, its share of the gains from international trade increases, and this welfare gain may partly offset the welfare loss (measured conventionally) associated with the cost of pollution control. Since its terms of trade improvement means, by definition, that those of its trading partners must deteriorate with associated welfare losses, it means that a part of the economic cost of pollution control in leader-countries will be imposed on lagging countries via shifts in the terms of trade. International trade thus may spread the cost of environmental management to other nations, whether or not the latter engage in environmental programmes of their own.

On the other hand, if the home country is a relatively large market the terms-of-trade effects of pollution control may turn out to be correspondingly less. In other words, the increased competitiveness of imports on the domestic market may cause foreign suppliers to raise their prices. Hence, both export and import prices may rise with a correspondingly smaller improvement in the terms of trade (if any at all).

Whereas the supply and price responses to environmental management may generate a terms-of-trade improvement for countries leading in the field of environmental control, demand-related elements may influence the terms of trade as well. If we are correct in presupposing that leading countries will develop into exporters of pollution-control hardware and technology, for which demand may subsequently develop abroad, this could also benefit the nation's terms of trade if it is reflected in higher export prices. But this may be of marginal importance and could easily be offset by higher input prices paid for pollution-control equipment and technology purchased from abroad. Lastly, there is the more general demand reorientation from pollution-intensive to less pollutive products which could, depending on a country's trade structure, lead to either an improvement or a deterioration of a nation's terms of trade.

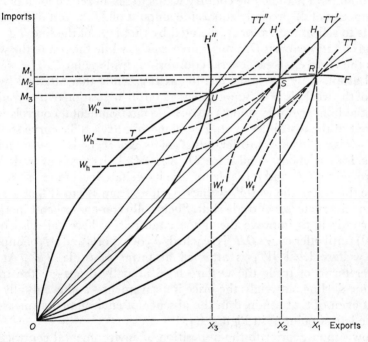

FIGURE 4.4   Environmental control and the terms of trade

Whether any terms of trade shift caused by environmental control leads to a net welfare gain depends for a particular country on the relevant starting-point – that is the pre-existing structure of tariffs, subsidies and other distortions of international trade that exist. This can readily be demonstrated with a standard diagram such as Figure 4.4. The vertical axis measures the quantity of imports the country is able to obtain M, in return for the quantity of exports it has to give up X, measured on the horizontal axis. Curve OH is the so-called free-trade 'offer curve' of the home country: how much of X it is willing to give up for how much of M at all possible M/X exchange ratios – given by the slope of a straight line from O to any point on OH. The higher the M/X exchange ratio – the terms of trade – the more of X it is willing to give up in return for M. The offer curve bends backwards because the marginal utility of X rises as more and more of it is exported, while the marginal utility of M falls as more and more is imported. Hence the incremental offer of X per unit of M falls throughout the length of OH. The corresponding offer curve for the home country's trading partner, the rest of the world, is OF and gives all possible amounts of M it is willing to export in return for X at increasingly favourable (for it) X/M exchange ratios.

There is one particular M/X exchange ratio, or terms of trade, where the amount of X the home country wants to sell in return for a particular amount of M precisely equals the amount of M the rest of the world wants to sell in return for X, denoted by the slope of the line TT. The home country exports OX, and imports OM, while the rest of the world does the reverse, at the general equilibrium trade point R. The welfare level attained by the home country is W_h, while that attained by the rest of the world is W_f.[9] Suppose we start from a position of free trade R, and the home country adopts cost-rising environmental controls while the rest of the world does not. The home country's offer curve shifts to OH' – it is willing now to offer only X_2 of its export goods in return for M_2 of the import goods – and since $M_2/X_2 > M_1/X_1$ its terms of trade have improved to TT' and it is able to raise its welfare level from W_h to W'_h while the rest of the world's welfare declines from W_f to W'_f as a result of the adverse terms of trade shift. Such pollution-control cost increases can continue to improve the home country's welfare (all else being equal) until offer curve OH'' is reached, X_3 of exports and M_3 of imports, and welfare level W''_h is attained at terms of trade TT''. At still higher terms of trade the welfare level actually drops – as the trade-volume decline outweighs the price improvement – and eventually falls short even of that attained in the absence of environmental measures, to the left of point T in Figure 4.4.

Now suppose, prior to the imposition of environmental controls, the home country maintained a complex of trade distortions such that the maximum attainable welfare level at point U (W''_h) had already been reached. In such a case, the terms-of-trade effects of pollution control would in all likelihood be negative. Alternatively, if tariffs and other trade distortions yield an intermediate trade point such as S, pollution-control costs may or may not produce an improvement in the nation's welfare. In assessing the effects of pollution control on the level of welfare of a country, therefore, a determining factor is what other kinds of trade distortions exist, and how they have *already* affected the terms of trade.

There are two further points. First, the less elastic the foreign offer curve, the greater will be the likelihood of an induced terms-of-trade improvement. A perfectly elastic foreign offer curve means the the home country is a 'price-taker' and can sell nothing abroad above the going price and can buy nothing from abroad below the going price – hence the terms of trade are fixed, and *OF* is a straight line. Secondly, pollution-control costs may affect foreign countries as well, in which case *OF* will shift to the right and the net terms-of-trade effect is indeterminate; it will depend on the relative price changes in the two sets of countries.

To summarise, international trade and comparative advantage will be influenced by environmental management in a fundamental sense. Pollution control will affect relative prices, which will be reflected in international trade flows. Countries with substantial environmental assimilative capacities for specific types of pollutants will develop a comparative advantage in products whose supply is relatively pollution-intensive. The resultant shifts in trade and production will also reflect differences in environmental preferences, and will tend to bring about a socially more efficient use of environmental resources on an international scale. Both the short- and long-term adjustments to new equilibria that incorporate environmental resources, however, depend in large measure on the policy instruments that governments use in environmental management. This will be the subject of the next chapter.

FURTHER READING

William Baumol, 'Environmental Protection, International Spillover, and Trade', Wicksell Lecture, Stockholm (1971).

R. C. d'Arge and Allen V. Kneese, 'Environmental Quality and International Trade', *International Organization* (Spring 1972).

B. P. Klotz, 'Trade Effects of Unilateral Pollution Standards', in *Problems of Environmental Economics* (Paris: O.E.C.D., 1972).

Anthony Y. C. Koo, 'Environmental Repercussions and Trade Theory', *Review of Economics and Statistics* (March 1974).

A. Majocchi, 'The Impact of Environmental Measures on International Trade: Some Policy Issues', in *Problems of Environmental Economics*.

Horst Siebert, 'Trade and Environment', *Beitäge zur angewandten Wirtschafts-forschung*, University of Mannheim, mimeo., no. 40 (1973).

Horst Siebert, 'Comparative Advantage and Environmental Policy', *Beitäge zur angewandten Wirtschaftsforschung*, University of Mannheim, mimeo., no. 43 (1974).

Horst Siebert, 'Environmental Protection and International Specialization', *Beitäge zur angewandten Wirtschaftsforschung*, University of Mannheim, mimeo., no. 44 (1974).

Ingo Walter, 'Resource Diversion and International Trade: The Case of Environmental Management', *Weltwirtschaftliches Archiv* (September 1974).

Ingo Walter, 'Environmental Management and the International Economic Order', in *The Future of the International Economic Order*, ed. C. Fred Bergsten (Lexington, Mass.: D. C. Heath, 1973).

5

Neutrality of Instruments: Pollution, Protection and Efficiency of Policy

The impact of environmental management on international trade and the location of production, as outlined in Chapter 3 and 4, has been examined under the implicit assumption that the internalisation of environmental externalities and its impact on competitive relationships between nations proceeds without government interference. In other words, as processes and products are modified to meet collectively-established environmental norms, the costs are fundamentally reflected in product prices or factor returns, and the international competitive effects – both short and long term – are allowed to work themselves out via normal competitive relationships within the context of the market.

This is fine in theory, and permits the formulation of some reasonably coherent cause-and-effect relationships that can serve as the basis for prediction. But it is not necessarily the way the world works, and the *techniques* which nations use to implement environmental policy are of central importance in gauging its international economic consequences.

DOMESTIC AND INTERNATIONAL POLICY RESPONSE

We have tried to emphasise that the process of economic and social adjustment to a new set of environmental standards is by no means a costless one. Jobs will be lost, plants will close, transport will be disrupted – all of which represents transitional burdens on society as a whole, but more particularly on those immediately affected. The size of the adjustment costs depends at least in part on the time available for the required changes to work themselves out : the more rapid the required adjustment, the higher will tend to be the resultant costs. Few will disagree that adjustment to new standards of environmental quality will eventually have to be undertaken. But there is a great deal of argument about how this adjustment will come about, how high the costs will be, and who will pay the price.

On the domestic side, economists have long argued that maximum efficiency and minimum economic distortion in applying environmental controls is achieved when these controls are enforced by means of effluent charges. The polluter is faced with a tax which is set at a level such that the cost of increasing pollution is greater, at the margin, than the cost of internalising it. Effluent changes are set at whatever level provides the needed incentive to reduce pollution to the desired level. Polluters, in turn, are encouraged to pursue environmental management in the most efficient possible way, and distortions in resource allocation are minimised as the polluter passes on the increased operating costs to the factor and product markets, respectively, in accordance with prevailing competitive conditions in each.[1]

Effluent charges are, of course, only one of the instruments available for pollution control, and together with enforcement of standards can be categorised under the 'polluter pays' principle (PPP), which has been accepted by member countries of the Organisation for Economic Cooperation and Development (O.E.C.D.) as the most appropriate implementation framework.[2] There are, however, a number of issues dealing with equity and cost allocation which suggests that the PPP will not be – perhaps *should* not be – universally observed if such possibly competing national priorities as income redistribution and regional development are to be met as well.

The principal economic dislocations of concern in environmental management involve the differential impact of pollution control on the production-cost structures of competitive suppliers operating under different political jurisdictions and environmental assimilative conditions. The latter may be regarded as given. The former may be minimised in the case of interregional economic disturbances by means of decisions at the national level that promote domestic co-ordination and harmonisation – given a judgement that the cost of such dislocations to the national economy outweighs the cost implicit in enforced uniformity. In the absence of a similar decision process at the *international* level – which may lack both validity and practicality – some degree of competitive impact is inevitable and probably desirable, as we have already noted. This essentially mandates cost internalisation along the lines of the 'polluter pays' principle, and departures from the PPP can be regarded as distortions of international competition with a negative impact on resource allocation, at least in the short run. Even if the PPP is followed, countries may be tempted to neutralise the resultant competitive pressure on domestic suppliers via offsetting import restrictions or export subsidies. Such countervailing trade-policy responses cannot be justified on economic grounds, but this hardly means that they will not be employed. These two policy issues will be examined in this chapter.

THE 'POLLUTER PAYS' PRINCIPLE: OBJECTIVES

Ideally, whatever international economic dislocations do emerge from pollution-control policies reflect valid differences in inter-country environmental preferences and assimilative conditions. They should reflect a more rational use of environmental resources on a transnational basis. Achievement of this objective presupposes that the techniques employed in environmental management do not *themselves* trigger significant distortions of international competitive conditions and the international allocation of production. Environmental control techniques should, in so far as possible, be trade-neutral. Thus, the document formalising acceptance of the 'polluter pays' principle in O.E.C.D. states quite explicitly:

> This principle means that the polluter should bear the expenses of carrying out . . . measures decided by public authorities to ensure that the environment is in an acceptable state. In other words, the cost of these measures should be reflected in the cost of goods and services which cause pollution in production and/or consumption. Such measures should not be accompanied by subsidies that would create significant distortions in international trade and investment.[3]

Accordingly, we shall outline briefly the salient characteristics of the PPP with reference to its role as a guideline, or *norm*, for national and international environmental policy.

Equity

Under the PPP, the cost of internalising environmental externalities is at least partly passed forward to consumers of final products, in proportion to their direct and indirect expenditures on those products. The ability to pass forward environmental-control costs depends largely on the relevant price elasticities of demand and supply. Charges associated with pollution control are thus distributed generally in proportion to the incidence of environmental damage-avoidance costs. They depend on the volume and composition of consumption of individual products, which satisfies conventional criteria of horizontal and, in part, vertical equity.* The question is whther departures from the PPP in the allocation of costs will sacrifice, or retain, the desirable equity characteristics of the PPP.

There is no unequivocal answer. Suppose, for example, tax-financed pollution control is viewed as an alternative to the PPP. If the products involved are standard consumer goods, the consumption of which generally parallels the incidence of taxation, it may not matter from an equity standpoint whether the PPP or tax-financed pollution control is applied – although some shift in the degree of progressivity seems inevitable. On the other hand, the PPP could have a *regressive* or *progressive* incidence in comparison with tax-financed pollution control, depending on the specifics of the national tax structure and the product mix involved. And the equity dimension of the PPP becomes even more complex when

* See Richard A. and Peggy Musgrave, *The Theory of Public Finance*, revised edn (New York: McGraw-Hill, 1973). Horizontal equity is defined as equal treatment of equals, while vertical equity is defined as unequal treatment of unequals in taxation.

suppliers of productive factors are considered, since they may also bear some of the costs of pollution control in the form of reduced earnings.

The precise input, output and competitive-structure characteristics of each industry determines the incidence of environmental-control costs under the PPP, and must be compared with the composite national tax structure in order to determine whether the PPP or tax-financed pollution control is more efficient as an allocative principle, from the standpoint of achieving a given equity target.

What would be required is a concordance of affected constituencies under the two alternatives, in the light of income-distribution goals set by society, to determine the implications of departures from the PPP from the standpoint of equity. Whether or not equity considerations favour the PPP thus remains indeterminate, but needs to be considered in any cost–benefit analysis of this particular issue.*

Demand patterns

A second advantage claimed for the PPP is that by forcing environmental damage-avoidance costs to bè reflected in product prices it will alter demand patterns in ways beneficial to environmental balance. Products whose manufacture generates significant environmental externalities will rise in price relative to less pollutive products. Consumers and producers will be induced to shift their purchasing decisions accordingly, and the resultant output mix may prove less pollution-intensive than the alternative.

The extent to which adherence to the PPP causes the kinds of beneficial substitution effects just mentioned depends on the relevant cross-elasticities of demand in consumption, and the corresponding input-substitution elasticities in production.† These parameters clearly will vary widely, (a) according to the degree of substitutability among the variety of products involved, and (b) according to the time-frame within which the adjustment can take place. Indeed, in some cases restructured demand will come about only very gradually – particularly in the area of basic renewable and non-renewable materials and fuels.

Regardless of the prospective magnitude of PPP-induced shifts in output, however, there can be no doubt that the direction of change favours a more rational use of environmental resources. Policy departures from the PPP which do not have this effect, therefore, may perpetuate resource misallocation. They may be intended to alleviate the transi-

* There are, of course, a variety of broader issues concerning the question of equity. How does equity *after* environmental control compare with its distribution *with* pollution? What about the issue of implicit rights? A broader treatment of this question is outlined in W. J. Baumol, 'Environmental Protection and the Distribution of Incomes' in *Problems of Environmental Economics* (Paris: O.E.C.D., 1971).

† That is, the sensitivity of consumption and input-use patterns to relative product and input prices.

D

tional costs of pollution control, but may result in perpetuating efficiency losses to society which cannot be ignored.

Residual damage

In many instances, efforts to assure environmental control are not complete, regardless of the techniques used in their implementation. The goal of zero discharge – even if it is deemed environmentally appropriate – may not be possible given the state of the art, or its social and economic consequences may be considered excessive. Consequently, residual environmental damage may be unavoidable, at least within conventional public-planning time-horizons. Although the issue depends heavily on the structure of 'rights', the point is frequently made that individuals and groups impacted by such residual damage should be adequately compensated and 'polluters should pay not just for their actual control costs, but also for the costs imposed on others by the pollution which is *not* eliminated'.[4]

Adherence to the PPP may facilitate the residual-damage problem. The PPP-induced demand shifts serve to reduce the extent of residual damage *at the source*, while the concept of residual damage removal in turn complements possibly favourable equity characteristics of the PPP. Perhaps more important, once the principle has been accepted that the polluter must pay for eliminating environmental damage, it follows that he must compensate those affected by damage which cannot be eliminated. Such compensation seems less likely where instruments are employed that represent departures from the PPP. There is also the point that the PPP will minimise residual damage by maximising incentives for the recovery of waste materials for resale, thus reducing the net cost of pollution control and reducing the volume of solid waste.

Trade Neutrality

Perhaps the most important advantage claimed for the PPP is that it tends to minimise international competitive distortions arising from pollution control. It thus promotes the flow of trade and productive factors in ways that coincide with the dictates of international competitive advantage and it maximises gains from the efficient use of resources – including environmental resources – as discussed in Chapters 3 and 4.

The PPP tends to promote, in each sector, production shifts in favour of countries with relatively large environmental assimilative capacities for the specific pollutants involved, and at the same time tends to favour production shifts in the benefit of countries where collective preferences dictate lower environmental standards. There is a parallel set of incentives relating to the movement of productive factors, which reinforces international competitive pressures on the trade side and encourages an additional efficiency-inducing shift in the locus of production. Application of the PPP also supports efficiency in the achievement of environmental standards by providing constant pressure to reduce the capital and operating costs of pollution control. We have already seen that assessment of the impact of environmental management on international trade and factor flows, especially in the short run, is predicated on adherence by major competitor countries to the PPP. The greater an intercountry deviation from the PPP, the less the neutrality of environmental instruments with respect to international economic relations.

The international competitive implications of the PPP depend heavily on whether the relevant environmental-control costs are in the nature of fixed or variable charges. If they are variable costs they will tend to influence the pricing and output behaviour of the firm rather directly, thereby passing part of the costs forward in the form of higher prices. The extent to which a price increase develops depends largely on the prevailing competitive structure in each industry – the lower the degree of effective competition, the greater the anticipated net price change. If it is true that industries subject to heavy international competition tend to be characterised by more competitive market structures, the impact of PPP-induced cost increases may be felt relatively more strongly in production cut-backs than in price increases. In the case of fixed costs, there may be little or no immediate price response – according to conventional microeconomic theory – and the burden of pollution-control costs will be borne initially by productive factors, principally in the form of reduced profitability of the affected enterprise.

To summarise, the PPP embodies a number of distinct advantages from the standpoint of equity, induced shifts in demand patterns, alleviation of residual damage and trade neutrality. It serves as a coherent rule governing the application of environmental policies, a rule without which chaotic conditions could well develop in the international competitive arena – with each country working to shield its producers as much as possible from adverse competitive trends, and in the process sacrificing many of the advantages of the PPP in promoting optimum utilisation of environmental resources on an international basis. In the case of departures from the PPP, therefore, the burden of proof falls on the advocates of such departures : it must be demonstrated that their benefits, in social or economic terms, outweigh the PPP-related benefits forgone.

DEPARTURES FROM THE 'POLLUTER PAYS' PRINCIPLE : OBJECTIVES

We have noted that the PPP has taken on the role of a *norm* in evaluating pollution-control instruments. Like many norms, it can only be adhered to without exception under certain conditions, for example in a static context, with costless economic and social adjustment and adaptation, and in the absence of conflicts among societal goals.* Free trade is a similar norm : it is based on conditions that cannot be attained in the real world, and hence free trade will never be – perhaps should never be – attained. This makes the norm no less important as a benchmark, and as a condition whose implications are well known and considered generally desirable. Against the above list of justifications for mandatory application of the PPP, one can develop a corresponding array of reasons why such adherence may not be entirely appropriate under all circumstances.

Transitional expediency

As national environmental policy is applied, the process of transition to a new and more viable balance between economic and environmental considerations may prove costly in several respects. Changes in production techniques or product characteristics may be mandated, which can involve severe dislocations at the level of the enterprise : production lines may have to be shut down; scale economies may be lost for a time; and workers may be laid off. Adjustment burdens may call the financial health of firms into question. A case can be made for public assistance to help meet transitional adaptation costs of this type. The public as a whole will benefit from adaptation which forces environmental balance, and hence the public as a whole should help defray the transitional economic burdens. This principle has been widely accepted in the form of 'adjustment assistance' under a wide variety of circumstances, ranging from import competition to the effects of rapid technological change. The affected productive factors may claim special aids when it can be shown that injury has clearly followed from environmental measures. To be acceptable as a departure from the PPP, such aid must be based on legitimate-injury criteria, must be clearly transitional in nature, and must indeed facilitate – not impede – actual economic disengagement and efficient adjustment to the new conditions.

Moreover, if the entire adjustment cost were in fact lodged with the firms and productive factors most directly involved, resistance to increase pollution abatement might be so severe as to jeopardise the environmental objectives sought. Depending on the political strength and economic size of the impacted sectors, postponement or even abandonment of environmental goals would hardly be out of the question.

The sharing of transitional adjustment costs through public assistance

---

* The social-benefit dictates in a given country might be in conflict with the international trade interests of other countries. In such cases, a decision has to be made, at the national level, whether domestic interest in departures from the PPP is more critical than the national interests of those countries affected by the departure and its subsequent feedback to the home country.

may not represent a permanent exception to the PPP. As in Figure
5.1(a), the percentage of environmental charges falling on final-product
prices – all else being equal – starts and ends at 100 per cent at the initial
and terminal target levels of environmental quality, but falls below 100
per cent in the interim along a time-path such as R. This makes possible
a hypothetical product-cost time-path such as T in Figure 5.1(b), instead of S. The former, indeed, may not be attainable if productive factors are displaced transitionally or even permanently. Closely related to

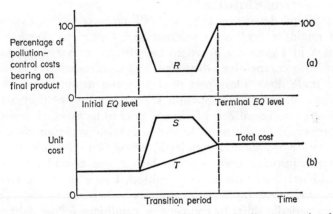

FIGURE 5.1 Transitional departures from the 'polluter pays' principle

the equitable *distribution* of environmental adaptation costs is the goal
of minimising the *size* of the costs themselves. Their magnitude is highly
industry-specific. Capital equipment may or may not be useful in production other than that for which it was originally intended. Labour
skills may or may not be readily transferable to different tasks. The same
is true of land inputs. One of the goals of environmentally-efficient adaptation should be to minimise such adjustment costs, and publicly-financed
programmes on a large scale may help to reduce the over-all adaptation
costs to society.

One of the most important determinants of structural adjustment
costs, as noted earlier (pp. 37–9), is the time element. A case can be
made, therefore, for individual exceptions from the PPP in order
to stretch out the adjustment interval and reduce its real cost to the
economy. This may be done, for example, by using graduated subsidies
that make it clear that eventual adjustment is mandatory, but permit
adjustment to occur in a more gradual and orderly way.

Adaptation costs may also be reduced by providing for environmental infrastructure at public expense. There are significant economies of scale, for example, in regional waste-treatment facilities, financed from public revenues. The region may benefit from reduced pollution and its people may be dependent on local jobs, and hence regional authorities may be as willing to finance environmental infrastructure investments as to finance local highways. Part of the cost, to be sure, will eventually fall on the polluting firm via increased taxes, but hardly sufficient to comply with the spirit of the PPP. To some extent, the cost allocation of infra-structure-type pollution-control investments may be aligned with the PPP through user charges. Financing of the residual may have to be considered necessary departure from the PPP.

Transitional departures from the PPP make sense too if the objectives are to minimise traditional international distortions. Price movements such as S in Figure 5.1(b) would be reflected internationally as an adverse shift in competitive advantage, and a corresponding abrupt alteration of trade flows. Only part of this impact would be permanent and productive resources in competitor countries would be drawn for export production into the affected industry, only to be expelled again once the transition ends. Furthermore, if several major competitor countries move to higher environmental standards, disruption of trade flows – and resultant adjustment costs – might be far greater under the PPP than if transitional departures were permitted. Unless timing of environmental measures were uniform, mandatory adherence to the PPP would result in periodic shifts in competitive conditions followed by partial or full restoration of initial competitive relationships, and the resultant two-way displacement of trade flows and productive resources could prove extraordinarily costly.

Whereas transitional departures from the PPP seem legitimate, even desirable – partly on equity grounds and partly on efficiency grounds – there remains the question of how long the transitional period may be. Since case-by-case variations in the time dimension are probably inevitable, advocacy of transitional departures from the PPP becomes operational only if a firm commitment is made at the outset to limit the duration of whatever aids are granted.

Risk coverage

In the course of formulating environmental targets and instruments, considerable uncertainty may be imposed upon business enterprises. Levels of environmental quality that are acceptable today may not be acceptable tomorrow. And those projected for the future may be – and frequently are – changed as society's preferences change. Businessmen are understandably hesitant to invest in pollution-control hardware or to alter operating procedures when these may subsequently prove inadequate and have to be modified at considerable cost. This is particularly important given the widely-held view that the capital cost of retrofitting existing plants to meet higher pollution standards far exceeds the incremental capital cost of achieving the same standards with new plants.

The risk element in environmental control is an important consideration, especially since the issue falls into the political sphere, and since there remains major uncertainty in the scientific community about the nature of environmental-damage functions. It might be argued that firms should insure themselves against such risk by charging higher prices and building up reserves. But the pressure of competition almost surely will preclude this. Besides, since much of this risk has its origin in the public-policy nature of the environmental-management problem, a strong case can be made that the public as a whole should – for purposes of equity – bear some of this risk in the form of transitional economic aids. If, for example, the rules of the game are changed *ex post*, it might not be considered an unacceptable departure from the PPP for government to defray some of the costs of resultant erroneous decisions made at the enterprise-planning level.

Technical obsolescence

Another potentially valid exception to the PPP, closely related to the one preceding, is coverage by governments of incremental costs arising out of technical obsolescence of pollution-abatement hardware. Under the PPP, firms may be reluctant to invest heavily in environmental-control equipment if there is a likelihood that technical innovation will produce substantially more efficient means of accomplishing the same thing in the foreseeable future. The firm may incur additional costs if it is forced to scrap equipment before it is fully depreciated, or additional opportunity costs if it continues to operate with old equipment when a new generation of hardware is already available. As a result, firms may seek in every way possible to delay action, and the achievement of environmental goals may be made considerably more difficult.

It may thus be possible to justify tax-financed assistance to firms facing redundant costs that can be ascribed to technical obsolescence. In effect, the public is assuring the firm that it will lose nothing by moving ahead on environmental control with all deliberate speed and, in effect, insuring the firm against technology-induced risk. In return, the pace of pollution abatement may be materially accelerated. While departures from the PPP may be accepted in order to achieve this objective, there are operational problems in defining cost redundancy induced by technological advance, and the problem may have to be approached with *ex post* assistance for re-equipment projects.

Acceleration of goal achievement

Another possible justification for departures from the PPP is to accelerate improvements in environmental quality, in order to compress the time-table that would obtain if the financing of pollution abatement rested solely with the enterprise – even if firms did go along willingly with stronger environmental controls. Achievement of environmental objectives combined with the preservation of economic viability may be a slow process indeed. A government that decides to compress its pollution-control time-table by means of aid from public fiscal resources has made an implicit judgement that the social benefits of the stream of environmental damage avoidance that results from acceleration, properly discounted, exceeds the applicable economic costs.

Here the time preference for environmental management is the determining factor. If the motive is indeed to accelerate pollution-abatement schedules – using public fiscal resources in the face of a host of competing needs for such resources – the sacrifice of PPP advantages may be considered unavoidable. Indeed, if subsidies are held to be incremental costs resulting from acceleration, there may be little real damage to the PPP. It can also be argued that the international competitive impact of accelerated pollution control using public assistance may not in the end be very different from much more gradual pollution control without such assistance.

Conflicting social and economic objectives

Almost inevitably, the goal of restoring and maintaining environmental balance will conflict with other objectives to society. Examples include (a) minimum unemployment, (b) maximum industrial production, (c) price stability, (d) upgrading the economic status of disadvantaged social groups, (e) income redistribution, (f) regional development of industry, (g) minimum effective transport costs, and so forth. The possibility of such conflict seems especially strong when the PPP is applied, and may reinforce some of the kinds of structural adjustments identified earlier.

When there is a conflict between pollution abatement and another social objective, there are two alternatives. Either goal may be sacrificed to the other, or the linkages that connect them may be severed – so that achievement of one objective does not automatically imply abandonment of the competing objective. This separation frequently may involve explicit or implicit subsidisation. Such subsidies, however, need not be applied to the environmental target, thus forcing a departure from the PPP. They may, instead, be applied to the competing social goal. In a conflict between regional development and environmental quality, for example, public assistance may be focused on the development target without violating the PPP. There are, of course, cases where such fine distinctions cannot be made, and where departures from the PPP attributable to conflicting social and economic objectives are inevitable.

Alleviation of accumulated damage

The question of environmental reparation of past accumulated damage – the *stock* of past pollution rather than the *flow* of current pollution – is an important one. The real beneficiaries of past pollution, according to the converse of the PPP, are the factors employed in the polluting industries and the purchasers of the output of those industries at the time the pollution occurred. It may not be appropriate to ask current productive factors and consumers to pay for reparation, since the two groups (present and past) are entirely different. Both tax-financed environmental reparation and the PPP involve a transfer of real income to a generation whose revealed preference for environmental damage avoidance was lower than that of the current generation. Consistent application of the PPP to the problem of environmental reparations may result in dramatic short-term shifts in costs, prices and productive-resource adjustments – all of which are temporary and may be seriously disruptive. This problem alone may be sufficiently important to justify departures from the PPP for reparation purposes.

Research and development expenditures

One type of departure from the PPP has become a recognised exception, in that governments have made an implicit judgement that its benefits outweigh its costs; this comprises research and development costs associated with environmental control. Scale economies in research and development activities may be significant. Centralised, government-sponsored research activity may generate the necessary technical advances more quickly and more efficiently than fragmented efforts on the part of individual enterprises. Once innovations have been generated, moreover, they tend to be diffused very rapidly, both nationally and internationally.

Research and development thus may benefit domestic *and* foreign suppliers in meeting environmental objectives with relatively short time-lags, both in the scale of technology abroad and in the development of industries producing innovative pollution-control hardware for export. International competitive distortions in this respect caused by non-adherence to the PPP thus may well be minimal, especially when viewed against the background of widespread tax-financed research and development in other sectors – such as aerospace, electronics, and so forth. As a departure from the PPP, tax-financed research and development appears to be non-controversial in nature and clearly delineated in scope.

Upgrading in-place industrial capacity

Another argument that may be used to justify financial assistance for pollution control is that the required resources exceed the financial capabilities of the individual enterprise. For infra-marginal firms, mandatory adherence to the PPP and enforced upgrading in the quality of capital equipment will tend to raise the fixed costs of the firm. Since there is no direct impact on marginal costs, profit-maximising behaviour does not indicate any immediate change in price or output, although it does tend to produce a reduction in profitability. Infra-marginality indicates that the firm can continue to operate indefinitely, and that factor owners will tend to bear part of the costs of pollution abatement. Fewer new resources may flow into the affected sector, and in the long run economic structure may change, but this is indeed one of the intentions of the PPP. The character of business behaviour, of course, may not follow the dictates of microeconomic theory. The firm may try to maintain a target rate of return on invested capital or follow a share-of-market or sales-maximising strategy, in which case the additional fixed costs may well have an impact on prices and output. In any case, for the infra-marginal firm – regardless of the incidence of the PPP-induced costs – it is very difficult to make a case for departures from the dictates of the PPP.

A different argument may apply in the case of marginal enterprises. The increased fixed costs may induce losses, which permit continued operations in the short run but eventually lead to shutdown. Transitional aid of the type mentioned earlier may be justified. If the net additional cost of re-equipment is entirely subsidised, no disruption of international competitive relations may be noted – since price and output tend to remain unchanged – but it nevertheless represents a potentially serious misallocation of resources. There seems to be little argument that pollution-control costs associated with new plant should not be subsidised by the public. Retrofitting of existing plant on a subsidised basis may, on the other hand, be justified under certain circumstances for marginal firms.

Cost-sharing

One of the serious practical problems encountered in the field of environmental management is the allocation of pollution-control costs associated with incremental industrial development in a region where acceptable levels of environmental quality have already been attained. For example, suppose in a given airshed existing stationary sources of air pollution have, over a span of several years, reduced emissions to 20 per cent of those prevailing in a given base period, and that this effort is in conformity with the PPP in terms of cost allocation. The new ambient level of air quality is acceptable to the authorities and, implicitly, to the populace. Suppose, now, a new plant is proposed for location within the airshed, creating new jobs, income and economic activity.

There are several alternatives : (a) permit the new firm to locate, but force it to conform to a zero-emissions standard; (b) forgo the new investment and deny permission to locate; (c) permit the investment and force all existing polluters to reduce emissions still further, so that the target level of ambient air quality can be maintained – with the new firm conforming to the new, tighter standards; (d) permit the new investment, and use public subsidies to reduce emissions of the new firm, existing firms, or both; and, (e) relax environmental standards and permit the new investment in conformity with presently allowable individual plant emission limits.

Each of these solutions is conceivable, and all except (d) conform to the spirit of the PPP. However, they are hardly likely to be adopted. Solutions (a) and (b) may turn out to be the same thing if zero emissions are impossible to achieve with existing technology and within given economic contraints. Option (c) is potentially feasible, but runs the risk of driving out existing firms, who may anticipate successive additional reductions in permissible emissions with future new investment in the region. Alternative (d) is also feasible and may be justified fiscally in terms of the growth dividends that the new investment is expected to bring. Option (e) is a very real possibility, but clearly defeats the purpose of environmental control.

If we exclude zero emissions and relaxed standards as viable alternatives, and also exclude the prohibition of new investment as politically irrelevant, we are left with the two cost-sharing alternatives (c) and (d). Option (c) is in conformity with the PPP, but existing firms find the rules of the game changed through no fault of their own and may face potentially disruptive cost increases and competitive disadvantages. Hence public assistance may be called for, and option (d) is the most likely outcome. Its violation of the PPP may be lessened if it is financed by taxes bearing on the firms involved or by fiscal levies that are eventually reflected in factor costs that have to be paid by the polluting enterprises.

Cost-sharing is a difficult problem in perspective of the PPP, all the more so because it is likely to be encountered rather frequently in practice. None the less, relative to the other alternatives, it may represent the indicated solution under given political and economic conditions.

To summarise, the above array of possible motivations for departures from the PPP is based on the concept that the social or economic gains in each instance may outweigh the damage inflicted on the desirable characteristics of the PPP, including its trade-neutrality. The intent must be to come as close as possible to achieving both sets of objectives simultaneously, and where this is difficult an explicit trade-off must be identified which will make clear the choices involved.

Conceptually, the 'theory of second best' applies here.[5] The goal is to minimise the gap between marginal social costs and marginal social benefits in all aspects of economic activity. Any policy measure which serves to narrow this gap, after all of its implications have been identified, must be considered desirable. According to the theory, a move toward international trade liberalisation may or may not be desirable, depending on competitive structure in the affected industries, factor markets, and so on. In the same way, pursuit of the PPP as a policy goal may or may not be desirable, depending on a wide variety of specific elements which must differ from one case to the next.

Lastly, if strict application of the PPP shows itself to be unacceptable economically or politically in a given country under given circumstances, the same conditions may prevail abroad as well. If major competitor countries are forced to depart from the PPP under similar conditions, again the international trade effects may be held to a minimum. The greater the inter-country synchronisation, whether or not through international organisations, of environmental standards and techniques, the fewer will be the competitive distortions that arise.

DEPARTURES FROM THE 'POLLUTER PAYS' PRINCIPLE : INSTRUMENTS

Having discussed in detail the social and economic *objectives* of adherence to – and departures from – the PPP, it is necessary to consider the *techniques* actually employed to bring about environmentally beneficial changes in economic activity. All may be considered departures from the PPP, but some will be seen as less distortive of international trade than others.

Capital grants

These represent an outright form of subsidisation by governments of productive enterprises. They may be awarded directly to the enterprise in order to reduce the capital outlays required for pollution-control facilities. As a result, depreciation charges and the firm's cost of capital per unit of output are lower that would otherwise be the case. Capital grants may also be awarded, *indirectly*, to local or regional pollution-control facilities. In terms of the international competitive implications and the objectives of the PPP, it would seem that capital grants are most objectionable in the short run if they are indirect and lead to an effective lowering of average variable costs. They may also be objectionable, even if no variable-cost reductions are involved, to the extent that they raise effective factor returns and in the long run draw additional resources into the affected industry or retain redundant productive factors.

Concessionary loans

Loans may be made to a firm for purposes of pollution control, either directly by government or indirectly by public authorities, at rates of interest and/or amortisation terms more favourable than those ordinarily available competitively from financial institutions. Credit guarantees may also be extended to the firm, permitting it to borrow at rates more favourable than would otherwise be the case. Interest subsidies may be used, whereby part or all of the incremental interest cost associated with pollution control is underwritten by the state. All such techniques effectively reduce the cost of capital to the individual enterprise, thereby lowering average fixed costs and raising the firm's profitability. Again, this may not impact on competitive conditions in the short run, but may do so in the long run.

Concessionary leasing

This represents another way of reducing capital costs associated with pollution control. The required equipment may be purchased by public authorities and leased to individual enterprises on terms more favourable than they would obtain if the firm had to acquire comparable equipment itself. The enterprise saves on capital requirements, and its costs may be lowered due to cheaper credit available to government agencies (and subsequently embodied in leasing costs) as well as outright below-cost leasing. Sale-and-lease-back arrangements may also be used, whereby the enterprise invests in pollution-control equipment, sells it to a public agency at cost, and leases it back on concessionary terms. Leasing of capital equipment in general appears to be growing rapidly in importance, and hence this form of implicit subsidisation may likewise grow in significance in the future.

Operating subsidies

Government aids may be applied in cases where costs associated with running pollution-control facilities are considered significant – perhaps beyond the capabilities of the individual firm. They may represent a transitional device intended to accelerate the achievement of environmental objectives. They may include training operational personnel, the cost of technical assistance, materials, testing expenses, and so forth. Governments may agree to defray a certain percentage of the operational costs involved, either permanently or as a temporary arrangement. Operating subsidies may defray fixed costs, but may also involve variable costs if the relevant expenses depend on the volume of output, and there may be a significant short-term impact on international competitiveness.

Effluent charges, either directly or in the form of other policy tools such as taxes, can also represent departures from the PPP if such charges do not reflect the real cost of removing the damage otherwise inflicted. In effect, the government subsidises the polluting unit. Industry will have lower variable costs than otherwise would be the case, and in the short run will be in a better competitive position – especially if similar industries in other countries receive no aid at all, or receive a kind of aid that affects fixed costs only. Research and development subsidies were discussed earlier as one basic departure from the PPP. For the individual enterprise, subsidised research and development carried on *externally* may reduce costs that otherwise would have to be borne by the firm itself. The savings primarily involve fixed costs. Such savings may be even greater if the subsidised research and development is carried on *within* the firm itself, and the government thus may defray an additional portion of common fixed costs. Its competitive implications operate largely on the long-range profitability of the enterprise and resource allocation.

Tax abatement

Tax relief is really nothing more than implicit subsidisation by government of capital or operating expenditures associated with pollution control. A certain percentage of capital investment for this purpose may, for example, be granted as a credit against taxes due. Or a 'tax ceiling' may be used which limits pollution-control costs to a certain percentage of value added, with costs in excess of this amount being offset by equivalent reductions in tax liabilities. The tax relief under such schemes may employ either direct or indirect taxes, and influence either fixed costs, variable costs or the profits of the enterprise. If, for example, the tax relief involves sales or value-added levies, the impact on price is similar to a reduction in variable costs. If it involves property taxes, on the other hand, the effect is similar to a reduction in fixed costs, and will impact principally on the profitability of the enterprise. The same is true if relief involves direct taxes. In both of the latter cases there may be long-run international competitive consequences via induced shifts in resource allocation, but there may also be short-run repercussions if the firms behave in other than a profit-maximising way.

Accelerated depreciation

This is a distinct form of tax relief associated with capital investment for pollution control. By writing off a pollution-control facility more rapidly than other assets, the enterprise can effectively reduce its current tax burden and employ the resultant savings for productive purposes. The savings are attributable to the discount factor in cash flow over time. Because it is associated with fixed capital investment, accelerated depreciation influences the fixed costs of the firm, thus having primarily longer-range competitive implications.

Access to tax-financed waste-treatment facilities

Enterprises may discharge liquid or solid wastes into facilities that are operated by municipal governments, local waste-management authorities or regional networks. Such facilities may be justified by economies of scale, which can drastically reduce the cost per unit of effluent processed, and the resultant reductions in variable costs at the enterprise level are often entirely warranted. The PPP in this instance assumes that user-charges are imposed on the enterprise equivalent to the *pro rata* cost of waste treatment attributable to its operations. This equivalence may be difficult to bring about in practice, especially when the waste-disposal facilities are financed via indirect taxes. To the extent that the enterprise finally pays less than its *pro rata* share of the costs, the difference between what it *actually* pays and what it *should have* paid amounts to a subsidy of variable costs – with direct impact on prices, output and competitiveness.

Cost-sharing in regional authorities

This technique is closely related to the foregoing type of potential departure from the PPP, except that whatever costs are imposed on the enterprise are likely to take the form of user-charges. These may vary according to the amount of effluent processed or solid waste generated, or they may take the form of time-charges. Governments may subsidise regional authorities from general tax revenues, and this will reduce user-charges well below what would be required to cover full costs. Without government subsidy, distortions attributable to regional authorities are likely to be less than for tax-financed waste-treatment facilities. Whatever distortions do occur will tend to make themselves felt by influencing the variable costs of the enterprise.

Cost-sharing within industry associations

A firm's pollution-control costs may be met partly from a pool of resources at the industry level. Such resources may be assembled from contributions by all members of an industry association, and may then be disbursed to individual enterprises on the basis of need. This may assist enterprises in regions especially impacted by environmental controls, or firms that may fall into the marginal category and be unable to raise the required resources themselves. Industry pooling of pollution-control funds may also be assisted by implicit or explicit government subsidies.

Standards relaxation and schedule extensions

Where production pollution or residuals pollution is involved, relaxation of pollution standards would presumably bear equally on both domestic and foreign goods sold in the national market. Where process pollution or raw materials recovery pollution is involved, on the other hand, both variable and fixed costs of each affected enterprise will be reduced. If relaxation is undertaken specifically to alleviate international competitive pressures attributable to pollution control, it can be considered a departure at least from the spirit of the PPP. However, such measures may, in most instances, involve transitional adjustment problems so that the distortion may well be removed within a relatively short period of time. None the less, short-term international competitive shifts could materialise.

General industrial aids

If the PPP is appropriate in the environmental sector, then presumably other kinds of social costs ought also to be fully reflected in final product prices. The fact is, of course, that they are not. Each nation maintains a complex of implicit and explicit subsidies which pervade competitive conditions in a wide variety of industries. They range from tax concessions, subsidised financing of property and plant acquisition, and relocation assistance to concessionary freight rates, export subsidies, government direct and indirect sponsorship or research and development costs, and maintenance of entire industrial sectors through defence procurement and related practices. Against this background it would not appear that government aids specifically for pollution control are of cardinal significance.

There is also the problem of distinguishing departures from the PPP contained in government aids primarily granted for other (unrelated) purposes. Regional development programmes, for example, may include provision for capital or operating subsidies involving pollution control, either supplied directly to enterprises or through regional authorities. Such subsidies, in whatever form, clearly represent departures from the PPP. It would, however, be extremely difficult to separate the non-PPP component from general or specific industrial aid policies. And even if this were possible there is some question whether it would be wise. Regional or industrial assistance programmes are going to be carried out regardless of the PPP, since they are governed by other social and economic priorities. It would appear preferable to see such projects carried out in ways that are environmentally sound, rather than to force neglect of the environmental issues by attempting to prevent such projects altogether on PPP grounds. Solution of this problem seems possible only if a 'general agreement on aids to industry' can be reached among the major industrial countries.

COMMERCIAL POLICY AND POLLUTION CONTROL

Earlier sections of this book have emphasised the point that international differences in environmental programmes will influence competitive conditions and trade flows, and that this influence can be traced to (a) differences in target levels of environmental quality, (b) differences in environmental assimilative capacity, and (c) differences in national approaches to pollution control and in the instruments used in their implementation. The latter emphasised adherence to, and departures from, the PPP. It is not unreasonable to conclude, on balance, that variations will inevitably arise in all three areas, and that this is certain to be reflected in international competitiveness, trade flows and economic adaptation.

It is possible, indeed probable, that the instruments of commercial policy will be employed to countervail this adaptation, or at least to soften its impact by slowing it down. If the social cost of adjustment is reduced thereby, it is possible to justify the latter on economic grounds. We have stated repeatedly that it is not similarly possible to justify the former – to neutralise permanently the influence of environmental factors on international trade. This does not mean, of course, that it will not be attempted or that it may not succeed in certain cases, with resultant misallocation of environmental and other resources at the global level.

For example in the United States, Section 6 of the Federal Water Pollution Control Act Amendment of 1972 (Public Law 92–5000) explicitly instructs the Secretary of Commerce to determine

> The probable competitive advantage which any article manufactured in a foreign nation will likely have in relation to a comparable article made in the United States if that foreign nation –
>
> (a) does not require its manufacturers to implement pollution abatement and control programs,
> (b) requires a lesser degree of pollution abatement and control in its programs, or
> (c) in any way reimburses or otherwise subsidizes its manufacturers for the costs of such programs;
>
> Alternative means by which any competitive advantage accruing to the products of any foreign nation . . . may be (a) accurately and quickly determined, and (b) equalized, for example, by the imposition of a surcharge or duty, on a foreign product in an amount necessary to compensate for such advantage; and the impact, if any, which the imposition of a compensating tariff or other equalizing measure may have in encouraging foreign nations to implement pollution abatement and control programs.[6]

There is a close similarity between external diseconomies related to environmental damage and conventional trade distortions in that they create a gap between social costs and private costs, as reflected in product prices, thus engendering a similar misallocation of resources and a gap between realised and potential social welfare.

There is another similarity in that both trade restrictions and pollution control are a matter of public policy, hence products of the same collective decision process. Tariffs, non-tariff barriers and pollution control thus can all be viewed – from the standpoint of domestic manufacturers – as part of a single protective structure. Effective protection is reduced (increased) with reduced (increased) tariffs and non-tariff barriers on internationally traded final products, increased (reduced) trade barriers applied to intermediate inputs, and increased (reduced) *internalisation* of domestic environmental externalities on both final products and inputs. Environmental externalities have a parallel on the export side in that they represent an implicit subsidy that results in an underpricing of goods sold abroad, a subsidy which is reduced as soon as internalisation of the external social costs begins to be enforced.

The net effective rate of protection of domestic industry provided by a nation's tariff structure is

$$\frac{t_j - \sum_i a_{ij} t_i}{1 - \sum_i a_{ij}}$$

where t_j is the tariff rate on a final product, t_i is the tariff rate on an input, and a_{ij} is the proportion of the final sales value of output j contributed by input i.[7] If we let n_j and n_i represent, respectively, the tariff equivalents of non-tariff barriers applied to the final product and each input, then the corresponding net rate of protection afforded by such distortions is

$$\frac{n_j - \sum_i a_{ij} n_i}{1 - \sum_i a_{ij}}$$

Since pollution-control costs g imposed domestically on producers of final products and inputs can only *negatively* affect the competitiveness of the former, their contribution to the net rate of effective protection is

$$\frac{-(g_j + \sum_i a_{ij} g_i)}{1 - \sum_i a_{ij}}$$

and the composite net rate of protection embodying all three variables is

$$\frac{t_j + n_j - g_j - \sum_i a_{ij}(t_i + n_i + g_i)}{1 - \sum_i a_{ij}}$$

How important are the cost effects of environmental norms in relation to tariffs and non-tariff distortions of trade? If, for example, a given product is already subject to quantitative import controls, then tightened national environmental standards will have little or no impact on domestic producers' competitive viability in the home market. If high effective tariffs or other levies already severely restrict imports, the additional effect-ive protection afforded by foreign pollution-control standards, or the loss of effective protection in the case of domestic environmental measures, may be marginal. One study of the importance of the *g* variable relative to the *t* and *n* variables in the industry profile of U.S. protection – abstract-ing from any environmental-control costs that may be embodied in import-ed inputs or final products (and which cannot be affected by U.S. policy) – showed that the direct pollution-control costs of the final-products industries are about 11 per cent of the nominal tariff rate. Over-all direct and indirect environmental-control costs are approximately 4 per cent of value-added, representing 27 per cent of effective protection afforded by tariffs and non-tariffs barriers.[8] This indicates, in a preliminary way, that the economic costs involved in pollution control are not insignificant *relative* to the degree of effective protection currently afforded U.S. industry. Continued trade liberalisation and tightened environmental con-trols envisaged for the future will further tend to increase the importance of this factor to the extent that corresponding costs are not simultaneously imposed on principal competitive foreign suppliers.

All the more likely that pollution control, especially its implementation via instruments that do not conform to the PPP, will be met by compensa-tory commercial policy action. Again a distinction must be drawn between *product* and *process* pollution-control measures and then possible trade-policy responses in the form of non-tariff barriers.

On the product-pollution side, the issue is quite simple: products that do not meet domestic standards may not be imported. Various techniques are available to enforce this dictum.

(1) *Embargoes*, which generally play a minor role in international commercial policy, have already been mentioned as potentially taking on substantial importance in connection with environmental activities. Automobiles that do not adhere to emission control or safety standards are already embargoed in some countries. It is not difficult to visualise extension of embargoes to such products as plastic and aluminium pack-aging materials, certain types of plastics, products containing certain chemicals, and even products such as newsprint which are not composed, to a specific degree, of recycled wastes.

(2) *Customs procedures* can be applied to restrict trade for environ-mental reasons, particularly when they are imposed in conjunction with licensing and other certification measures. It may well be, for instance, that certain products considered environmentally sensitive will be subject

to automatic import licensing, with the licence awarded only after all of the requirements of the importing country have been satisfied. So long as the degree of rigour applied to imports does not exceed that applied to home-produced goods, one cannot object to this procedure. Nevertheless, there is substantial scope for misuse in any licensing and certification scheme, and it may easily be applied in a highly protectionist manner – either as a matter of policy or on a discretionary basis.

(3) *Consular formalities* may also be employed. Environmentally sensitive imports could be required to obtain consular clearance and compliance certification, which might include inspection of manufacturing facilities. This system induces additional costs, delays and uncertainties, and provides ample scope for misuse in a protectionist manner.

Problems currently encountered in *state trading* and *discriminatory government procurement* may grow when the requisites of pollution control go into effect. Public procurement, which already discriminates heavily in favour of domestic suppliers in most countries, may be limited to domestic goods when imported products are deemed harmful.

Even if environmental standards for imported goods are no more stringent than for home-produced goods, and enforcement of such regulations can lead to substantial costs and uncertainties on the part of foreign suppliers. Unless there is clear-cut mutual acceptance of certifications concerning the salient environmental characterisitics, as well as mutual acceptance of inspection and other procedures, serious trade distortions may result.

A number of other international competitive distortions may arise in response to pollution-control efforts. These include selective import prohibitions, variable import changes and advance deposit requirements. On the export side as well, restrictions may be imposed on products whose supply is deemed damaging to the domestic environment – timber represents perhaps the most striking example.[9]

On the process-pollution side, environment-induced trade barriers are likely to involve compensatory import charges – particularly when environmental measures abroad depart significantly from the PPP and/or domestic measures are wholly or partly implemented by punitive treatment or rigorous enforcement of standards. One may even envisage the general imposition of countervailing duties based on the *ad valorem* equivalent of domestic pollution-control charges applied to all products where this issue is deemed troublesome, whether or not the imported goods were in fact produced under similar conditions of environmental stingency.[10] Such charges would not be inconsistent with exisiting trade rules (Article III. 1 of GATT), which are concerned only with the principle that imported goods be treated the same as domestically produced goods. They would also require rebate of the charge on exports, in order to avoid penalising home-produced goods in other countries applying a similar system. The scope for implicit protection in any such arrangements is obvious.[11]

This type of scheme is very similar to the application of border taxes and the 'destination principle' of adjustment for international differences in indirect busines taxation, currently in widespread use. It would demand a complete schedule of compensatory environmental adjustments paralleling the national tariff schedules for affected products. The incidence of these charges would vary widely among different kinds of goods, and would eliminate all environmental incentives for the international reallocation of production. It would also be exceedingly complex and difficult to administer in an equitable manner. For example, a domestic firm which succeeds in reducing the incidence of pollution-control falling on its products as a result of existing norms would benefit substantially in the face of a continuation of equalisation charges on competitive imports and rebate on its exports. Furthermore, elaborate investigative machinery would be required to set compensatory rates, including appeals procedures for the affected industries. Changes in these rates could trigger significant policy responses on the part of foreign governments. The system would also have to be adopted by all of the major competitor countries applying environmental measures, in order to avoid inequities, and hence its establishment would be complex indeed.

Aside from the industries most directly affected by pollution-abatement standards, the cost incidence of countervailing import charges would be felt in a wide variety of user-industries as well. As a practical matter, therefore, compensatory surcharges and rebates would take the form of rough approximations or flat rates covering a variety of different manufacturing activities, and would involve the danger of serious overcompensation or undercompensation with respect to specific industries and products.

The problem becomes even more complex when this kind of system is used in conjunction with pollution taxes, and when pollution-abatement measures applied by domestic industry result in a reduction in the tax incidence. Logically, any import surcharges and export rebates should then be reduced along with the degree of conformity with environmental standards and the concomitant reduction of associated effluent taxes. In the international context this would place at a relative disadvantage precisely those suppliers progressing with environmental control, but work in favour of laggards or those producing under less rigorous standards. Retention of environmental equalisation duties and export rebates under such conditions would be undesirable from a pollution standpoint and clearly inconsistent with existing GATT rules.

Compensatory commercial policy arrangements of this nature can easily evolve into *de facto* non-tariff distortions of international trade and lead to falsification of international competitive relations – e.g. if the surcharge/rebate is deliberately increased beyond justified levels to favour domestic industry. Moreover, there is sufficient room for misinterpretation on the part of trading partners, particularly by those favouring alternative solutions to the international competitive aspects of environmental control and those less concerned with the issue as a whole. This presents a constant danger of retaliation.

If the PPP is universally adopted, or at least adopted among all of the industrial countries, it should not be difficult to avoid the development of general commercial policy measures imposed for environmental reasons on the process side. Any pressure for compensatory protection is likely to be roughly in proportion to prevailing differences in environmental standards, but may be highly industry- and product-specific. If, however, significant supplier-countries adopt major departures from the PPP, then offsetting import levies or quantitative restrictions can be expected in the affected importing countries for the sake of 'fair' competition. These could, like existing anti-dumping and countervailing measures, be aimed only at offending suppliers and might persist until a determination has been made that the problem has been resolved.

Such charges are provided for under GATT to offset export subsidies and access to this device is becoming easier. The likelihood is that basic rules covering countervailing charges and subsidies will be negotiated in the near future and departures from the PPP must be assessed accordingly.[12]

EFFICIENCY OF POLICY

We have attempted in this chapter to link environmental policy alternatives to their international economic implications and, in turn, to the possible reactions in the field of commercial policy. The intent has been to outline the options available as well as their characteristics in terms of the *efficiency of policy* – the attainment of environmental objectives at minimum cost to society within an acceptable time-frame – all within a dynamic growth context pervaded by myriad unrelated distortions and widespread conflicts among policy objectives.

Equal emphasis was placed on the importance of the PPP as an operative norm to reduce international competitive distortions, and on *departures* from the PPP – to reduce domestic adjustments costs or to distribute them more equitably. Certainly departures from the PPP must be based on flexible procedures – procedures which are operative in a dynamic system where the objectives of environmental policy, the available instruments and (most importantly) the economic context may differ substantially over time. If the PPP is to survive in the real world, such a general conclusion is not very helpful, except in that it aids in focusing on the complexity of the issue and the inherent need to make some compromise in the formulation of policy in this area.

Among the various objectives of the PPP, the trade neutrality of environmental policy appears to be of overriding importance, particularly given possible applications of compensatory trade barriers. In the case of a given industry or enterprise, the degree of international competition – as indicated by the relevant demand, supply and substitution elasticities – determines the sensitivity of trade flows to direct and indirect cost increases attributable to environmental measures. It does not really matter whether such international competition occurs in export markets or in the domestic market.

The majority of instruments involved in departures from the PPP influence *fixed* costs of enterprises, and hence tend not to influence competitiveness in the short run. Instruments which affect variable costs – such as operating subsidies – should be avoided to the extent possible in any departures from the PPP. Fixed cost-reducing techniques do, however, influence intermediate-term competitiveness and patterns of resource allocation. This also re-emphasises the critical importance of the time dimension in determining the acceptability of departures from the PPP. If short-run competitive considerations and the probability of offsetting commercial-policy action are of principal concern, then less importance needs to be attached to socially desirable departures from the PPP involving primarily fixed-cost reductions, so long as they are not fixed on intermediate-range international competitive objectives under the guise of environmental management. In the very long term, in any case, it may not matter very much whether resources are diverted to environmental control via price increases or via alternative mechanisms.

One of the points that has been emphasised is that it is not very productive to attempt to 'unbundle' general aids to industry in order to identify environment-related components as possible departures from the PPP. General aids may be subject to political or economic priorities which exceed those of environmental control, and forced separation of environmental safeguards (even if subsidised) may well be counterproductive. Moreover, in cases where conflicts emerge between environmental quality and competing social and economic goals requiring public assistance, such subsidies should – to the extent possible – be related to the non-environmental objectives.

The importance of departures from the PPP depends in part on the nature, magnitude and distribution of non-environment-related aids to industry, as well as competitive distortions such as tariffs and non-tariff barriers. When viewed in this context, departures from the PPP may not appear particularly significant. It may not be wise to prohibit certain exceptions to the PPP which carry with them clearly desirable environmental gains, while at the same time ignoring non-environmental trade distortions whose benefits may be much more questionable.

Lastly, a number of ways were pointed out whereby environmental policies may lead to barriers against access to international markets. In certain respects, particularly in forcing conformity of products with national environmental targets, such barriers are entirely legitimate and constitute an integral component of national pollution-control policy. In other respects, attempts to compensate through trade barriers for international differences in pollution-control costs cannot be justified on economic grounds, even though they may well accelerate the achievement of domestic environmental targets.

FURTHER READING

J. H. Cumberland, 'The Role of Uniform Standards in International Environmental Management', in *Problems of Environmental Economics* (Paris: O.E.C.D., 1972).

General Agreement on Tariffs and Trade, *Industrial Pollution and International Trade* (Geneva: GATT, 1971).

Charles Pearson and Wendy Takacs, 'International Economic Implications of Environmental Control and Pollution Abatement Programs', in *United States Economic Policy in an Interdependent World*, Compendium of Papers, vol. 1 (Washington, D.C.: Government Printing Office, 1971).

Ingo Walter, 'Pollution and Protection: U.S. Environmental Controls as Competitive Distortions', *Weltwirtschaftliches Archiv* (March 1974).

Ingo Walter, 'Environmental Control and Patterns of International Trade and Investment: An Emerging Policy Issue', *Banca Nazionale del Lavoro Quarterly Review* (March 1972).

6

Environmental Management and Multinational Corporate Operations

Discussions of the international economic implications of environmental management generally focus on the 'nation', which pursues certain environmental policies and programmes in accordance with collectively-determined social objectives, under particular environmental conditions, while other 'nations' either do the same or behave differently. This sets into motion international commercial and financial flows, which in turn influence the achievement of national economic and social goals including environmental balance. This abstract view of the nation as the principal actor or decision-maker contributes to analytical neatness in the discussion, and often enables us to discern the probable direction and magnitude of the economic adjustment and adaptation that will have to result. But it also glosses over the reality of thousands of decision-makers, producers and consumers, who react in different ways to policy stimuli – and who will, in the final analysis, determine the outcome.

One of the most important actors in the international economy is the multinational corporation (MNC), which maintains production and sales facilities in two or more countries, either under direct ownership or with some substantial element of managerial control.[1] A large and growing proportion of international trade and investment activity is undertaken by MNCs and their growth as a dominant force is hardly likely to slacken. For this reason, an examination of how MNC management may react to international differences in environmental policy is of considerable importance. Emphasis will be placed, in part, on decision-making with respect to the location of production, and especially on international investment flows resulting from environmental policies and programmes.

MULTINATIONAL ENTERPRISE

It may be useful to begin with a brief review of what multinational corporations are and how they operate.[2] In addition to the aforementioned ownership and control characteristics, the multinational enterprise ideally operates its productive, distributive and research and development facilities as integral parts of a more or less cohesive transnational logistical network. This implies the existence of a unified management and planning system in which interdependence of costs, competitiveness, technology, procurement, marketing, profitability and decision-making is clearly recognised.

The behaviour of management and the control of operations are the principal criteria in distinguishing enterprises that are truly multinational from those which merely operate foreign subsidiaries as independent profit centres in the form of appendages with substantially separate and autonomous decision systems. This is one reason why the line between multinationals and other firms is somewhat unclear, and one of the grounds for the confusion that often surrounds the issue. The distinction is not unimportant because the impact of the multinational enterprise on national economies is in large measure dependent on its transnational systems approach to management and decision-making.

A multinational firm is often identified with a given 'home' country in terms of ownership and management – although ownership of the parent corporation may be held by individuals and institutions in many countries and a number of foreigners may be found in top management. Generally, MNCs are identified with the manufacturing sector, although the services sector is increasingly involved as well. Frequently, the affiliates of multinational firms will assimilate comfortably into the economy, society and culture of the 'host' country – particularly where these are industrial nations – and frequently will take on the public image of a domestic firm. While ultimate control is invariably exercised by corporate headquarters, management ranks are normally filled predominantly by local personnel, often operating with considerable autonomy.

Foreign direct investment by multinational enterprise has grown substantially more rapidly during the past decade or so than either world trade or world production. To cite some illustrative figures, U.S. direct foreign investment in manufacturing during the 1960s increased at an average annual rate of about 11.6 per cent measured by book value and 12.3 per cent measured by sales of foreign affiliates, compared with growth rates of 9.3 per cent for world trade and 7.0 per cent for world industrial production. In the same period, the share of the manufacturing sector in U.S. foreign direct investment rose from 32 per cent in 1959 to over 40 per cent in 1970, and there was a growing tendency to acquire *existing* foreign firms, which frequently seems to be a characteristic of purposeful corporate planning in a multinational context.[3]

To a significant extent, the competitive advantages that the multinational corporation seems to enjoy can be traced to the fact that it is indeed multinational: it is in a position to make a careful analysis – virtually disregarding political frontiers – of the cost of labour, capital and other productive resources, human skills, size, growth and proximity to markets, and a host of related factors. It continually reviews its present and prospective product-mix, and determines *what* can best be done *where* in the context of a global or regional production-distribution system. Sometimes it acts in a manner identical to its local competitors in a given host country. Sometimes it assembles or makes components from imported or local materials and sells them in the host country or sends them to another country for further processing. Sometimes it produces nothing at all in the host country and maintains only a marketing operation. Occasionally local operations are limited to the research and development function, for which the firm itself is the sole customer.

The essential point is that by operating intra-firm logistics on a global scale, the multinational firm can significantly lower costs by taking advantage *internally* of the traditional gains from international trade and investment – by allocating productive factors more rationally and sharing these gains with its customers (in the form of lower prices) and its suppliers of labour, capital and other resources (in the form of higher prices). One of the symptoms of this process is a tendency for international trade to shift from finished to intermediate products.

Aside from allocating production internationally in order to minimise factor costs, the multinational firm can also trace its competitive advantage in the international market-place to the fact that it creates efficiency itself. It typically represents a highly effective collector, transferer and assimilator of information concerning the market : demand, supply, technology, transport, and so forth. In this way it overcomes lack of knowledge – one of the major impediments to competition in the international market-place. The multinational corporation, in addition, tends to be an innovator in the development and application of modern management techniques which it then applies, where appropriate, in each of its operating units. Methods that don't work get discarded : those that do are rapidly adopted globally as a matter of company policy. Not least important, multinationals tend to be highly innovative in production, distribution and new-product technology – again disseminated rapidly to the subsidiaries of the firm – and this often provides a competitive lead based on know-how in the various markets they serve.

A basic issue is whether the multinational firms' unprecedented capabilities for increasing efficiency and improving resource allocation in the international economy always redound to the benefit of the nations involved – or whether it frequently uses these same unique advantages to restrict competition and, by exercising monopoly power, retains for itself many of the benefits that are supposed to accrue to the international economy generally. That this in fact happens is beyond doubt. The extent to which it indicts the multinational firm as an institution potentially inimical to the public interest is still open to question. Multinational enterprise does seem to speed up the process of international adjustment, however, through rapid and efficient transfer of goods, services, technology and factors of production. Since the cost of economic adjustment depends in part on the time-frame within which it occurs, MNC operations may impose costs on national economies quite apart from any exploitive behaviour that may be involved.

Environmental assimilative capacity and pollution-control policies and programmes enter into MNC decision-making like any other demand- and supply-related element. Hence, they can be expected to influence the way the firm operates and how it serves international markets, taking due account of the environmental externalities involved. If national environmental policies were clear cut, consistent and predictable, analysis of management's response and assessment of the resultant investment and trade flows would be a reasonably straightforward matter. Unfortunately things are not quite this simple and the question of environment is closely associated with the general issue of multinational corporate social responsibility.

SOCIAL RESPONSIBILITY AND POLITICAL VULNERABILITY

If it is agreed that the internalisation of environmental externalities cannot be left to the interplay of market forces, and that the formation and implementation of environmental policy is a matter of collective decision-making at national and regional political levels, the matter of corporate social responsibility in environmental affairs ought to resolve itself. The enterprise is a 'rule-taker'; it may try to influence the establishment of environmental standards during the course of political decision process as much as it can, but once the rules are established, it must abide by them. In this view, the firm cannot do less, but it need not do more. Indeed, it should not do more, since corporate executives have no mandate from the public to make decisions as to where the environmental trade-offs ought to lie. The firm is entirely passive, and the question of 'social responsibility' is essentially a non-issue.

At the other extreme is the argument that the enterprise should, indeed must, develop policies and programmes to involve itself actively in matters transcending narrowly-defined corporate operations. It must do more than it is required to do by law or by the market in a variety of fields that include such diverse issues as worker safety and job satisfaction, consumer protection, employment and promotion of disadvantaged social or racial groups, dealing with foreign countries that are politically out of favour, as well as restoration and maintenance of environmental quality.

One argument for active social responsibility of business is that conventional political decision machinery really is not all-encompassing – that it *presupposes* a certain degree of social responsibility on the part of all elements in society including business firms. The collective decision process works in a variety of ways *other* than through legal and administrative channels, including what may be termed 'public opinion', although this is often ill-defined and subject to interpretation. Definition of the collective will in this manner actually may be more efficient, particularly in an area such as environment where uncertainty is paramount and progress must often be achieved through an extended process of trial and error. It may also be more efficient in an operational sense, if the enterprise is able to set its own goals and timing, and move ahead in ways that it considers to be most desirable in terms of internal cost effectiveness. The problem is, of course, that there is no assurance that a consistent definition of socially responsible action will emerge in any particular instance, or that compliance will be reasonably consistent among firms or industries. If it is not, then economic distortions could easily emerge which might partly or wholly offset the intended social gains.

A less extreme view is that corporate social responsibility is good business, and represents an integral part of the firm's social contract with the community at large. Society undergoes constant change, and if it is to survive and prosper as an institution the business sector must adapt as quickly and efficiently as possible. If the goal of the enterprise is to maximise long-term shareholder wealth, it cannot long remain out of touch with prevailing social trends without seriously compromising this objective. One study has formulated the social responsibility of business as three concentric circles. The inner circle forms the traditional role of business in producing income, jobs and economic growth. The middle circle encompasses the need to 'exercise the economic function with a sensitive awareness of changing social values and priorities' including environmental conservation.[4] The outer circle covers even broader, more amorphous and ill-defined social responsibilities that transcend the traditional role of the corporation, but where business may perform more efficiently than other social institutions.

It is this view that has been adopted by top management in many major enterprises and translated into corporate philosophy, organisational structure, operations and performance. They have opened up a wide variety of communicative channels to employees, consumers and community neighbours as well as stockholders, suppliers, governments, labour unions and various interest groups, recognising that

> A company functioning in the midst of a dynamic society may be compared to a living organism striving to live and develop within its environment. Relationships are extremely complex. The world around is at once sustaining and threatening. Multiple causes and multiple effects are continually at work. To be insensitive, even to the subtleties, could be disastrous. It becomes necessary for the corporation's own existence that it be highly responsive to the environment within which it lives.[5]

Moreover, the increasing number of very large corporations with broad market power and influence on society have brought with them a corresponding increase in social responsibility and accountability.

Enlightened self-interest on the part of corporations has been actively promoted in many countries by governments and by the courts. Tax treatment of corporate donations for education, culture and the arts is often favourable, for example, as are such tax policies as accelerated write-offs of pollution-control equipment. We have already noted the concept of 'negative proof' in consumer-protection cases, under which a new product must be proven safe by the manufacturer prior to public distribution – rather than requiring the injured party after the fact to prove damage by an allegedly defective product. Governments have provided other incentives, such as contracts, cash subsidies, concessionary loans, credit guarantees, and the like, as well as disincentives such as taxes and penalties in a 'carrot and stick' attempt to mould corporate behaviour.

Governments may also permit consortium arrangements among business firms to alleviate social problems such as pollution more efficiently. These could reduce competitive disadvantages of socially responsible policies and permit larger-scale social ventures – although such arrangements can easily run foul of anti-trust policies. Lastly, there is the possibility of hybrid public–private enterprises which may focus the strongest aspects of government and private enterprise on major socio-economic priorities. In this way, access to tax revenues, political mandate and general accountability in the public sector might be coupled with management ability, research and technology, and business systems analysis in the private sector.

Also, social responsibility is not necessarily poor business even in the short run. Firms looking ahead within the context of social change are more likely to stay ahead of the market and anticipate the evolution of demand for goods and services in the future. The social activities themselves may create new markets, and the design and production of pollution-abatement systems and related technical and process changes is a prime example. Investors themselves are becoming increasingly sophisticated about a firm's net social contribution, and this assessment, accentuated by the views of security analysts, is likely to affect the margin between the market price of traded corporate stock and the book value of its assets. While evaluation of corporate social responsibility is still in its infancy, increasing efforts are being made to develop extensive and reasonably objective 'social audits' of business firms in some countries.[6]

Of course, corporate social responsibility is not without its limits. There are many firms which lack the size and the expertise to go very far in this direction, and all firms are heavily occupied with their mainstream business which often renders the definition of a balanced position rather difficult. Also, public expectations of what a firm can and should do are not very well-defined and in a state of flux, and this raises the possibility of excessive expectations and subsequent backlash in public sentiment if they are not fulfilled. The problem is to 'minimize the dual danger of under-response and resulting public dissatisfaction, or of over-response which could lead companies well beyond their competence, bring about destructive rivalry rather than healthy competition with other institutions, and stretch corporate capabilities so far as to sap performance in the mainstream business'.[7]

All of this is multiplied in complexity for the multinational enterprise which must operate viably in a number of national states; each enterprise faces a unique set of social and environmental circumstances. The regulatory framework differs, as does the way government formulates and implements policy. Expectations and public opinion differs, and what is considered socially responsible in one country may be viewed as unacceptable in another. Should the firm conform strictly to the behavioural requirements imposed upon it by government in each host country? Should it go beyond this and accept social responsibility in a variety of fields in conformity with the prevailing climate in the countries in which it operates? In that case, how does each subsidiary determine its own mandate and integrate it into the over-all policies of the parent corporation? Or should it adopt the strictest requirements it faces *anywhere* for all of its global operations – or simply apply those of the home country of the parent firm – and how would this influence its competitiveness in the various markets it serves?

These are difficult questions, and they are made even more difficult by a wide variety of other political and legal conflicts surrounding the multinational enterprise, particularly between the firm and host countries. Perhaps the most difficult of these is outright nationalism: that firms operating in a given country ought to be staffed, managed, controlled and owned by nationals of that country. Nationalistic views are ubiquitous, and are appealed to whenever political, social or economic conflicts involving multinational corporations arise – some for entirely legitimate reasons.

There is the problem, for example, of foreign subsidiaries of MNCs being subject to host-country laws yet at the same time having to abide by home-country regulations (legal extra-territoriality) in such areas as anti-trust policy and East–West trade. Carried further, there is often the nagging suspicion that the multinational firm may at times act as a political agent for its home government, either because this is endemic to the system or in return for national political support when the firm gets into trouble. Then there is the problem of taxation: by using imaginative pricing policies the multinational firm is frequently in a position to minimise its over-all tax burden by taking its profits in low-tax countries. When a host country tries to redress what it regards as an inequity, political problems often arise. Another hot political issue is extra-territoriality of *decision-making*: when decisions fundamentally affecting the local economy – including cessation of operations – are made thousands of miles away at corporate headquarters with little or no regard for its broader impact on the host country. The multinational firm may also exploit its market power to drive local competitors out of business, or dominate large segments of local industry.

To a large extent, political conflicts between host countries and MNCs arise from a misunderstanding of how multinational business really operates, and how it can best be used in the national interest. Some are convinced that multinational firms will do exactly what they can get away with: no more and no less. In many advanced countries what the firm can get away with is clearly limited – by anti-trust laws, by the big labour collectivities, by national economic policies, and by social, environmental and consumer-orientated measures. When the firm moves into a different environment some of these countervailing forces may not exist or may be poorly developed, and the enterprise adopts policies that would never be tolerated at home and which sooner or later lead to political difficulties in the host country. Multinational enterprise is by its very nature extremely adept at operating under different sets of rules.

This view places responsibility largely on the host country to make rules that best fit its own social, economic and political goals. The multinational firm will then indicate whether it wants to play by those rules. If not, the country can seek alternative ways of accomplishing what the firm would have done. If so, the country may be successful in harnessing the unprecedented organisational, technological and operational capabilities of the multinational corporation to achieve national goals in the most efficient possible manner. A less rigid view would, as we have seen, place upon the firm itself some of the responsibility of acting in the best interests of the host society.

Still missing in national efforts to maximise the benefits provided by the multinational enterprise – to harness its energies in pursuit of maximum economic welfare – is some degree of international consistency in the rules governing its operations. Such rules have more or less dominated international trade and finance for decades, and they have contributed immeasurably to the evolution and maintenance of a viable international economic order. No such rules govern international investment or other aspects of MNC operations, and this policy vacuum is the source of much uncertainty and conflict both on the part of firms and of governments. Agreement on some basic issues, such as non-discrimination in national policies affecting foreign and domestic firms, would go a long way toward meeting this need. However, there remains a great deal of disagreement on the nature of such rules – and whether they are desirable at all – so that the prospects for progress in this important area of policy are not at all bright.

ENVIRONMENTAL FACTORS IN CORPORATE LOCATIONAL DECISIONS

Given the organisational and operational characteristics of the multi-national enterprise, and the relevance of the social responsibility concept to corporate planning, how will the MNC react to environmental management pursued with great diversity among the nations of the world? Like any other resource, environment tends to be used in productive processes in relation to its cost to the enterprise – the cost of disposing of production wastes into the atmosphere, bodies of water and on land, as well as the visual, audible and other types of pollution associated with industrial activity. In the absence of pollution control, therefore, the impact of the quality of the environment within which production takes place on corporate operations is likely to be relatively small, and limited to the technical requirements (for example adequate water supplies) of the production process itself. It is likely to have little, if any, influence on corporate forward planning and particularly on plant-siting decisions.

The advent of pollution control changes all of this by placing a positive cost on use of the environment, either through the enforcement of standards, effluent taxation or other policy instruments that conform to the 'polluter pays' principle. A rational firm will then use environmental resources in accordance with their relative cost and marginal product, as in the case of any other productive resource. At a given plant site the firm has no choice but to pay whatever cost of pollution control is required of it. Its options are limited to transferring the plant's production elsewhere, shutting down entirely if the costs become excessive under given competitive conditions or shifting plant output into less-pollutive production if this is a viable option.

The firm, of course, has other choices which involve shifts in the location of production, either by adding plant capacity at new sites or shifting existing capacity to locations where environmental assimilative capacity is greater or environmental preferences are more modest. Given interregional and international differences in environmental assimilative capacity and/or collective preferences as reflected in environmental targets, decisions affecting the location or relocation of industrial facilities will and should be influenced accordingly.

Options available to the individual firm thus hinge on: (a) the importance of pollution control as a cost and competitive element; (b) the existence of differences in interregional and international pollution-control standards; (c) differences in labour availability and quality, public services, transport costs and proximity to markets; (d) the nature of the firm's own logistical network, the character of its product and its rate of growth in required productive capacity; (e) the social and political framework, including the availability of investment incentives

E

and the nature of investment controls, tax policies, etc.; and (*f*) the availability of raw materials and intermediate inputs with the production process.

There is as yet very little evidence that would indicate the possible future impact of environment-induced international shifts in industrial location, although there is some evidence that this has indeed been occurring interregionally within industrial economies. In the United States, for example, a number of political jurisdictions have begun to discourage industrial location and new investment following an implicit cost–benefit assessment that the negative environmental consequences of such investment substantially outweigh the attendant static and dynamic economic gains.[8] Particularly affected are the pollution-intensive facilities. Also affected are public-sector investments such as power plants, highways and airports.

A prime example is the German B.A.S.F. Corporation which, bowing to local pollution-control requirements, abandoned its plan to build a 100-million-dollar petro-chemical complex at Port Victoria, South Carolina.* Additionally, it accelerated the shutting-down of a unit at Wyandotte, Michigan, because the cost of retrofitting this plant to meet new environmental standards was deemed excessive. Other examples include prohibitions by the State of Delaware against new port facilities and refineries, application by the States of Montana and Arizona of standards to preclude aluminium- and copper-smelting operations, and even broader measures by the State of Oregon to freeze or restrict a wide variety of economic activity and substantially slow the region's industrialisation. A similar pattern emerges at the municipal level.

It is tempting to generalise that regions in the United States adopting anti-development policies for environmental reasons tend to be characterised by relatively high incomes and favourable historical development patterns. Such regions might be expected to adopt such a position in the growth-versus-environment trade-off. The political balance in other regions of the United States, particularly in the South, appears to be quite different and represents a fundamentally different evaluation of the alternatives. The result may be substantial growth in the importance of environmental considerations in decisions regarding industrial location and interregional investment flows and a shift in economic development and commercial trends within the nation as a whole.

If the United States is taken as an example of a large economically integrated area with diverse environmental resources and (within limits) diverse environmental controls at the state and local level, then the perceived influence of environmental factors on U.S. plant location may be

---

* Although nothing in this case suggested that a U.S. firm would not have encountered precisely the same obstacles, a suspicion that discrimination was somehow involved lingered on in Europe.

indicative of what may happen internationally as well – although the factors involved are a good deal more complex. We would thus expect environmental pressures to promote a gradual shift of pollution-intensive forms of economic activity from higher- to lower-income regions domestically and from higher- to lower-income countries internationally, with the range of activities affected gradually widening over time. If this indeed develops, it will have notable implications for the development process, patterns of international trade and commercial policy.

Any such impact on the international economy will tend to be felt initially at the industry level and progressively spread to broader ranges of economic activity. Firms that find preferred sites at home excluded for environmental reasons have available alternatives which encompass both alternate domestic and foreign locations, and there are bound to be certain international locational spillovers attributable to local or regional environmental control.* As domestic environmental awareness and cost assessments increase in leading countries, these spillovers will tend to grow, with certain foreign locations appearing progressively more advantageous relative to domestic locations, and environmental considerations increasing in importance relative to other factors determining locational decisions. Since inter-country variations in ecological awareness are generally likely to exceed interregional domestic variations, and since the imposition of homogeneous environmental control standards internationally is likely to lag well behind domestic harmonisation, the scope for the extent of international locational spillovers will tend to be both significant and long lived. There may indeed be instances where the export of pollution through capital investments abroad becomes national policy in certain economic sectors, with possible benefits for both the capital-exporting and capital-importing countries. But the political sensitivity of this issue will tend to ensure that any such policy will be applied with a great deal of circumspection.

As noted earlier, little information is available thus far on the sensitivity of industrial location decisions to international differences in environmental conditions. If emerging differences in pollution-control standards in fact reflect differences in environmental assimilative capacity and social preferences – and if environmental impacts are indeed localised with minimal transfrontier effects – then any resulting locational shifts and capital flows will tend to narrow the gap between marginal social costs and marginal social benefits on a global scale, and thereby serve the general welfare and efficient utilisation of the environment. But it is much too early to obtain an accurate picture of the variables involved in this calculus, or to make defensible forecasts – except that the impact

* This discussion is based on Ingo Walter, 'Environmental Management and Optimal Resource Use: The International Dimension', in *Das Umweltproblem in Okonomischer Sicht*, ed. Herbert Giersch (Tübingen: Mohir (Paul Siebeck), 1974).

will tend to be longer term in nature, often inseparable from other factors affecting international locational decisions.

Foreign investment decisions on the part of multinational enterprises are by their very nature highly complex and highly specific to the firm and industry involved. We have already taken note of variables such as relative labour costs, labour skills, growth of the local market, access to raw materials, proximity to major markets and related factors that have to be taken into account. There are also numerous policy variables that often may be no less important in corporate decisions. These include registration and screening procedures for new investments, required by the host country. Tax considerations are also important, as are tariffs which the firm will have to pay on imported inputs or would have had to pay if the local market had been served from abroad. Government incentives such as tax holidays and various types of subsidies may also be of significance in locational decisions. The same is true of government policies on ownership and control of local industry, including joint ventures and past incidence of internalisation and expropriation. Exchange controls will also influence international direct investment, especially with respect to the remission of interest, dividends, royalties, and the like.

All of these policy variables figure into *any* investment decision by multinational enterprise, although the precise mix and weighting of factors will vary widely from case to case. There are also some systematic differences between investments intended to produce for the domestic market in the host country on the one hand, and investments intended to produce largely or wholly for export on the other. Investment incentives provided by the host country, for example, tend to be considerably more important in the latter rather than in the former.

Within this complex decision framework environmental questions obviously play a role, but it is a role that can easily be swamped by other factors. How important is it? Several elements are involved.

First, environmental costs for most industries do not represent a major element of production costs, amounting to less than 5 per cent of sales in virtually all industries – not including the pollution-control costs embodied in inputs such as electric power, raw materials and intermediates. Hence, the competitive advantage to be gained by locational shifts are relatively marginal and are readily overridden by suboptimisation in other sectors.

Secondly, to the extent that some domestic suppliers remain as competitors, abiding by strict environmental norms, governmental reaction to locational flight into 'pollution havens' may be expected, joined by labour groups and others opposed to the export of jobs. This may take the form of highly differentiated import controls as between basic raw materials and successively higher levels of processing, and block some of the gains expected from locational shifts.

At the same time serious and potentially embarrassing questions will be raised about the social responsibility of business flight to pollution havens with regard to its impact on the domestic economy and the environment in recipient countries and global environmental balances. Given the aforementioned vulnerability of the MNC to charges of corporate irresponsibility this is something it can ill afford.

Thirdly, although less rigorous environmental standards may initially have induced investment in a given host country, a point will eventually be reached when ecological balance will become a major concern to these as well, and the same kinds of conflicts may arise that prompted the initial location decision. These tensions may well be magnified at that point because the polluting firms are foreign owned. This may be one reason why executives often view pollution havens with a good deal of scepticism.[9]

Lastly, the incremental cost of building a new 'clean' plant may be relatively low at least when compared with retrofitting old plants and this may largely determine the incentive to alter plant siting for environmental reasons. Moreover, once favourable environmental characteristics of modern plants have been demonstrated, local opposition to new or expanded facilities may well wither away. It seems reasonable to suspect, therefore, that only when environmental considerations block expansion in a particular locale, or impede the supply of vital services such as transport, do they play a major role in plant-siting decisions.

This seems to be borne out in the Japanese case[10] where pollution factors figure prominently in the efforts of the aluminium industry, for example, to locate new capacity abroad – together with the availability of raw materials and cheaper electric power. Difficulties in finding environmentally-sound refinery sites have forced the petroleum industry to look abroad as well, particularly in Indonesia. In the pulp and paper industry, 'Great difficulty in obtaining factor sites in Japan due to pollution as well as heavy reliance upon overseas lumber have prompted plans for production in the U.S. and Brazil and importation of the products to Japan.'[11] In other sectors as well pollution is noted as a major reason for the decentralisation of industry within Japan and to neighbouring parts of Asia. As part of a dramatic proposal for remodelling the Japanese islands, the government in 1972 proposed that 'economic and human flows must first be readjusted. Relocation of industries is the basic measure to that end. Under the measure industrial plants in overcrowded areas will be moved to sparsely populated areas, while construction of new plants will be encouraged in areas other than the Pacific coastal belt.'[12] Much of this is to be accomplished by 1985, with appropriate environmental safeguards and employing a variety of government incentives.

Even if relocation of production for environmental reasons is limited to relatively few sectors with severe pollution problems, and where other decision variables either do not present serious impediments or also favour relocation into more favourable areas, the economic effects may still be quite substantial. There will be initial capital flows, followed by the shipment of capital goods and accompanied by the transfer of technology and managerial skill. There will be positive employment effects in the host countries along with the standard kinds of backward and forward linkages to other sectors of the economy. Trade flows will also be affected. Firms locating abroad for environmental reasons may serve the home market and third markets from the new location, thereby raising home-country imports and reducing exports of the products in question although, as noted, trade shifts in inputs may move in the opposite direction. Processing may be done closer to the sources of raw materials, particularly in developing countries, resulting in a rise in the average value of their exports. One would expect, for example, pollution considerations to contribute to the development of refineries and petro-chemical plants in petroleum-exporting countries, with high-value product rather than crude oil entering trade channels. Metallic ores, lumber and certain chemicals may be similarly affected.

To summarise, just as international trade may contribute to the efficient use of environmental resources so, too, may international investment. However, the plant-location effect of differential environmental resources and policies may have only a marginal impact in all but a few industries where pollution represents a true bottleneck to expansion or rationalisation of production. In other cases, the environmental considerations simply may not be sufficiently important, relative to other factors, to have a determining influence – particularly given the multinational corporations' sensitivity to questions of social responsibility. Where an impact is felt, nevertheless, the indications for international trade and investment flows may be substantial in certain industries.

Clearly, the multinational firm will have a comparatively wide range of options available because it can shift production to minimise pollution costs usually without simultaneously increasing operational difficulties and encountering prohibitive increases in costs from other aspects of its operations. Environmental control will thus affect the relative profitability of alternative investment opportunities on a multinational scale, and of alternative operational decisions. At the same time, it has already been pointed out that the homogeneous environmental regulations provided by a central government at the national level are absent internationally at least for now. This lack will extend the range of realistic options available to the MNC and will amplify its responses to them. Lastly, since international investment decisions affect employment and economic activity in both home and host countries, locational 'flight' induced by environmental controls will raise serious questions of social responsibility and extra-territoriality of decision-making.

ENVIRONMENTAL FACTORS IN CORPORATE OPERATING DECISIONS

As part of its growing concern with social responsibility, management in multinational corporations has become increasingly aware of environmental issues and policies in the various countries in which they operate. The 'corporate environmental manager' is a position frequently found today in major firms, charged with over-all responsibility for minimising environmental damage associated with company operations and achieving compliance with national and local pollution requirements.

One study involving 130 interviews with corporate executives dealing with environmental matters revealed that such individuals have two primary areas of responsibility: 'to persuade corporate management at all levels to think about solving environmental problems and to determine how these problems will evolve with changing conditions in the next five to ten years'.[13] This clearly is an amorphous mandate, and it seems evident that the qualifications of such individuals, their competence in environmental affairs, the resources placed at their disposal and their influence on top management differs dramatically among firms.

Much of the task seems to be educational in nature, encouraging engineers and planners to think of plant-siting decisions in environmental terms, and similarly with use of materials, product design, plant operations, and so forth. The aforementioned study found some chemical firms adopting a 'materials balance approach' to pollution control, accounting for every input and every output and maximising recovery of by-products. Others developed internal checklists that in effect represent detailed environmental impact statements exploring pollution consequences of company operations and new facilities. One firm developed comprehensive pollution guidelines, stated in the form of corporate policy at the highest level, to be implemented in its world-wide operations, while another impressed upon employees the need to consider environmental factors as seriously as productivity, quality and safety. A European MNC has assigned corporate environmental affairs to one of its directors who, with the assistance of a senior engineer, inventoried the company's world-wide anti-pollution activities, centralised pollution-control research and services, set up a communications and advisory network linking all operating units and levels, established environmental impact review of all new capital investments exceeding one million dollars, and set up links to industry, national and international environmental groups.[14]

What this indicates is that many MNCs take their environmental responsibilities seriously enough to have it influence their corporate operations. Whereas this concern might not yet have permeated long-range planning and formulation of fundamental directions of corporate activity, it does seem to have been recognised as legitimately influencing the operating characteristics of the firm. Another comparative study of European multinationals confirms that, thus far, 'environmental objectives have not emerged too sharply in companies' long-term goals, with perhaps a few exceptions in the cases of certain large corporations, and in the case of Sweden in general'.[15] An attitude of 'wait and see' seemed to be prevalent with respect to basic policy decisions, with considerable effort devoted to public relations activities to improve the environmental image of the firm. Moreover, there was again wide variance among firms in the impact of environmental factors on corporate operating decisions.

Several other interesting findings emerged from the latter study. First, anti-pollution factors have become important elements on developing a brand image and in product promotion. Secondly, firms seem to place top priority on protecting themselves against their own pollution. Thirdly, a number of firms have taken steps to draw up detailed environmental impact analyses before launching new products, particularly in the field of packaging. Fourthly, in combating pollution, a number of firms have discussed new ways of doing things, and this has led to more general improvements in operating efficiency through innovation and has hence reduced the net cost of pollution control. Fifthly, a great deal of anti-pollution activity is undertaken by specialists and by consulting firms under contract, opening up a major new industry, and has resulted in significant corporate diversification into pollution-control activity – including patenting and licensing of processes successfully used within the firm. Indeed, the market for pollution-control equipment and know-how, as well as the sale of recovered materials, is considered by many firms an important element of environmental activities.

Both among European and U.S. enterprises, pressure for environmental protection has tended to promote inter-firm collaboration and co-operation. For example, the European oil firms have established a survey bureau called Conservation of Clean Air and Water for Western Europe (CONCAWE) for this purpose; the Union of German Cement Manufacturers has formed an anti-pollution 'Dust Commission'; while in Sweden a single Institute for Research on Air and Water Pollution serves both government and industry.[16] Such associations may serve as channels of communication between firms and governments, pool industry-wide information, monitor legislative and administrative action, reduce duplication among firms, and (not least important) attempt to influence government environmental policy and provide greater credibility in public relations efforts. Inter-firm collaboration, as noted earlier, can easily run foul of anti-trust policy in some countires, particularly the United States, as indicated by the fact that European affiliates of U.S. automobile firms failed to join in a collaborative anti-pollution venture established in 1973 by the European automobile industry (see Chapter 9).

In addition to collaboration in the environmental field, there also have emerged associations to assist in the financing of pollution-control investments. Sometimes there are regional or industry pooling arrangements but they also include new financial institutions set up specifically for this purpose. An example is the Industrial Group for Environmental Protection (GIPADE) and the Interprofessional Group to Finance Anti-pollution Investments (GIFIAP) in France, and backed by several financial houses which float anti-pollution bond issues the proceeds of which are loaned out to industry. Chemical Bank and Chase Manhattan Bank of New York, the Banque de Paris et Pays-Bas and Crédit National in Paris, and the First Pennsylvania Bank of Philadelphia are examples of banks that participate actively, either alone or in consortia, in anti-pollution financing.

MULTINATIONAL CORPORATE TRANSFER OF ENVIRONMENTAL TECHNOLOGY

One explanation for the success of multinational firms in the international economy focuses on technological gaps. Even in the early days of foreign business activity in tropical agriculture and extraction of fuels and raw materials, the justification of such operations was based on the fact that local enterprise had neither the capital nor the know-how to exploit available indigenous resources. To be sure conflicts arose from time to time and sometimes involved serious international political strains. But by and large foreign firms were welcomed in host countries which felt that, all things considered, they had more to gain than to lose.

This pattern of multinational corporate involvement based on flexibility, skill and know-how carried over into the industrialisation era. Foreign firms were welcome to manufacture locally products which otherwise would have to be imported, and for which technical capabilities were lacking domestically. Direct foreign investment frequently represented a mandatory component of the national growth strategy, whether based on import substitution or export expansion. This partly explains the active involvement of multinational firms particularly in developing countries, which clearly is not based on taking advantage of cheap indigenous labour for use in export production.

What happens when the know-how gap narrows? The multinational firm becomes increasingly vulnerable as the apparent benefits to the host country decline : the country may have generated the necessary expertise itself, or can buy it from abroad on a contract basis. The entry of local firms may sharpen the competitive environment, and may cause shifts in public policy biased against the foreign-owned subsidiary. The end result can be a significant diminution of the multinational firm's control over its own operations. As the pressure mounts, the firm is increasingly forced to search for new ways to widen the know-how gap and reestablish its value to the host country. If it cannot provide the new goods or new expertise that would maintain its allure, or it has no special control over export markets or sources of key imported supplies, it must count on gradual encroachment on its autonomy. The result may be greatly increased government participation in its operations, even nationalisation or expropriation. In such cases multinational firms find themselves constantly striving to keep the technological gap wide enough to justify their own existence in a cost–benefit balance as viewed from the perspective of host countries preoccupied with their current (not past) contributions to social welfare.

Pollution control falls under this same heading, and influences the costs and benefits of direct foreign investment to the host country. We have already pointed out that environmental technology transfer within MNCs is extremely rapid and efficient if it is deemed appropriate in a particular country setting. Two possibilities exist : first, if the host country raises environmental standards and the MNC has already met those standards in other countires, it may be able to comply more quickly and more efficiently than indigenous firms. Hence, it may achieve for itself a competitive advantage in the form of lower pollution-control costs. Secondly, the MNC may introduce more advanced pollution-control techniques in new or existing plants in a particular host country before such facilities are required by government. This again may give the MNC a competititive edge once stricter requirements are set, and in addition may bolster the firm's image in the area of social responsibility. To extend the latter point, a demonstration effect may make itself felt, once government notes that things can be accomplished in an environmentally sounder way, and pollution-control programmes pioneered by the MNC may become a benchmark for the remainder of the economy.

To summarise, the international economic dimensions of environmental management are closely interconnected with the managerial behaviour of the multinational enterprise, which dominates a large and growing share of economic interchange among nations. By obtaining a sound grasp of MNC operating and planning behaviour, it may be possible to ascertain in much greater detail and accuracy the implications of environmental control for international economic relations – particularly with respect to the siting of new production facilities and the transfer of environmental technology.

FURTHER READING

Committee for Economic Development, *Social Responsibilities of Multinational Corporations* (New York: C.E.D., 1971).
Jacqueline A. de Larderel and Anne-Marie Boutin, 'How Do European

(and American) Companies Really Manage Pollution?', *European Business* (winter 1972).

John H. Dunning (ed.), *Studies in International Investment* (London: George Allen & Unwin, 1969).

Thomas N. Gladwin and John G. Welles, 'Environmental Aspects of Multinational Corporate Operations', in *Studies in International Environmental Economics*, ed. Ingo Walter (New York: Wiley, 1976).

Robert G. Hawkins, 'The Multinational Corporation: A New Trade Policy Issue in the United States', in *The United States and International Markets*, ed. R. G. Hawkins and Ingo Walter (Lexington, Mass.: D. C. Heath, 1972).

Charles P. Kindelberger (ed.), *The International Corporation* (Cambridge, Mass.: M.I.T. Press, 1970).

Philip W. Quigg, 'Organization for Global Environmental Management', *Columbia Journal of World Business* (May–June 1972).

John M. Stopford and Louis T. Wells, *Managing the Multinational Corporation* (New York: Basic Books, 1973).

Raymond Vernon, *Sovereignty at Bay* (New York: Basic Books, 1971).

Ingo Walter, *Environmental Control and Consumer Protection: Emerging Forces in Multinational Corporate Operations* (Washington, D.C.: Center for Multinational Studies, 1972).

Ingo Walter, 'A Guide to Social Responsibility of the Multinational Enterprise', in *Dimensions of Corporate Social Responsibility*, ed. Jules Backman and Ernest Block (New York University Press, 1975).

John G. Welles, 'Multinationals Need New Environmental Strategies', *Columbia Journal of World Business* (Summer 1973).

7

Transfrontier Pollution

One of the most perplexing issues concerning the international economic dimensions of environmental management has to do with transfrontier pollution (TFP), which is perhaps of more direct policy relevance and immediacy than some of the more indirect questions – such as trade implications – that we have already discussed in considerable detail. The latter arise from international differences in *national* pollution-control programmes. TFP relates to the direct impact of pollution caused by economic activities undertaken in one national state on the welfare of people living in another. It is a matter, therefore, of transboundary externalities which require negotiated settlement between governments.* As a problem of international conciliation, TFP as an issue is distinctly multidisciplinary in character, requiring the skills of lawyers and political scientists as well as economists and ecologists – as part of a 'package' of political and economic issues to be resolved in inter-government negotiations. Moreover, there may be considerable slippage between identification and definition of a TFP problem and its eventual resolution.

THE NATURE OF TRANSFRONTIER POLLUTION

Transfrontier pollution concerns any environmental externalities that cross international political boundaries as a result of natural water flows and atmospheric motion, the two primary transmission mechanisms. It also concerns earth resources not claimed by any single nation, such as the atmosphere and the oceans, but which affect the quality of life in every nation. Consequently, TFP can be highly localised and limited to a specific lake or a river, or it may be extremely broad in character and capable of settlement only be means of equally general international agreements. Problems usually centre on coastal areas and seas, international rivers and lakes, airsheds that cross national boundaries and urban or industrial frontier zones. Moreover, TFP may be continuous – as in the case of noxious effluents from a manufacturing plant – or it may be dis-

* One useful definition is the following: 'any discharge of matter (or release of energy), in the territory of one country, which is propagated by natural forces and causes damage in the territory of another country'. See O.E.C.D., Environment Committee, *Transfrontier Pollution Cost Sharing* (Paris: O.E.C.D. Document AEU/ENV/72.17, January 1973).

crete and exceptional, as in the accidental discharge of oil due to marine collision or grounding involving a tankship.

Another important characterisitic of TFP is that in the majority of cases relatively few parties are involved. Hence conflict resolution based on bilateral or multilateral bargaining and compensation – either in terms of fiscal transfers or via concessions in areas unrelated to the environment – is possible between the affected parties. Monetary compensation between polluters and pollutees at the national level is often discussed in conceptual terms, but its complexity is such that it is rarely the solution of choice. This is not true of TFP. Whereas at the national level administrative and judicial instruments to deal with environmental problems are usually well established, they are frequently absent at the international level. Hence, the joint bodies to frame solutions, settle conflicts and finance remedial action almost always have to be created *de novo*, frequently on an *ad hoc* basis.

Very little is known about the costs associated with TFP or its abatement. Estimates for the O.E.C.D. countries indicate that environmental damage attributable directly to TFP is of the order of perhaps a billion dollars annually, with net savings potentially deriving from pollution control estimated to be in the tens of millions of dollars.[1] On economic grounds alone, this would seem to justify increased attention to the problem.

There are two types of TFP: the first is *one-way* where pollution originating in one country damages one or more other countries, but without significantly damaging the country of origin; the second is two-way (*reciprocal*) with pollution originating in one country causing damage both to itself and to others. Figure 7.1 illustrates the environmental interactions that may exist between two countries, i and j. On the right-hand side of the diagram are purely internal pollutive flows, the centre depicts purely one-way flows, while the left-hand side depicts reciprocal

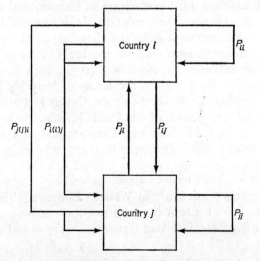

FIGURE 7.1   Types of transfrontier pollution

flows. Such distinctions are, of course, rather simplistic. Almost every case of TFP imaginable is probably reciprocal in nature, so that the problem of differentiation is one of degree, not kind. But if it is stated in such terms, and allowing for international variation in perceived impact and political reactions to it, the distinction becomes quite important and may govern both incentives to take remedial action and the form such actions may take.

In the following discussion we shall focus on the concept of 'rights' – (both the right to pollute and the right to a clean environment), the economic consequences of TFP and its alleviation, the allocation of those costs, instruments for TFP management, as well as some broader issues concerning oceanic and atmospheric pollution.

ENVIRONMENTAL RIGHTS

One of the critical issues in TFP – and environmental management in general – is the issue of 'rights'. Who has the right to pollute? Who has the right to a cleaner environment? What happens when nations' concepts of their own environmental rights come into conflict? Clearly, there are both economic and legal dimensions of this issue, and neither is subject to straightforward resolution.

Domestic legislation in most countries seems to assume implicitly an unlimited right to pollute any environmental resources, air and water, from which it is not specifically excluded on the basis of territorial claims. However, this principle of unlimited national environmental sovereignty is no longer intact, and a number of legal decisions and international agreements have held that a nation cannot use its own territory in such a way as to damage others.

In the area of air pollution, there is for example the Trail Smelter Arbitration, which involves TFP originating in Canada and damaging residents of the United States. The resolution of this case provides some guidance to settling damages payable by the offending state.[2] Legal precedents and international agreements exist for marine TFP as well, and include the Geneva Convention on the High Seas (1958), the Geneva Convention on the Continental Shelf (1964), the General Assembly Declaration of Principles Governing the Sea-Bed and the Ocean Floor, and the Subsoil Thereof, Beyond the Limits of National Jurisdiction (1965), and the Geneva Convention on Fishing and Conservation of Living Resources on the High Seas (1966). Throughout, there appears an expression of the view that the right to pollute is limited – a theme that is carried through at the regional level in decisions and agreements among individual governments particularly in Western Europe and North America. Additional examples concern international radioactive pollution – most notably in the Nuclear Test Ban Treaty of 1963 – and noise pollution through the I.C.A.O. Convention on International Civil Aviation of 1949.[3]

More generally, the Declaration on the Human Environment, agreed to at the United Nations Stockholm Conference in June 1972, states explicitly that nations have the responsibility to 'ensure that activities within their jurisdiction or control do not cause damage to the environment of other states or of areas beyond the limits of national jurisdiction'.[4] Although not binding on national governments, this statement clearly indicates the direction of international law with respect to TFP.

The idea that the right to pollute internationally is limited thus appears to be growing in force. The inference is that the pollutee, or victim, countries also have rights to a clean environment. Allocation of these rights between polluter and victim is thus a matter of international *equity*, and there are few principles either in law or in economics that are very helpful in guiding decisions in this respect – quite apart from questions of enforcement once general principles have been agreed upon.

For the source country, the incentive to pollute is clear. It depends upon the opportunity costs of (*a*) secondary-materials recovery; (*b*) domestic environmental damage caused by deflection of effluents away from TFP; (*c*) forgoing or curtailing the pollution-causing economic activities; (*d*) shifting production to other locations; and (*e*) internalising pollution within the emitting productive units. Hence the environmental condition of a river, lake or airshed that transcends national boundaries 'will be set by a nation that is reducing to a minimum the total costs of pollution, including in the term "costs" both the expenses of dealing with wastes in some other way and the damaging from not enjoying a cleaner environment.'[5] In spite of the growing thrust against TFP in international law, the likelihood is that nations will continue to pollute one another, simply because it is in their immediate economic self-interest to do so and because possible political or economic sanctions are not of overriding concern.

IMPACT AND POLICY-RESPONSE: ONE-WAY TRANSFRONTIER POLLUTION

Under conditions of one-way pollution by an 'upstream' country (*U*) which impacts on a 'downstream' country (*D*), the former assumes the right to pollute up to whatever level it finds domestically acceptable, and the pollution – reduced by the amount of dilution that occurs in transit – affects the victim country without regard to the latter's environmental preferences. The TFP augments whatever pollution is generated internally in *D* and determines the prevailing level of environmental quality in that country – and/or the cost of attaining a given degree of pollution control. Either way, there is an effective transfer of real income from *D* to *U*. Given the existence of environmental management programmes in both countries, under the 'polluter pays' principle both consumer real income (via product prices) and factor income will be higher in U and lower in D than without TFP. In the absence of pollution control, the quality of the environment will be worse in D and better in U than without TFP – again, a transfer of real income calculated so as to encompass aggregate welfare incorporating environmental quality.

Clearly it is in the interest of the downstream country to convince the upstream country to reduce its TFP while at the same time attempting to control its own pollution to the extent possible, although the level of pollution experienced, and the aggregate costs, including damage and abatement, will inevitably be higher than without TFP.[6] The upstream country, meanwhile, will tend to remain passive and leave the initiative up to the victim. The bargaining position of D, if limited to the TFP issue alone, is weak indeed.

If we suppose that the complex of relations between the two countries is such that both agree to discuss the TFP issue, and both agree that the quality of the environment must somehow be improved, the bargaining objectives are as follows:

Downstream country	*Upstream country*
(a) reduced TFP damage;	(a) continued TFP;
(b) increased TFP compensation from U;	(b) minimum or zero TFP compensation to D;
(c) reduced inducement to control TFP payable to U; and	(c) maximum contribution to pollution-control costs from D; and
(d) downgrading rights of U to continued TFP due to precedent.	(d) minimise limitations on future rights to TFP.

Relative bargaining power will determine *which* country realises *which* objectives, and each country will muster all of the claims, assertions and data it can in support of its position – all against the background of national sovereignty.

Given imperfect information about the nature and severity of TFP – and the inherent tendency in bargaining to take extreme positions and to ignore facts – the outcome of such a 'bargaining-and-rights' approach is highly uncertain, and can encompass a wide variety of trade-offs. There are, however, some alternatives.

One is the 'cost-sharing' approach.[7] It recognises that in the case of TFP, unlike pollution control at the national level, no institutions or instruments exist which may be used to redistribute income in order to compensate for the economic effects of pollution itself or of pollution abatement. Instead, general principles or guidelines have to be developed which, if politically acceptable, can serve this function adequately. The cost of pollution control to achieve acceptable levels of environmental quality are pooled for both upsteam and downstream countries, and agreement is reached on the share of costs to be paid by each. As in the 'bargaining-and-rights' approach cost-sharing involves conflict, as each nation strives to minimise its share of the pooled costs and to set standards that minimise its share of environmental damage plus pollution-control costs.

A third proposal envisages that 'the upstream country alone bears the cost of pollution control (whether it is carried out upstream or downstream) in order to achieve the optimum level of pollution, when this can be defined, or when it cannot, a target level which is mutually satisfactory'.[8] Claimed advantages of such an international version of the PPP include : (a) concordance with the evolving international legal definition of environmental 'rights'; (b) non-acknowledgement by the upstream country of residual damage in the downstream country, obviating compensation payments; (c) compromise between inherent interests of the upstream and downstream countries; and (d) conformity with application of the PPP at the national level. Its main disadvantage is that no allowance is made for relative bargaining strength, and hence there is only a slim chance that such a solution would be adopted easily by *both* parties in a particular case of TFP. Once such an arrangement is agreed upon, a principle that 'who changes must pay' would be applied, placing the burden of alleviating *incremental* pollution squarely on the offending country.

Yet another proposal is the so-called 'mutual compensation principle', which involves mutual taxation of two countries that cannot easily agree on damage costs or pollution-control costs. The polluting country pays, into a common fund, a tax based on the polluted country's own estimates of damage caused, and the latter pays into the same fund a treatment tax based on the cost of pollution control estimated by the polluting country. The first tax will hopefully encourage the polluter to reduce TFP, while the treatment tax is designed to encourage the polluted country to estimate damage costs as realistically as possible. In short, 'the country requiring more intensive treatment must compensate by paying a higher treatment tax, whereas the country requiring a higher level of pollution compensates by paying a heavier pollution tax'.[9] A joint agency would record cost estimates, collect taxes and deduce the acceptable level of pollution. Net transfers under the scheme can, of course, shift over time, and there is no mechanisim for determining environmental targets on an *a priori* basis. A schematic of the process of agreement under the mutual compensation principle is presented in Figure 7.2.

A related set of proposals takes a somewhat more elaborate approach to the TFP problem, and again calls for the polluting country to bear the cost of removing TFP and the polluted country to bear the residual damage cost, with the target level of environmental quality subject to bargaining.[10] Moreover, fiscal transfers between the two countries may be required

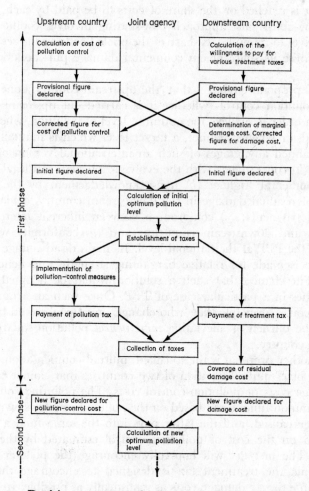

FIGURE 7.2 Decision process under 'mutual compensation' principle for resolving transfrontier pollution

Source: O.E.C.D., Environment Committee, *The Mutual Compensation Principle: An Economic Instrument for Solving Certain Transfrontier Pollution Problems* (Paris: O.E.C.D. Document AEU/ENV/73.12, 17 September 1973).

to finance pollution-control measures undertaken abroad. The polluting country should alone bear the full cost of overstepping the agreed environmental limits but, by analogy, the polluted country should alone bear the cost of reducing those limits below the jointly agreed level. Emphasis is also placed on assembly of basic pollution and cost data as well as the establishment of joint administrative and planning agencies.

All such proposals have been criticised on the grounds that they consider only a very restricted set of possible ways of handling the TFP problem, and that they will probably prove inept in a world subject to constant change and uncertainty.[11] The problem is that TFP conflicts of interest are all variants of the same basic proposition : 'either the polluter compensates the pollutee for damages done or the pollutee bribes the polluter to stop his pollution'.[12] Solutions all require the definitive establishment of property rights, defensible estimates of environmental damage and pollution-control costs and development of institutions to reconcile international differences. They are complex in character, and contain strong political, economic and legal elements set against the backdrop of national sovereignty. Solutions will clearly have to be approached on an *ad hoc* basis – as in the Trail Smelter case cited earlier – and must involve a diversity of institutional arrangements.[13]

IMPACT AND POLICY RESPONSE : ONE-WAY TRANSFRONTIER POLLUTION

Reciprocal TFP is in some ways an easier problem to resolve than simple one-way TFP. The reason is, of course, that the polluting country itself feels the direct consequences of its own action, which diminishes the cost–benefit gap between it and the victim country with respect to the pollution-control process. There is at least partial coincidence of both rights and damages. As a result, the bargaining conflicts are less, and the likelihood of compromise solutions is correspondingly greater.

Suppose two countries border on a common lake, which is divided in two by a causeway forming the political frontier. Each country, acting rationally, will minimise the combined cost of environmental damage and pollution control in accordance with its own environmental preferences – with possibly quite different levels of water quality in the two halves of the lake. Now suppose the causeway is removed and the waters of the lake allowed to mingle, resulting in substantial TFP and a single level of water quality for both countries – worse for one country and better for the other – identifying one as the net-polluter and the other as the net victim. The victim country may now reduce its pollution sufficiently to restore the water quality it previously enjoyed, while the polluter country may increase its pollution somewhat in the face of improved water quality. Such an action–reaction cycle will eventually lead to a stable equilibrium, but not one representing an optimum for both.*

The alternative is a programme of joint action, which is likely to be arrived at much sooner than in the case of one-way TFP. If their joint aim were to minimise combined damage and damage-avoidance costs, and tastes and costs differ, then such action will induce one country to shift resources from pollution control to other sectors, while the other

* This discussion follows Scott, *Transfrontier Pollution: Are New Institutions Necessary?* pp. 27–33.

country does the reverse, with a fiscal transfer between the two. Both may enjoy a cleaner environment than with independent action, and combined abatement costs may be lower. This is only one possible alternative, but the fact of interdependence facilitates agreement on joint action.

There are a variety of other problems related to two-way TFP. For example, what happens when one country is clearly dominant in terms of control of the joint environmental resource or simple political or economic power? What happens when three, four or more countries share the same resource? Is joint action in such cases facilitated or made more difficult, given the increase of information requirements and uncertainty?

Perhaps the most significant instance of concrete action in the face of two-way TFP concerns the Great Lakes of North America, which form a sizeable part of the boundary bwteen the United States and Canada. The Great Lakes basin forms the largest body of fresh water in the world, contains 30 million people, generates one-half of the Canadian and 20 per cent of U.S. G.N.P. and is used for transportation, recreation, energy, cooling, commercial fishing and wildlife, as well as domestic and industrial waste disposal.[14] Environmental damage incurred, particularly in the lower Lakes (Erie and Ontario) includes eutrophication, oxygen depletion, bacterial and visual contamination, accumulating solids, waste oil and thermal pollution, toxic materials and organic contaminants. The symptoms include foul-tasting and odorous water, disappearance of certain species of fish and certain micro-organisms, mercury contamination of fish, destruction of wildlife, oil accumulation on beaches, and so forth. Pollution originates from both the Canadian and American shores, but predominantly from the latter, roughly of the order of nine to one. Extensive studies have shown that TFP is indeed involved.

As early as 1909, the U.S.–Canadian Boundary Waters Treaty was signed to settle and prevent disputes concerning the Great Lakes and the international section of the St Lawrence River, later implemented by the formation of the International Joint Commission (I.J.C.) of six members, three from each side.[15] Its functions include approval of new uses affecting the boundary waters, and investigating as well as deciding issues referred to it by the two governments. The I.J.C. is a permanent tribunal, and its mandate is based on clearly stated 'rights' of the two countries with respect to the Great Lakes. In 1964, the United States and Canada requested the I.J.C. to undertake a major study of pollution in Lake Erie and Lake Ontario, as well as the St Lawrence River – its nature, its origins and appropriate remedial measures. The Commision submitted its report in 1970, which resulted in joint ministerial meetings in 1970 and 1971 to design and implement anti-pollution measures. These include 'common water quality objectives, better treatment of municipal and industrial wastes, a phosphorous control program, a contingency plan to deal with emergencies, and a program for further studies'.[16]

These general objectives were then used to design a series of specific environmental instruments and standards.

The cost of the Great Lakes programme is substantial, totalling almost 1.6 billion dollars in terms of 1968 dollars, of which a little under 1.4 billion dollars represents the U.S. share. Evidently no explicit cost–benefit analysis was undertaken by the I.J.C., and decisions seem to be entirely based on technical and pragmatic considerations. But by tackling a serious problem in a serious manner, the I.J.C. has scored a breakthrough in dealing with TFP of a two-way nature, even if the solution leaves something to be desired in terms of economic reasoning. Perhaps this is a case where the net cost of performing the indicated economic cost–benefit analysis outweighs the suboptimisation inherent in a more pragmatic approach.

RESOLVING ISSUES OF TRANSFRONTIER POLLUTION

Apart from the instances of one-way and two-way TFP cited above, both of which involves the United States and Canada, the incidence of TFP seems to be concentrated where zones of industrial concentration transcend national political frontiers, and where a large number of relatively small countries dominate a particular geographical area. As Table 7.1 shows, most of the instances that have been cited as examples of TFP so far – and have been the subject of some sort of mutual consultation – are located in Western Europe. One-way TFP is limited to rivers and certain air currents, while most of the remaining problems involve reciprocal TFP of lakes, seas, coastal zones and regional airsheds.

Also TFP is not always a relatively discrete problem in its own right, which can be clearly separated from other economic and political objectives. Just as the latter can be used to influence the shape of TFP policy, so the problem of TFP can be used as a pretext to achieve non-related national or regional objectives. For example, Indonesia and Malaysia have threatened to deny free passage in the Strait of Malacca – serving as a major artery for 50,000 vessels per year, of which over one-third are tankers – citing the danger of coastal pollution as the reason. While the need for better navigation aids and close monitoring of pollution is granted, proposals to exact a toll of 5000 dollars from each tanker and 3000 dollars from each freighter seem to indicate that the real motivation is power and prestige rather than environmental management. If accepted, such arguments applied to the 114 other straits in the world would represent a disaster for international shipping.[17] Again, it is a matter of rights: the rights of riparian nations to protect themselves from environmental damage versus the right of innocent passage and freedom of the seas. It is hardly surprising, though, that this conflict would be complicated by a variety of other national motivations.

Table 7.1 Examples of transfrontier pollution

Resource	Countries involved	Specific environmental problem
A. *River/waterways:*		
Rhine	France, Germany, Netherlands, Switzerland	Salt and thermal pollution
Saar	France, Germany	Industrial/municipal effluents
Moselle	France, Luxemburg, Germany	Same
Ems–Dollart	Netherlands, Germany	Effluents from the Netherlands
Meuse	Belgium, Netherlands	Drinking water supplies for Netherlands
Escaut	Belgium, Netherlands	Same
Danube	Germany, Austria, Eastern Europe	Industrial/municipal effluents
St John	Canada, United States	
B. *Lakes:*		
Constance	Germany, Switzerland	Drinking water for southern Germany
Leman	France. Switzerland	Municipal effluents
Lugano	Switzerland, Italy	Same
Maggiore	Switzerland, Italy	Same
Great Lakes	Canada, United States	Industrial/municipal effluents
C. *Seas:*		
North Sea	Bordering countries (8)	Same
Baltic	Same (8)	Same
Mediterranean	Same (15)	Same, plus accidental discharge
D. *Coastal zones:*		
Mediterranean	Italy, France, Spain, Yugoslavia	Effluents from coastal towns
North Sea	Norway, Sweden	Industrial/municipal effluents
E. *Air:*		
Scandinavia	Sweden, Denmark, Norway, Finland, United Kingdom, Germany	Acid rain
Netherlands	Netherlands, Germany	Sulphur dioxide from rural area
Saar-Lorraine	France, Germany, Luxemburg	Pollution from iron and steel industry
Benelux industrial zones	Belgium, Netherlands	localised industrial pollution
St Clair–Detroit	Canada, United States	Responsibility for nuclear accidents

Source: O.E.C.D. Environment Committee, *Outline of Program on Transfrontier Pollution* (Paris: O.E.C.D. Document AEU/ENV/72-7, Annex, 24 March 1972).

Whatever instruments are adopted to deal with TFP, there are certain criteria that may be used to guide policy-makers in designing solutions which are both economically efficient and equitable.

Economic guidelines

A good instrument will ensure the maintenance 'of an optimal pollution level over time through recourse to the least costly strategies of pollution abatement . . . and must promote use of the best methods of pollution control in whatever area they are applied (organization of transfers and purchase of treatment facilities)'.[18] Efficient management of TFP implies that : (a) decisions be made according to an implicit cost–benefit calculus and/or a collective decision process; (b) TFP control be undertaken at those locations where the objectives can be accomplished at least cost; and (c) provision be made for modification of both processes and objectives as conditions change over time. Economic efficiency may well mandate the creation of a joint mechanism charged with the task of decision-making, monitoring, planning, implementation and control, as well as an effective channel for fiscal transfers between countries.

Political guidelines

A good instrument will tend to contribute to smooth international relations, a factor which depends in part on the degree to which it departs from concepts that have been accepted at the national level. Specifically, it should discourage countries both from adopting extreme positions for negotiating purposes and from over-estimating the economic and social costs of environmental damage and pollution-control costs. At the same time, it should discourage recourse to the mass media and emotionalism in bargaining, and should balance costs and benefits for the participating countries. It should, in so far as it is possible, take the form of an extension to the international level of policies already adopted at the national level – for example the PPP – and should not require significant transfer of sovereignty to an outside agency. Lastly, it should involve creation of a task-orientated agency with a mandate limited to the TFP problem, and should not require mediation or arbitration by a third country or international organisation.[19]

Social guidelines

Perhaps the most difficult aspect of TFP control, as we have seen, involves the problem of equity. In general terms, 'a good instrument should first enable excessive pollution to be avoided and secondly allow the victims to be thoroughly, reliably and promptly compensated. While the instrument's preventive and deterrant character is more important than its remedial aspect, this latter feature must not be neglected.'[20]

All three sets of guidelines must be applied in selecting instruments to

combat TFP. The range of possible instruments includes the following:
(a) the 'pollution charge', involving taxation proportional to the amount
of pollution and rebates proportional to reduced pollution below an agreed
level; (b) the 'treatment charge', whereby the victim pays the polluter
for treatment below an agreed level of environmental quality and receives
compensation for pollution above this level; (c) the 'optimal line charge',
which is proportional to the treatment level and whose rate is equivalent
to the marginal cost of environmental damage at the optimal pollution
level; (d) purchase and sale of 'certificates' entitling the holder to discharge pollutants into the environment, between victim and polluter
countries; (e) sale of environmental rights, assigned by the countries involved to an international agency, back to the polluter at a price equivalent to the cost of treatment avoided; (f) mutual compensation, involving simultaneous use of treatment and pollution changes, as discussed
earlier; and (g) other instruments – including shared responsibility, tax
credits, concessionary interest rates, redistributive charges and lump-sum
subsidies – which make an attempt at proportionality but may not be
economically efficient as some of the foregoing techniques.*

Another class of instruments has been termed 'threshold instruments',
and involve simple compensation between polluter and victim when
pollution exceeds an agreed level, with a view to keeping over-all TFP
below this level. These are quasi-economic instruments linked to legal terms
such as 'abnormal', 'excessive', 'abrasive' and 'accidental'. They focus
on outright damage payments between countries, with the polluter com-
pensating the victim for 'excessive' impairment of environmental quality,
and includes collective compensation where risk of accidental pollution is
involved. They may involve substantial transactions and information costs,
and invariably require the assignment of guilt. They also include such
techniques as marshalling the pressure of public opinion through a variety
of channels – as used frequently where endangered animal species are involved – although the potential costs in terms of political tension may render this technique of questionable value in specific instances of TFP. Closely
related are diplomatic and economic pressures that can be brought to
bear, but these run the same kinds of risks of violating the political guidelines noted above.

The conceptual discussion of measures designed to deal with TFP is,
of course, at times quite far removed from reality – although it does
provide guidance to socially and economically efficient solutions. This
may be due to the fact that countries are already taking unilateral remedial
action and have no desire to rock the boat; or because countries are
fearful of undermining their own negotiating positions and compromising
their environmental 'rights'; or because the fiscal transfers might be poli-

* This classification scheme follows O.E.C.D., *Instruments for Solving Transfrontier
Pollution Problems*, Annex 1, which contains a full analysis of each set of instruments.

tically unacceptable at the national level. Such factors serve to complicate the TFP issue, even if the direction of sensible policy is reasonably clear. The outlook, then, is for slow progress, interspaced with periodic international conflicts as symptoms get recognised, or exceed the existing level of tolerance, and international political reaction develops. Principal industries affected may include agriculture, electric power, iron and steel, non-ferrous metals, chemicals, petroleum and particular kinds of manufacturing activity.

An example of a concrete proposal for establishing a foundation for resolving TFP issues is the O.E.C.D. 'Action Proposal on Principles on Transfrontier Pollution' of 1974. Member countries obligate themselves to prevent and control TFP, harmonise policies and devise a long-term policy to improve environmental quality in TFP zones. They commit themselves to prevent increases in existing TFP and to reduce it within a yet-to-be-specified time-frame. Specifically,

> countries should as far as possible seek a fair balance of rights and obligations as regards the use of shared or common environments. Countries should among other things :
> (a) take account of :
> − the nature and quantities of pollutants,
> − levels of existing pollution and the present quality of the environment concerned,
> − the assimilative capacity of the environment as established by each country concerned,
> − activities at the source of pollution and activities and uses sensitive to such pollution,
> − the situation, prospective use and development of the zones concerned from a socio-economic standpoint,
> − the need for a land-use planning policy consistent with the requirements of environmental protection, and
> − relevant environmental quality objectives and mutually agreed standards;
> (b) draw up and maintain up to date in a suitable framework :
> (i) lists of particularly dangerous substances regarding which efforts should be made to eliminate polluting discharges, if necessary by stages, and
> (ii) lists of substances regarding which polluting discharges should be subject to very strict control.[21]

In addition, TFP should not be subject to less severe legal and statutory provisions than domestic pollution, and levels of TFP should not exceed acceptable domestic levels. The PPP, if it is applied domestically, should also be applied in cases of TFP. There are also provisions for exchanges of information and design of 'early warning' identification systems, and the proposals envisage the establishment of joint bodies and international commissions wherever appropriate.

TRANSFRONTIER POLLUTION, INTERNATIONAL TRANSPORT AND OCEAN DUMPING

One sector where questions of TFP have already had a major impact on the international economy is transportation – frequently one of the principal determinants of trade between nations. Affected products include fuels, ores and other basic raw materials, lumber, cereal grains and similar bulk commodities. Since the cost of transport is generally higher in international trade than in domestic trade, the foreign sector tends to be disproportionately sensitive to environmental-control policies that affect the transportation industry. This sensitivity takes several forms.

First are marine safety requirements. Apart from the general need for improved marine safety, a series of collisions involving tankships and resulting in oil spills have, in the recent past, greatly increased pressures in this direction. Investments in anti-collision hardware and improved crew training, together with tighter enforcement of exisiting regulations have and will continue to raise shipping costs – both directly and as a result of delays attributable to more cautious traffic control, particularly in congested areas.

A related problem concerns maximum size limitations. Economies in bulk transport are achieved primarily by increasing vessel size. But the risk of environmental damage likewise grows with average vessel size, although not proportionately because of the reduced number of ship movements required to handle a given amount of cargo. Pressure seems to be mounting to set limits on maximum vessel size and, unless countered by advances in the safety area, may raise transport costs significantly above what they otherwise would be.[22] As we noted earlier, legal responsibility for accidental marine pollution is still being argued, but the trend is clearly toward increased liability for the ship owners, charterers and shippers. This is raising marine insurance premiums and hence shipping costs. Full liability for environmental damage, however measured, could have a major impact.

Environmental concerns are also affecting standard shipboard operating procedures. Examples include the flushing and cleansing of tanks at sea, sailing under ballast, disposal of shipboard sewage and dumping of solid wastes. In each case the answer lies either in the provisions of onboard treatment plants or in performing the necessary operations in port. Both are expensive in terms of capital requirements, as well as port charges average running times and other variable costs, and will raise the cost of sea transport. Moreover, fear of environmental damage has closed several coastal areas to development of ports, particularly for tankships, and most drastically on the U.S. east coast. This will require either suboptimal re-routing of supply flows or the development of offshore facilities at high cost, both of which will raise transport charges. At existing port facilities, stricter anti-pollution requirements in cargo handling procedures will have a similar effect.

From a policy standpoint, one of the transport-related issues that has received the most attention is waste-oil pollution of the seas. It has been estimated that pollution from ships accounts for about 10 per cent of all pollution of the seas. It also accounts for about half of the ocean pollution caused by oil, the remainder caused by land-based sources. A convention negotiated by the International Maritime Consultative Organisation (I.M.C.O.) in 1973 performs the following tasks: (a) prohibits the dumping of plastics and limits the discharge of other garbage at sea; (b) prohibits or regulates the discharge of chemicals at sea; (c) prohibits the discharge of oil and petroleum derivatives in the Mediterranean, Baltic, Black and Red Seas and in the Persian Gulf and within 50 miles of land; (d) promotes the construction of shipside reception stations for waste oil and chemicals; (e) requires that all tankers be out-fitted with on-board holding tanks for oily waste within three years, and that all tankers of over 70,000 tons built after 1975 be equipped with fully segregated ballast tanks; and (f) provides for compulsory arbi-tration of disputes.[23]

Strong leadership forcing a tough I.M.C.O. position was taken by the United States and Soviet Union, with the United Kingdom taking the most conservative position. Although accepted by 71 nations (with three abstentions), enforcement procedures will remain weak even after ratifi-cation, since unless the offence occurs in territorial waters prosecution can be brought only by the country whose flag the offending ship flies – which in many cases seems rather unlikely.

Transport-related environmental problems, whether involving TFP or not, are certainly not limited to the oceans. The Alaska pipeline contro-versy is only the most visible of a growing array of actions against the environmental consequence of this particular form of transport. The dis-ruption of domestic energy supply logistics caused by environmental re-straints will spill over on to the international trade sector and may lead to rather substantial economic dislocations. Fortunately, there are relative-ly few air-pollution problems arising from marine and air transport. Particulate emissions from gas-turbine exhausts have already been men-tioned, applying both to marine and aircraft propulsion units, and can be remedied fairly easily. Emission from steam-turbine and diesel vessels do not seem to be a serious problem, and evidently can be alleviated without significant impact on shipping costs.

With the exception of supersonic aircraft environmental control in international transport is unlikely to have a major over-all impact on the physical volume of international trade in the near future – particularly in the critical area of fuels – because they represent a relatively small component of final price and may be submerged by continuing demand growth in the face of steadily more apparent supply limitations. But they will raise the landed value of traded products, which includes transport costs, and may occasionally seriously disrupt normal flows of commerce among nations.

We have touched only briefly in this chapter on pollution of global common-property resources such as the atmosphere and the oceans. Both properly fall under the heading of TFP, and can only be resolved by means of broad international agreements which are binding on the signatures and which encompass essentially all of the world's nations. Pollution of the oceans has grown particularly rapidly in importance as the sea and the sea-bed developed into a critical source of basic materials and food.

Certainly one of the principal problem areas is ocean dumping – the discarding of municipal and industrial wastes, sewage sludge, radioactive materials, and so forth, in international waters. There is clearly a conflict here between freedom of the seas and the need to protect the oceans from environmental deterioration, and the conceptual problem fits into the general framework of two-way TFP, discussed earlier. Furthermore, the uncertainties characteristic of all environmental problems are even more serious in the case of ocean dumping because its effects on animal and plant life, its diffusion through ocean currents, and its indirect impact on man through the food chain, are all subject to scientific controversy.*

To conclude, we have in this chapter attempted to outline the problems of TFP in relatively broad scope. It is perhaps one of the easiest problems to which economists can apply the tools of their trade, yet certainly one of the most difficult in terms of contributing to solutions that make sense and are realistic. The international economic consequences of TFP are considerable, both in terms of its direct impact of environmental damage and pollution-control cost-avoidance and in terms of the economic dislocations that may result in the event of serious conflict.

FURTHER READING

Most of the work on the legal and economic implications of transfrontier pollution (TFP) has been done by members of the staff and consultants to the Environmental Directorate of the Organization for Economic Cooperation and Development in Paris. Some of the initial studies are collected in the volume *Problems in Transfrontier Pollution* (Paris: O.E.C.D., 1974). Additional studies, including those cited in the notes and references to this chapter, are released periodically in document form by the Environment Committee of the O.E.C.D.

* The 1974–5 United Nations Conference on the Law of the Sea, held in Caracas and Vienna, has not shed very much additional light on this issue.

L. M. Alexander (ed.), *The Law of the Sea: The Future of the Sea's Resources* (Kingston: University of Rhode Island, 1971).

Barry Commoner, *The Closing Circle* (London: Jonathan Cape, 1971).

Economic Commission for Europe, *E.C.E. Symposium on Problems Related to the Environment* (New York: United Nations, 1971).

H. W. Helfrich (ed.), *The Environmental Crisis* (New Haven: Yale University Press, 1970).

A. D. Scott, 'The Economics of International Transmission of Pollution', in *Problem of Environmental Economics* (Paris: O.E.C.D., 1972).

U.S. Department of Commerce, *Environmental Control Seminar Proceedings: Rotterdam, Warsaw, Bucharest* (Washington, D.C.: Government Printing Office, 1971).

Ingo Walter (ed.), *Studies in International Environmental Economics* (New York: Wiley, 1976) especially papers by R. C. d'Arge, C. Pearson, L. Ruff, R. Stein and J. Butlin.

8
Trade, Environment and Economic Development

One of the open questions arising out of the international economic dimensions of environmental management is its implications for the developing countries. These nations, encompassing two-thirds of the world's population, are faced with a host of serious problems and conflicting policy priorities – over-population, hunger and malnutrition, unemployment and underemployment, illiteracy, rural–urban imbalance and chronic poverty – many of which can only be solved by economic growth in the conventional sense. They require the absorption of larger proportions of the labour force in productive employment and increased efficiency in the use of scarce productive resources. Hence, one would hardly be surprised if, within the social welfare function that faces them, ecological questions generally assume a subordinate role for policy planners in developing countries.

Under present conditions, they simply may not be able to afford not to aim at maximum possible economic growth, and may have to reject out of hand anything which could interfere materially with this objective. They may be unable to concern themselves at this juncture with the fine points of industrial location, air pollution or despoilation of the land, and a certain degree of environmental degradation may well be accepted as a necessary cost of the otherwise efficient achievement of their primary objectives. Ecological balance may seem a luxury that they cannot afford at the present stage of development, although it may well be recognised that excessive postponement of concern with this issue could give rise to major problems later on.

ENVIRONMENT AND INDUSTRIAL EXPANSION

This does not deny that the developing countries have some very serious environmental problems of their own. Because of the limited capabilities of coping with environmental problems and the tendency to put conventional development objectives ahead of environmental safeguards, the results have periodically been 'environmental horror stories', where the environmental consequences of economic development have far exceeded what would have been tolerated (at least today) in the advanced countries. Examples that have been cited include dramatic losses in Peruvian cotton crops after the introduction of pesticides, phosphate mining in the central Pacific rendering an entire island uninhabitable, destruction of farming by tribes in Central Africa as a result of the environmental consequences of the Kariba Dam, stripping of Haitian mahogany forests for export, and so forth. Such cases are often blamed in large part on foreign firms, aid-granting institutions and governments that provide developing countries with technology without adequate concern on the part of either side with the environmental consequences.[1]

Even as certain environmental consequences are more damaging in developing than in developed countries, there is also the opposite argument that some of the effects of environmental pollution sometimes may be *less* dramatic in developing countries because their environmental assimilative capacity may be relatively higher. Hot, dry climates may reduce the impact of certain effluents from production processes. High rainfall levels may reduce the impact on air quality of some types of emissions. Low population densities reduce the effects of all types of pollution on the basis of *per capita* immissions, and large undeveloped tracts of land may render marginal encroachment by industry of comparatively minor significance. And the people themselves may operate under entirely different conceptions of the quality of life; they may be concerned more with elementary survival, nutritional adequacy and health than the environmental side-effects of the means of achieving these very fundamental goals.[2]

On the basis of such dramatic differences in environmental assimilative capacity and social priorities, one would expect environmental-control policies in the developing countries to differ fundamentally from those applied in the more advanced economies. This could manifest itself in different pollution-control standards and time-tables. With the marginal social benefits of pollution-intensive industries exceeding their marginal social costs in the developing countries, one would expect them to welcome development of these sectors, even with some damage to the environment. One would also expect them to have a relatively durable comparative advantage in the international markets for certain pollution-intensive product groups.

That there are differences of view on environment between developed and developing countries became clear during the course of a conference on this subject held at Founex, Switzerland, in June 1971.[3] Some spokesmen from developing countries indicated quite clearly that more industry was welcome even if it meant more pollution, while others voiced a much greater concern for environmental balance. One participant summarised the tenor of the conference as follows:

To a large extent, the current concern with environmental issues has emerged out of the problems experienced by the industrially advanced countries. With these problems developing countries, too, will be increasingly concerned. But the major environmental problems of developing countries today are essentially of a different kind. They are pre-dominantly problems that reflect the poverty and very lack of develop-ment of their societies. In other words, their environmental problems are those that can be overcome by the process of development itself. If we can say that in advanced countries development has been a *cause* of environmental problems, it is possible to argue that for develop-ing countries development may be a *cure* for environmental problems. It should be added, however, that concern with human environment does provide new dimensions to the development concept in that a new emphasis is not to be placed on the attainment of social and cultural goals as part of the development process.[4]

Environmental protection in the developing countries, to the extent that it moves ahead, will at the very least have a different emphasis than in the advanced countries. First, because the accumulated environmental damage is likely to be much less, emphasis will tend to be on *prevention* rather than *reparation*, with perhaps some exceptions in such areas as Sao Paolo in Brazil and other major urban centres. Secondly, effort will be concentrated on soil conservation, land reclamation, the use of fertiliser and pesticides, and so forth, partly because of the agrarian struc-ture of most developing economies and partly because such efforts pro-vide the scope for labour-intensive activity. Thirdly, a top priority will be the separation of storm and sanitary sewers, a serious problem in many countries subject to heavy tropical rainfalls, in many towns and cities for health as well as environmental reasons. Moreover, some of the environ-mental research in the advanced countries, particularly in weather moni-toring, marine pollution and information gathering, may be of direct benefit to the developing countries.[5]

ENVIRONMENT AND DEVELOPING-COUNTRY TRADE

The hypothesis that environmental preferences are lower and environ-mental assimilative capacity is higher in developing than developed count-ries is a convenient one to begin with. It leads directly to certain conclusions regarding international trade and investment flows involving the develop-ing nations, many of which are potentially beneficial to the poor countries. But any such hypothesis is bound to be vastly overdrawn. Just as there are wide differences in environmental policy among advanced nations, so too are there bound to be corresponding differences among even the poorest of countries. Concern with the environment may be one thing in Thailand, but quite another in neighbouring Malaysia or in Indonesia.

Furthermore, almost all developing countries have zones of industrial concentration, where commerce and industry locate in high-density metropolitan areas, in many of which environmental conditions match those found in the most advanced countries in terms of ambient levels of pollution and congestion. And, as we have already noted, sanitary conditions frequently represent a serious health hazard. This by itself may raise concern with environmental quality and its implications for human welfare. Nevertheless, it seems reasonable that emerging patterns of environmental management among the developing countries will differ quite systematically from those in advanced countries, and that this will have significant implications for international trade and investment flows.

There are several ways in which environmental management in the advanced countries may influence trade in the developing nations. First, with respect to process pollution, if the developed countries pursue more rigorous environmental policies than the developing countries, a differential movement in the prices of their respective products can be expected to emerge. Prices of export- and import-competing goods and services can be expected to rise in the developed countries relative to those in developing countries. Hence, the less-developed countries (LDCs) may obtain an edge in competing for markets in such countries' exports in third markets and in their domestic markets. This competitive advantage will differ widely among various traded product groups.

This may or may not lead to important shifts in trade flows favouring the developing countries. It depends on their ability to supply in volume the products in question within the bounds of their own environmental policy constraints. On the export side, this may lead to diversification by widening the range of products that can reasonably be expected to compete in foreign markets. On the import side, it may reduce the price-competitiveness of foreign goods, and enhance the market position of domestic import-competing goods. Pollution-control differences between developed and developing countries may thus promote export diversification and import substitution, both of which are standard policy objectives in economic development.[6]

Secondly, still covering process pollution, the same price movements that may produce a favourable impact on the *volume* of trade of the developing countries will tend to cause a deterioration in their *terms* of trade. They will have to pay more for imported manufactured and semi-manufactured goods, including such major imports as refined petroleum products, chemicals, pharmaceuticals and fertilisers, as well as food products and consumer durables. They may also have to pay more for capital equipment (as well as motor vehicles) built to environmental specifications in the advanced countries for which no need yet exists in the developing nations.

Even if such environmental 'overbuilding' can be avoided, research and development charges and other joint costs of environmental control will still be allocated to exports to the developing countries, thereby raising product prices. Any such terms of trade deterioration means that the

F

LDCs have to produce a larger amount of export goods in order to obtain in return a given amount of import goods and this, all else being equal, represents a real-income transfer from developing to developed countries. Fortunately, all else is not equal, and the competitive improvement in the flow of LDC trade (possible only if the terms of trade is allowed to deteriorate) may generate sufficient benefits in terms of employment of resources and developmental linkages to more than offset this potential cost.

Thirdly, developing countries may also benefit from the impact of environmental management on international trade in pollutive products. Again, internalisation of the environmental costs will require relative price changes, and less-damaging goods will be substituted for more-damaging goods. In both cases, we can expect a restructuring of international demand patterns away from environmentally-damaging goods which increase relatively in price and toward less-damaging goods whose prices fall relatively. To the extent that developing countries are major exporters of 'natural' products that compete with synthetics, for example, they should stand to benefit with respect both to the terms and volume of trade. Indeed, the positive terms-of-trade effect with respect to pollutive *products* trade may serve as an important offset to the negative implications of environmental control with respect to pollutive *processes* for LDC terms of trade.

The three propositions just noted are, of course, subject to a variety of qualifications. Capital goods may indeed be subject to modification for less-pollutive or more-pollutive operations as conditions require – either through designed changes or via 'add-ons' – so that the price paid by the developing countries, for imports of such equipment, need not rise dramatically for pollution-control reasons. Furthermore, a great deal depends on whether the PPP is followed in the advanced countries. If, for example, pollution abatement is subsidised by governments, both the adverse terms of trade and positive volume of trade shifts will be less than if the PPP is followed closely. For the developing countries, moreover, restrictions on pollutive products in the advanced countries may or may not bias consumption patterns in their favour, depending on the pollution characteristics of domestic goods relative to substitutes in developing and third countries. There is also the problem of intermediate goods. As the pattern of consumption and production changes in the advanced countries to reflect removal of environmental externalities, import patterns will invariably shift, and this may or may not benefit suppliers in developing countries. It is also important, lastly, to remember that not all developing countries will be in a position to take advantage of whatever favourable trade shifts may emerge, and the more advanced among them (for example, Singapore, Taiwan, South Korea, Mexico, Brazil) will be in a better position to undertake the sophisticated production processes that are no longer acceptable in industrial countries on environmental grounds.

Over all then, the international competitive effects of environmental management should be largely favourable to the developing countries. In the short run they should benefit from favourable shifts in the trade balance. In the long run, they will have a comparative advantage in the production of environment-intensive goods, and will benefit from shifts in both final-goods demand and intermediate-input demand away from more-pollutive and toward less-pollutive products. In certain highly demand-orientated sectors such as tourism the position of the developing countries should be especially favourable, with increasing tourist flows to the 'unspoiled' developing-country resorts caused by pollution and over-crowding at competitive resorts in advanced countries.[7] There is, of course, an inherent conflict in the encouragement of tourism and the pollutive consequences of industrial development, as well as the environmental problems raised by tourism itself, which require careful planning if the maximum over-all benefits are to be achieved.

Another link between environmental control and developing country trade concerns natural resources and trade in secondary materials. Perhaps more than other sectors, the extractive industries in advanced countries are under severe environmental pressure.

First, it is becoming increasingly costly in terms of environmental degradation to recover and transport raw materials and fuels. Examples include strip mining for coal, recovery of shale oil, offshore drilling, pipeline construction, and so forth. At the same time, increasing political awareness of this problem, combined with generally rising standards of desired environmental quality, compounds its impact on the logisitics of crude-material supply. This includes iron ore, copper, bauxite and other mining activities – recovery and transport of virtually all raw materials and their primary processing. Raw material exports from the developing countries may thus be advantaged – both in quantity and price. Also, perhaps more important, primary processing may increasingly have to be done in the developing countries. This has the advantage of increasing the value-added of LDC exports, and generating more favourable developmental linkages than arise out of crude-materials exports only. At the same time, the pollution content of such exports is apt to be quite high, so that the developing countries may be able to apply at least basic environmental safeguards without materially narrowing their competitive advantage.

At the same time, we should note that materials-recovery and recycling is an important and permanent aspect of environmental policy in the advanced countries.[8] Increasingly, the fact that the supply of the world's natural resources is finite is making an impression on developed-country planners. Rising prices of fuels and raw materials underlines this fact, as does heated international competition for long-term, assured supplies of renewable and non-renewable natural resources.

Meanwhile, the advanced countries are increasingly faced with a solid-waste problem that cannot be solved by conventional means. It makes a great deal of sense to try to close the materials 'loop' by recovering as many resources as possible from production and consumption wastes. Examples are paper, textiles, aluminium, sulphur, lead, mercury, steel, copper, and so on. While efficient and cost-effective collection and separation techniques – particularly for municipal garbage – are still under development, we have seen that the volume of potentially recoverable resources is enormous. Already these resources are entering the channels of international trade, and we know that the materials-recovery loop is heavily transnational in character.

Recovered materials will, of course, compete in world markets with virgin materials and, to the extent that these represent exports of developing countries, their export prices and foreign-exchange earnings may be depressed as a result. It is as yet too early to tell the extent to which this factor may be important, or to assess the long-term implications for the developing countries.

Prospective competition for LDC exports from recycled materials will take time to develop, and current price–cost relationships and technical constraints will almost surely prevent a short-term impact. None the less, recurrent shortages of primary commodities and general price increases, together with the increased cost of waste disposal, will eventually affect the growth of primary-materials exports, and technical breakthroughs may result in periodic disruptions. In such cases, a way of providing an early warning to the developing countries, perhaps together with adjustment assistance, may be an appropriate activity on the part of international organisations.

To summarise, it may not be unreasonable to expect the net impact of environmental management on the trade of developing countries to be favourable. They will have to pay more for their imports, almost certainly but their exports seem likely to gain more than proportionately in international competitiveness. In part, this is due to the general substitution of less-pollutive for more-pollutive final and intermediate goods, where the LDCs may be in a relatively strong competitive position. In part, it may be a result of fundamental variations in environmental preferences and assimilative capacities, which could be more durable between developed and developing countries than among the developed countries themselves.

TRADE AND DEVELOPMENT POLICY

We have noted in Chapter 5 that countries may be tempted to neutralise the international competitive impact of pollution control on their industries by applying compensatory import restrictions of various types.

The developing countries may be affected by such measures precisely because of trade advantages attributable to their greater environmental assimilative capacity and/or modest environmental preferences. We have already said that compensatory trade barriers are quite clearly unjustified on economic grounds if the environment is considered a productive resource which can and should affect international comparative advantage in production, resource allocation and trade. Several types of policy responses to the trade effects of environmental control may nevertheless have certain implications for the developing countries.

Firstly, it is clear that products which themselves pollute, in normal use or as consumption or production residuals, will be subject to national standards. Imports which do not meet these standards will be banned from national markets. Examples we have cited earlier include automotive emission standards, pesticide residues in food products, sulphurous fuels, non-biodegradeable packaging materials, and so on. Argument may centre on what standards are reasonable and proper, but there can be no argument about nations' sovereign right to impose whatever standards are deemed desirable – so long as they do not discriminate against imports. Developing country suppliers of imports must therefore either strive to meet whatever standards are set or they must withdraw from the market. The developing countries, which have frequently had serious problems with quality control and health-safety standards in international trade, may be especially hard hit by environment-related product standards. A variety of examples may be cited: the United States banning DDT in domestic use affects imports of food products from the developing countries. Many developed countries have moved to eliminate lead in fuels, which affects such developing nations as Bolivia. Mandatory reduction in the sulphur content of heating fuels have tended – at least before the 1973–4 oil crisis – to shift petroleum trade from Venezuela to North Africa, Nigeria and Indonesia.

Secondly, we indicated earlier that environmental product standards may be used as pretexts for outright protection in the form of non-tariff distortions.[9] Standards may discriminate between domestic and foreign goods; or they may be enforced in a biased way. Import inspection procedures may destroy part or all of individual shipments at the customs frontier. Provision in the law may require inspection during manufacture, with non-recognition of foreign inspection procedures. These are only a few examples of how such standards can easily be abused, but they make the point.[10]

The possibility that policy measures in the advanced countries could adversely affect exports of the developing countries was explicitly recognised in the 1972 United Nations Conference on the Human Environment. Among the 109 specific recommendations emanating from the Stockholm conference were the following, bearing specifically on this issue : (a) the world's wealthy nations would not invoke environmental matters as a pretext for discriminatory trade policies; (b) the General Agreement in Tariffs and Trade and the United Nations Conference on Trade and Development would be allowed to monitor and assess tariff and trade barriers resulting from environmental policies; (c) financial and technical assistance would be provided to help poor countries remove such obstacles to their exports; and (d) appropriate measures for compensation would be provided where environmental standards have a negative effect on developing nations' exports.[11] Thus, one of the principal concerns will be safeguarding market access for developing-country exports against non-tariff barriers related to pollutive products in so far as these measures are indeed discriminatory against imports.[12]

Developing countries have also voiced concern about the possibility of compensatory process-related import restrictions in the advanced nations aimed at their exports. Such 'safeguard' mechanisms, either providing for compensatory import duties or setting quantitative limits on the volume or growth of imports permitted, are likely to be highly arbitrary in their administration, and as much motivated by protectionism as by a desire to provide interim competitive relief from domestic environmental-control costs. And there is also the possibility of more general policies involving compensatory import duties and export rebates, with a view to imposing on imported goods sold in each country the same environment-control burdens as fall on locally produced goods. We have tried to emphasise that such policies cannot be justified as a way of evening out environmental advantages and disadvantages, quite apart from serious difficulties that would be involved in the equitable administration of such a scheme. But they remain of serious concern to the developing countries.

To a large extent, the importance of potential compensatory trade barriers applied for environmental reasons on exports of developing countries will depend on the policy instruments applied for environmental management in the advanced countries. The greater the reliance on the PPP, the greater will be the danger of compensatory restrictions. If, on the other hand, countries adopt widespread derogations from the PPP, the adverse implications for import-competing suppliers will be less.

If commercial policy reactions flow from environmental management efforts, the developing countries are very likely to bear a disproportionate impact, whether such measures are justified or not. Consequently, it will be important for the developing countries to identify at an early stage which products of export interest to them might be affected by import charges or other trade restrictions in the developed countries – both process-related and product-related. They can then work within established international organisations as GATT and UNCTAD to forestall to the extent possible the imposition of such barriers. Otherwise, the expected beneficial trade-volume effect of environmental control may not in fact materialise, and its adverse terms-of-trade effect may dominate.[13]

INVESTMENT FLOWS AND TECHNOLOGY TRANSFERS

We have pointed out that environmental management may, on balance, serve to enhance the international competitive position of developing countries, at least to the extent that it is not offset by compensatory barriers to market access designed to shield import-competing suppliers. Favourable trade shifts are only one way in which the developing countries may benefit from a general movement toward pollution control. Another is via capital flows, already discussed in general terms in Chapter 6. We pointed out that one of the unique characteristics of the environment is that it cannot be moved. A country that is short of labour can either import labour or it can import labour-intensive goods, and will probably end up doing both. The same is true for a country that is short of capital. But when a country's environment runs out of the capacity to assimilate production-related pollutants, that country has only one option, and that is to import goods that absorb these resources in production elsewhere. Environment represents an *immobile* resource, and the only way to use it efficiently is to shift *other* productive factors in order to bring this about.

From the standpoint of the firm, we have noted that environmental control generally represents an element of production cost, like any other, and the objective is to minimise this cost. As environmental quality standards rise, so does the cost of compliance. Besides applying the most advanced pollution-control techniques, there is nothing the firm can to to lower costs attributable to this source of existing sites. Meantime, it may be under pressure of competition from imports that are produced under more favourable environmental conditions, including some of the developing countries. It can, of course, move to another site, one where environmental assimilative capacity is higher and/or environmental standards are lower. If this makes sense, then the firm's actions in effect represent a flow of mobile resources – labour and capital – as well as technology and managerial know-how from an environment-scarce area to an environment-abundant area. This process may be interregional or international, as we have seen, and is rather likely to involve developing countries.*

As a result of international investment of this nature, environmental resources are being used more efficiently within the context of collective preferences determined at the national level. So long as there are no international environmental spillovers this kind of resource mobility is to be encouraged as an activity tending to raise the level of world welfare,

* This discussion is based on Ingo Walter, 'Environmental Control and Economic Development: The Issues Reconsidered', *Intereconomics* (March 1974).

defined so as to incorporate environmental quality. And since the environmental-balance gaps between the developed and developing countries may be both wide and durable, the latter can expect to benefit considerably, if indeed such flows do materialise.

Aside from the induced inflow of private investment, host countries can expect a 'package' of resources favourable to economic growth, including spilled manpower, managerial know-how, entrepreneurship and technology transfer. Under the circumstances, it is likely that resultant direct foreign investment will be export orientated and hence produce both positive income and balance-of-payments effects. It may also involve positive backward and forward linkages into the host economy and generate a variety of 'intangible' development benefits such as labour-force training, promotion of service industries, improved education and medical care, and so forth. Under some circumstances, such investment may be based on local availability of raw materials as well as on local environmental resources, thus raising the domestic value-added of the host country's exports. It is hardly unreasonable, for example, to expect the relocation of refinery capacity in oil-exporting countries, thereby shifting exports from crude to refined products and even petro-chemicals. The same might be possible in the case of other non-renewable resources, such as ferrous and non-ferrous metals, and even renewable resources such as timber.

Also within the environmental planning of the developing countries themselves, it may sometimes be advisable to welcome foreign investment in environmentally-sensitive industries. The foreign firms may have much greater financial and technical resources than small indigenous operators, as well as valuable experience in other countries with respect to environmental conservation, particularly in such industries as timber, where large, integrated foreign firms may be in a favourable position, with appropriate host-government pressure, to carry out environmentally-sound logging practices and reforestation.

When international investment in developing countries is clearly related to pollution, it can be expected to come under attack from certain elements in the source countries. Aside from allegations of exploitive behaviour on the part of the firms involved, charges will be levelled at the host developing countires, accusing them of short-sighted behaviour, repeating the environmental errors of the industrial nations, contributing to global pollution, and so on. In part, such accusations may stem from the negative employment, income and payments effects that may bear on the source countries of the investments, but the 'pollution-haven' argument will be the focus of the debate.

To carry the point one step further, the developed countries may argue that production abroad should meet the same environmental standards as at home. If it does not the goods entering international trade may be considered products of a 'sweated environment', and thus the source of unfair competition for domestic output subject to much stricter standards. Representations may be made for the developing host countries to adopt the same environmental standards, with the implied or explicit threat that failure to comply could result in compensatory action on the commercial-policy front. At the same time, the firms themselves may face sanctions – which may include capital controls – to prevent the initial shift in the location of production or to make it less attractive.

Again, if we consider environmental assimilative capacity to be a legitimate supply factor and agree that social preferences can and will vary between sovereign national states, any interference with environment-induced international movements in productive factors cannot be justified on economic grounds. This does not mean that such measures will not be undertaken, or that the 'pollution-haven' argument will not be used to provide justification for protectionist measures totally unrelated to the environment. This is an area where the developing countries need to guard their vital interests most jealously. Whether they will in fact do so remains to be seen.

Some of the arguments against pollution havens, of course, cannot be taken lightly by the developing countries involved, and particularly the allegation that they are being short sighted in welcoming pollutive investment bears scrutiny. It is often stated that retrofitting existing plants for pollution control may far exceed in cost the procurement of environmental 'add-ons' in the first place. If the marginal cost is indeed within reason, it may well pay to design anti-pollution capabilities into new productive facilities against the day when environmental damage in areas of industrial concentration becomes a significant factor even in a developing-country context.

Certainly, the problem of whether or not to welcome pollutive industrial investment into developing nations is an agonising one and there are no simple answers. The solution does not lie in imposing on LDCs the kinds of detailed and rigorous environmental regulations that exist in some of the advanced countries. Nor does the solution lie in a *laissez-faire* approach. What is needed is a careful analysis of the social and economic cost–benefit type that takes into account all of the positive and negative implications that can be identified given the existing state of the art. The options have to be clearly and carefully laid out, and the ultimate choice has to be made in accordance with the needs and objectives of the individual developing nation involved. Even then, it is certain that the choices made will differ from one developing country to the next.

Much of the pollution-related investment in developing countries will involve multinational corporations. As we have attempted to show in Chapter 6, MNCs represent an enormous resource that the developing countries can use to maximise social gains if the institutional arrangements are adequate, and if there is sufficient bargaining leverage on the

LDC side. Given its head, with absent or weak checks and balances, the MNC can also become a serious force opposed to the national interest in developing countries.

We have already established that the MNC is the most efficient channel that exists for the international transmission of environmental know-how. It typically operates in a large number of countries, some with strict environmental controls and some with lax standards. As the lagging countries begin to impose stricter norms, the MNC can simply transfer, *within the firm*, knowledge that it has already applied elsewhere. The transfer is rapid, efficient and immediately usable. At the same time, it is not clear whether MNCs will, as a matter of course, apply common environmental safeguards throughout their global operations. Chances are that they will not, and even if the firm were to apply common environmental practices, this would clearly raise the cost of production facilities and burden the host developing country with a higher required return on capital.

Moreover, whenever environmental standards are raised in the developing country, the MNC will clearly have an edge over local competitors. It has in all probability already met those standards elsewhere, and may be able to do so at lower cost than indigenous firms having to acquire the know-how *de novo*. To the extent that such firms do apply common environmental practices internationally, any competitive disadvantage this causes may eventually be more than offset by the 'demonstration effect'. In other words, the MNC may show the host country that it is possible to do things in ways that are less damaging to the environment. The host country may then apply stricter pollution standards, and the MNC may already have anticipated those standards.

Another element not to be overlooked is the role of environmental management as a factor affecting MNC–developing country relations. We know that a host of real and potential conflicts exist between the interests of the MNC and the LDC, and will probably continue to exist. Environment adds one more source of potential conflict, and can increase the vulnerability of the firm to nationalistic pressures as well as quite legitimate sanctions on the part of the host government. Finally, these same firms are under pressure in the advanced countries for seeking to avoid high labour costs and profit taxes. Capital flight to developing countries in order to avoid tough environmental standards, however rational this may appear, will call still further into question the social responsibility of the MNC and threaten restriction of its operations – which in turn may be detrimental to the interests of developing countries. In short, the multinational enterprise will be as heavily involved in international environmental issues affecting the developing countries as it is in other aspects of international economic relations. It may be used as an efficient transferer of know-how, but it may also serve as a source of potential conflict in this area.

DEVELOPMENT ASSISTANCE AND THE ENVIRONMENT

Just as environmental considerations may influence private investment in developing countries, so it may also have a bearing on inter-governmental- and international-organisation development assistance. Certainly, public aid grants and loans provide an effective vehicle for the advanced countries to impose their views concerning the environment on the developing countries.

A specific project in a developing country financed by external loans involves long-term burdens in meeting interest charges and debt amortisation schedules. To support itself, the project must generate sufficient real income to throw off the required transfers to meet debt obligations, and in addition generate sufficient foreign exchange through expanded exports or reduced imports to make the debt-service transfers possible. If it does not, the burden is shifted to the rest of the economy, and if performance here is equally unsatisfactory, then default or debt-rescheduling may be in prospect, with serious consequences for future external financing. A given project – whether it be in the public or private sector – will be more costly if it incorporates appropriate environmental safeguards than if it does not. And yet the incremental investment will yield neither the real goods and services nor the foreign exchange needed to justify itself in terms of future debt-service requirements.

Some developing countries may be understandably reluctant to invest in pollution control to achieve benefits at very high cost to themselves, benefits which they may not regard as sufficiently important to justify the environmental burden. This view clashes directly with the position of some in the developed countries that environmental standards should where possible be harmonised, that global environmental consequences may arise that in any case are subject to considerable uncertainty, and that the developing countries would be wise to build pollution-control capabilities into new facilities from the outset. To this latter point, developing nations frequently reply that this makes little sense when the social discount rate (relating the value of *present* to *future* real income) is as high as it is. So the debate continues and may add fuel to any North–South confrontation over environmental issues in the future.

Nevertheless, developing countries will increasingly have to prepare 'environmental-impact statements' in support of projects for which external financing is sought. These statements consist of careful analyses and projections, to the extent that the state of the art permits, of the environmental consequences of a given project and their respective causes. Such statements do involve time and effort, but they greatly reduce environmental uncertainty and minimise unforeseen consequences – they are already required by the World Bank as part of project appraisal. The question is how such statements will be used in evaluating loan or grant applications in the donor countries or institutions, and it is here that serious conflicts may well arise.

The Aswan Dam is a case in point. Its principal purposes are hydro-electric power and flood control. Its environmental consequences are much more complex. Silt no longer washes on to the land downstream of the dam and has to be replaced by manufactured fertiliser. Nutrients in the water at the Nile's mouth have declined; the sardine catch dropped from 18,000 tons in 1965 to 500 tons in 1968, and the reduced sardine population has affected a variety of larger species as well. The level of salinity in the eastern Mediterranean has increased, with salt water also spreading into the Nile Delta – affecting farmland and water supplies. The more rapid water flow below the dam has caused serious problems, requiring an additional series of smaller dams to slow it down. In Lake Nasser above the dam, silt is accumulating at a rate of 100 million tons annually, while the relatively stagnant water has bred snails that spread schistosomiasis and has increased the incidence of malaria. Lastly, evaporation of lake water may influence the climate of the region, while seepage into groundwater may result in other environmental consequences as yet unknown.[14] In short, the Aswan Dam seems to be an economic success but an environmental disaster. Some of the environmental consequences might have been foreseen, others perhaps not. In the balance, however, the social and economic costs and benefits must appear in a different light in retrospect than was anticipated beforehand. Surely a detailed environmental-impact analysis could have contributed to a more favourable outcome.

Environmental safeguards, however, cannot be limited to project appraisal alone, but must, instead, become an integral part of the development strategy and an apparatus of individual countries. As one observer expressed it :

> Ecological factors and expertise should be included in pre-investment surveys and in all planning, decision-making and action phases of development. The training of development experts must be improved. More support is needed for research into how adverse effects can be eliminated. More experiments are needed with intermediate technology and ecologically sound techniques adaptable to tropical and arid zones. The costs involved must be written off against the long-term benefits accruing from more effective and rational use of resources.[15]

As early as 1971, lending officers of the World Bank were alerted to the environmental repercussions of projects financed by that institution, and appropriate organisational changes were instituted with a view to helping developing countries avoid some of the adverse environmental consequences of industrial development. The general feeling was that the cost of prevention is far smaller than the cost of environmental reparation later on – if this is possible at all. A representative question went as follows :

How far should a development finance agency go . . . in promoting projects that use natural gas or petroleum as a source of energy, knowing that combustion of these fossil fuels adds to the carbon dioxide in the atmosphere? Could this be offset, at a cost, by increasing the forest area of countries, such as South Korea, that have been practically denuded of trees, nature's means of reducing CO_2 ; and, if so, how would we justify to a board of directors an investment in growing forests in one country to offset atmospheric pollution by CO_2 originating largely in other parts of the world ?[16]

The answers are not readily apparent, nor is the extent to which such international bodies should take it upon themselves to safeguard global environmental resources at the expense of more specific and immediate developmental needs of client countries.

Quite apart from the environmental aspects of development projects themselves, and the acceptability of safeguards to countries that are the sources of capital, there is the prospect that development assistance in general may be endangered. Aid, whether in the form of grants or loans, has rather clear-cut fiscal implications and represents claims on the tax-generated revenues of donor countries. As such, aid for development is given a place in the rank ordering of public-expenditure priorities in the advanced countries. It competes with welfare, medical care, education, defence, public works and other spending activities. Environmental control adds another spending priority that may not have existed before and as a result development assistance may be pushed even further down the list than it already is. Indeed, developing countries have made a major point of this issue, under the implied assumption of one-for-one environment/aid trade-off.

This line of argument has tended to be counterproductive. Proponents seem to forget that government budgets are not necessarily closed-ended – that aid must also compete with increased domestic and defence spending, and with private consumption and investment priorities (and lower taxes). And, more often than not, aid is argued on its own merits and how it fits into a country's general foreign-policy objectives. The potential variance from these sources surely outweigh possible competition from environmental management.

Furthermore, environmental control does not necessarily mean increased government spending – true only if the government directly or indirectly subsidises environmental efforts themselves or the underlying research and development. In point of fact, the fiscal implications depend on the environmental techniques employed. Enforcement of standards involves only administrative costs on the expenditure side, but may engender reduced tax revenues as firms' costs rise. Application of pollution taxes or auctioning-off of pollution permits may actually raise government revenues.

ENVIRONMENTAL REPARATIONS AND GROWTH CONSTRAINTS

Another intriguing argument put forward by the developing countries goes as follows. In the process of getting where they are, the industrial nations have seriously damaged their environment. The developing countries have not yet impaired their environment. The environment is the common property of all the world's citizens. Therefore, the industrial countries have taken something away from their own peoples *as well as* those of the developing world. The former can be taken care of by environmental control, and must be paid for by the developed countries. The developing nations, since they have no environmental control costs of their own, should be paid reparations by the developed countries in order to promote their own economic growth in a manner conducive to maintaining environmental quality.

The basis of this argument is that developing countries have been tangibly damaged by developed-country industrialisation. But to many in the advanced countries it is unacceptable – especially when some of the LDC benefits in areas such as public health are considered which could not have been achieved without developed-country industrialisation. It is felt that the developed countries *should* indeed assist the developing world in maintaining environmental quality in every possible way and prevent recurrence of some of the same mistakes, but the opportunistic demand for 'reparations' is at best counterproductive.

Nevertheless, the developing countries have a point when they insist on maximum caution with respect to TFP. Like all countries, they represent 'owners' of global common-property resources and 'consumers' of environmental quality, and hence have a stake in what others do to despoil those resources. Secondly, they can expect a certain degree of international pressure where they are alleged to have originated TFP, particularly in altering the ecology of rivers and seas. Certainly not least important, wildlife is considered a common-property resource, and all nations have an interest in saving endangered species – predominantly situated in developing countries – from extinction.

Also, individuals and groups in the advanced countries are not lack for diversionary arguments. 'Environment at any price' advocates have begun speculating about the future and have concluded that we cannot go on the way we have; that growth should be slowed in the advanced nations and that the developing countries should moderate their own desire for development. If this line of reasoning is politically irrelevant in the advanced countries, it has faced an even worse reception in the developing world. LDC spokesmen often react vehemently to suggestions that growth should be throttled for the sake of environment. It certainly does not help matters, and probably hinders the developing countries in thinking constructively about environmental management within the framework of what is possible.

To the extent that resources are increasingly devoted to environmental control, economic growth – as measured in the production of non-environmental goods and services – will slow automatically.[17] This retarding effect will be felt more severely in countries with low environmental assimilative capacities and/or high levels of desired environmental quality, and less severely in countries where the opposite conditions prevail. It so happens that most developed countries fall into the first category and most developing countries fall into the second. Hence the growth effects of environmental management tend to serve as an equaliser, helping to redress the imbalance in real-income levels between developed and developing countries.

Policy measures may also be undertaken by individual developed countries and international organisations to assist the developing nations in environmental protection. One recent study suggests the following:

> The possibility of giving to developing countries, on especially favourable terms, technical assistance and know-how in the field of pollution control and resource management should be studied. In cases where the natural carrying capacity of the environment in developing countries is reaching its limits, consideration should be given to incorporating into industrial projects created with foreign aid the necessary anti-pollution facilities. The very difficult problem here would be to ensure that such extra costs are met through supplementary funds on favourable terms – funds that are really additional to the overall flow of development assistance.[18]

To summarise, on the basis of differences in assimilative capacity and societal preferences regarding the environment between developed and developing countries, it might not be inappropriate to project that, on balance, the pollution-control issue may help rather than hinder the developing countries' position in the international economy. This may well prove to be a transitional phenomenon, but it may also in the interim assist them toward sustained and orderly export-led growth and the eventual achievement of economic balance. Indeed, stringent environmental control in the developed countries may favour both export promotion and import substitution in the developing economies by increasing the relative competitiveness of their imports. While the terms-of-trade effect of pollution control may well be negative, the positive competitive and capital-flow effects may be sufficient to shift the over-all balance in their favour.

Nevertheless, the developing countries have several distinct concerns on the environmental front, some imagined and some real.[19] They are worried that preoccupation with environmental management in the industrial countries will divert financial and real resources from needed economic assistance for development. They are concerned that the developed countries will try to pressure them into adopting and enforcing environmental norms entirely inappropriate to their societies, including adverse project appraisals in bilateral, multilateral and international organisation aid and lending programmes because high levels of environmental safeguards are not being met. They feel that they can adapt production facilities to their own environmental conditions, but fear that misdirected altruism and paternalism in the developed world will impede beneficial 'capital exports with pollution'. At the same time, the developing countries are hoping for special assistance in meeting some of the economic and social problems arising out of their ultimate need for environmental management. This includes aid for restructuring their national economies to meet environmental standards set elsewhere, and might be accompanied by an early warning, impact-cushioning form of technical assistance and prior consultations on new departures in environmental policy.

FURTHER READING

Thomas L. Blair, 'The Environmental Crisis in the Third World', *Intereconomics* (February 1972).

General Agreement on Tariffs and Trade, *Industrial Pollution Control and International Trade* (Geneva: GATT, 1972).

Marshall I. Goldman, *Ecology and Economics* (Englewood Cliffs, N.J.: Prentice-Hall, 1972).

Michael L. Hoffman, 'Development Finance and the Environment', *Finance and Development* (September 1970).

Horst Siebert, 'Environment and Regional Growth', *Zeitschift für National-okonomie*, no. 33 (1973).

Shigeto Tsuru, 'Aid, Investment and the Environment', paper presented at a Columbia University–United Nations Conference on Development and Environment, mimeo. (15 April 1972).

United Nations Conference on the Human Environment, 'Environment and Development: The Founex Report', *International Conciliation* (September 1971).

United Nations Conference on Trade and Development, 'Impact of Environmental Policies on Trade and Development in Particular of the Developing Countries', Geneva: UNCTAD document TD/130 (13 March 1972).

Ingo Walter, 'Environmental Control and Economic Development: The Issues Reconsidered', *Intereconomics* (March 1974).

International Environmental Policy

From the outset, one of the points emphasised in this book is that nations are substantially independent and sovereign in the shaping of environmental policies. Except where transfrontier pollution (TFP) is concerned, the achievement of environmental balance at the national level – involving a more or less unique set of trade-offs and instruments – is a matter for the national political decision process. The solutions can, will and probably should differ internationally, and we have been mainly concerned with identifying and outlining the international economic implications of such differences as may arise.

We have emphasised this 'environmental-independence' approach to the subject because that is the way things presently seem to be going. There are, at this writing, no effective international institutions that have the ability to influence national environmental policies, and none seem in the offing. Those international environmental institutions that do exist either are limited to research and inter-governmental negotiation, or are focused on very specific TFP isssues, as indicated in Chapter 7. This state of affairs is not necessarily ideal, of course. After all, if we are correct in saying that many countries eventually will emerge with generally similar target levels of environmental quality anyway, why not hasten the process of convergence along – and thereby avoid some of the international economic disruptions that would otherwise arise in the interim? Adjustment costs thus avoided might well exceed the interim deviations from social optima that would be involved at the national level. It has, after all, been shown that international agreement can be reached on specific aspects of environmental policy, such as the 'polluter pays' principle (PPP) hammered out in the O.E.C.D.

In this concluding chapter, we shall turn to the question of formulating international environmental policy, indicate some of the organisations that are or might be involved, and identify some of the areas where additional research seems badly needed.

INTERNATIONAL ENVIRONMENTAL CO-ORDINATION AND HARMONISATION

Several types of international uniformity in environmental standards may be identified. First, there are uniform product standards, whereby nations agree on a set of prescribed operating or residual characteristics that

G

goods must attain before they are permitted for sale in the market-place. Examples that have been mentioned include automotive emissions levels, biodegradeability standards for detergents and packaging materials, and so on.

Secondly, an attempt may be made to achieve uniform *ambient* environmental quality targets, that is to say the degree of concentration of pollutants in the receptor medium, such as an airshed or a body of water. In such a case, the environmental assimilative capacity of the receptor medium will determine the volume of pollutants that can be absorbed per unit of time without exceeding the target ambient level of environmental quality.

Thirdly, harmonisation and co-ordination may be aimed at the level of *emissions* from pollutive processes. This includes end-of-pipe measurements of the composition of sewage or industrial effluents injected into bodies of water regardless of the assimilative capacity of the receptor medium.

Lastly, it may be deemed necessary to gear international efforts to achieve uniformity at environmental immissions of pollutants, particularly toxic substances, by human beings or other forms of animal and plant life. It has been pointed out, for example, that, in the case of human beings, 'the environmental significance of a residual to a human receptor depends upon the equilibrium concentration level within the blood stream, which in turn is a function of complex variables, such as intake, body weight, metabolism and similar relationships'.[1] Hence, immission standards may focus on the maximum permissible exposure by the human organism to individual pollutants.

To what extent do uniform environmental standards seem desirable or necessary in each of these four areas?

With respect to environmental performance, operating characteristics and disposal of products entering international trade, uniformity does not seem necessary or desirable from the standpoint of countries where the products are sold. International differences in environmental characteristics and preferences would seem to reject the need for substantial homogeneity in product standards. Little or no TFP is involved, and the environmental characteristics of products directly affects the price, so that the relevant trade-offs are readily apparent. Countries will set standards for products saleable in the domestic market – as is already done for product safety and health standards – and non-compliance simply means exclusion from the market. That wide differences have emerged in environmental product standards is quite evident in the automotive industry, for example.

On the other hand, uniformity in environmental product standards may be quite desirable from a production standpoint. This would avoid shortened production runs in accordance with different national design specifications, and would safeguard economies of scale that otherwise could be lost, as we noted in Chapter 3. How important this argument is, relative to the resultant product price and quality effects, remains to be seen. It depends at least in part on the ease with which product specifications may be changed during production. In some cases, including automobiles, environmental safeguards often involve 'add-ons', which are in any case undertaken by manufacturers with optional equipment and with international variations in technical and safety specifications. In other cases, such as containers, it may be considerably more difficult. Over all, it would appear that the arguments for international uniformity in environmental product standards are not very telling, and a good case can be made for continued heterogeneity.

On the other hand, uniformity in environmental product standards would reduce the danger of such standards being imposed for outright protectionist reasons. It would also reduce an inherent conflict between the twin objectives of a cleaner environment and freer international trade. Within the O.E.C.D., for example, there seems to be considerable agreement that an effort should be made to devise uniform product standards where these may be required for the prevention of non-tariff barriers, or to promote achievement of environmental goals, or to reduce adaptation burdens for industry. Certainly in the area of toxic substances, it is felt that uniform product standards are desirable.[2]

What about uniformity in *ambient* environmental quality targets? We pointed out in Chapter 7 that, where TFP is at issue, clear agreement of the affected parites on a target level of ambient environmental quality is generally necessary for solution of the problem. In the case of one-way TFP, this target does not need to be the same for both countries, and only agreement on a target for the receptor (victim) country is necessary for a solution to be reached. Uniformity is, however, desirable – and probably necessary – in the alleviation of two-way TFP as in the case of a boundary lake if continuous interflow of pollutants within the common environmental resource exists.

If there are no explicit and measurable environmental transfers between countries, the case for uniformity in environmental targets is greatly weakened. Nevertheless, the argument could be made that uniformity in ambient environmental quality targets will help to reduce international differences in pollution-control costs and hence their possible effects on international competition. However, in terms of efficient use of environmental resources on a global basis, this seems a weak argument indeed. With reference to Figure 1.1 (p. 20), with uniform targets the *DEQ* functions for all countries would be the same but the *EDF* functions would continue to differ, both in position and shape. Consequently, the diversion of productive resources to environmental control would continue to trigger short-term international competitive effects as well as longer-term shifts in comparative advantage, but these would not be as severe. Moreover, uniform environmental targets still would not guarantee uniformity of pollution-control instruments, and additional disturbances would certainly arise from this source.

Nevertheless, there has developed a view that at least some movement toward uniformity in environmental quality targets may be justified under certain circumstances. In the O.E.C.D. there seems to be some sentiment in favour of fixing basic minimum environmental quality targets acceptable to all countries, perhaps combined with a programme of gradually raising these minimums over time. Beyond this, the O.E.C.D. finds justification for uniformity in environmental targets only in border areas where significant TFP may be involved, as discussed above, and in the case of economic or political unions which decide to adopt common environmental objectives.[3]

There would appear to be even less justification for international harmonisation of *emissions*, simply because any such standards would take no account whatsoever of environmental assimilative capacity. Extremely high volumes of pollutants injected into certain environmental receptors may do little or no damage, while much smaller volumes of pollutants impacting on others may cause massive disruptions. Only in the case of extremely toxic substances or radioactive materials, where diffusion via the food chain or other mechanisms is involved or threatened, does international uniformity in the form of prohibitions seem to make sense.

The same point can be made for environmental *process* standards, which prescribe the production processes from which the emissions result. If it is rarely legitimate to harmonise emissions, then it is virtually impossible to justify harmonising the *means* which lead to such emissions. Even if certain emissions criteria could be agreed upon, there is still a great deal to be said for leaving countries, industries and firms free to find the most cost-effective processes to achieve these targets.

Lastly, a much stronger case for harmonisation and standardisation can be made for the emission of toxic substances affecting the health and welfare of human beings. Such standards, given definitive medical and biological evidence, might be widely accepted by all nations and lead to a removal of the contaminant in question. An example that has been cited in this connection is radiation, where there has already been a marked reduction of emissions in the form of curtailed atmospheric nuclear testing, and where pollution-control efforts promise to be even more effective as evidence mounts on the long-run consequences of radiation for human beings.

On the other hand :

To the extent that scientists remain unable to agree upon a relatively narrow range of biological safety in environmental standards, the case for uniform international environmental standards will be weakened. The case for uniform standards would also be weakened by divergent international attitudes concerning the value of human life, appropriate rates of discounting the future, and other basic value differences . . . .[4]

One might add that environmental considerations can easily be over-ridden by conflicting goals, including military strategy, and this may prove to be a problem in the future. On the other hand, successful nego-tiations on the environmental front may go forward in parallel with inter-national accommodation and conciliation in other sectors.

Increased uniformity in international environmental policy is certainly required in the *definition and measurement* of pollutants. At the present time, there seems to be a great deal of confusion in this highly complex technical area, with the result that international discussions frequently must concentrate on finding common definitions of terms and criteria rather than moving directly toward resolution of the problems at hand. Institutions such as the International Standards Organization (I.S.O.) have long attempted to remove differential standards as barriers to inter-national market access and trade, and there seems to be no reason why they should not actively extend their efforts into the environmental field as well. Certainly, international agreement on measurement of environ-mental quality seems a prerequisite both to assessments of the economic impact of pollution control and to utimate convergence on common stan-dards where these may be appropriate.

In summary, then, we find relatively little explicit justification for uni-formity in environmental standards among nations, with several impor-tant exceptions. One involves TFP, where under certain conditions a strong case for harmonisation and co-ordination of standards can be made. Another involves the establishment of uniform limits for biological exposure to toxic emissions. Lastly, uniformity may be desirable in the establishment of minimum quality levels for air and water world wide, but this may not be very helpful in actually moving toward the achieve-ment of such minimums or allocating the costs involved.

INTERNATIONAL ENVIRONMENTAL CO-OPERATION

Policy developments in the field of pollution control have been rather limited at the international level, partly because the required transnational forums have not existed. Some progress has been made in bilateral negotiations – as between the United States and Canada and between Germany and Switzerland – where two-way TFP has affected national interests. Far less progress has been made on a multilateral level, with the possible exception of the O.E.C.D., in part because of the problem of mutuality of interests – with some countries concerned with a particular environmental issue and others not – and because the requisite degree of supranational concern does not yet exist. One can expect that most progress in the intermediate term will be made on an *ad hoc* basis through regional negotiations of countries directly concerned with individual instances particularly of transfrontier environmental despoilation. In addition, the European Economic Community may obtain a certain degree of supranational authority in this field, although very little progress appears to have been achieved thus far.

Certainly the most extensive and promising efforts in the field of international environmental co-operation has been undertaken in the O.E.C.D. Member countries have generally accepted the concept of notification and consultation among each other concerning environmental measures applied by individual countries and the obligation to justify such measures. As early as 1971, for example, an 'early warning' procedure for chemical substances and heavy metals potentially dangerous to the environment was adopted. Moreover, a major programme of research and discussion has been devoted to defining the nature of the environmental 'problem', identifying policy options open to governments, and evaluating their prospective impact on national and international economic variables. This has contributed to the development of common language of environmental affairs and a rapid diffusion of the state of the art among member nations. Perhaps most importantly, the O.E.C.D. has focused on developing an international consensus on the principles of cost allocation resulting from environmental-protection measures and has succeeded in reaching agreement on the PPP. The principal intent here was of course to minimise possible conflicts between nations resulting from the effects of environmental policies on international competitive relations.

Organisationally, the O.E.C.D. efforts centre on the Environment Committee, set up in 1970 to pull together all of the work in this field. As noted in Figure 9.1, there are four sector groups, whose areas of responsibility are, respectively, air management, unintended occurrence of chemicals in the environment, water management and the urban environment. In addition, there is a subcommittee of economic experts, and the Environment Committee works closely with such other O.E.C.D. groups as the Oil Committee, the Energy Committee and the Industry Committee on specific issues of joint interest. Some of these (as of 1972) are noted in Figure 9.1. Secretariat functions are provided by the Environment Directorate, using internal staff and outside consultants – and particularly the Central Analysis and Evaluation Unit, which is charged with taking an over-all view of the environmental issue and relating to the economic and social development of the member countries. This includes the development of new research methodologies as well as empirical studies and co-ordination between sector and *ad hoc* groups.[5]

O.E.C.D. activities in the field of environment appear to be well

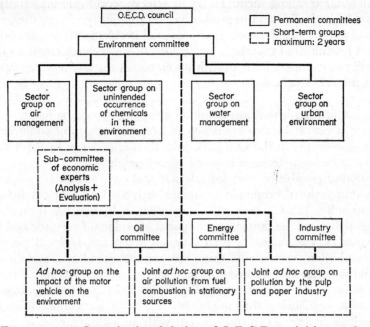

FIGURE 9.1   Organisational design of O.E.C.D. activities on the
environment

Source: O.E.C.D. Observer, no. 53 (August 1971) p. 3.

organised, well managed and well funded. They have focused from the
outset on learning the facts about environmental problems, in so far as
they can be known, and exchanging information among the various
national states – at the sectoral and the general level – both as a cross-
fertilisation process and to indicate what kinds of national decisions are
likely to have international repercussions. On the other hand, with the
exception of environmental cost-allocation principles, little headway as
yet seems to have been made in terms of harmonising environmental
policies through international agreement.

The O.E.C.D. forum, nevertheless, lends itself as well to additional
efforts that may involve environmental co-ordination and harmonisation.
As one observer notes :

International agreement on emissions standards must be achieved first
on a regional basis, and the OECD is the logical place to begin. It is
the only intergovernmental organization that embraces all the technically advanced nations of the non-Communist world. It is not too soon to
start negotiating uniform standards for OECD countries and a time-

table for reaching them. To try to achieve worldwide uniformity now
would be foolish and unproductive. In a majority of countries, people
and poverty are the great environmental problems; waters are polluted
not by industrial chemicals but by human waste. Such countries simply
will not tolerate adding to their development costs, except perhaps on a
highly selective basis.[6]

The implication is that any common standards should be hammered out
among a reasonably homogeneous and cohesive group of countries such
as is represented in the O.E.C.D. *first*, then adhered to by other nations
as they advance in terms of economic development.

Another possible avenue for international environmental co-operation
is within regional economic groupings such as the European Economic
Community (E.E.C.) Economic integration in Europe has from the outset gone beyond the simple establishment of regional free trade and factor
movements, encompassing such issues as social and regional policy, tax
harmonisation, creation of European product standards, and so on. It
would seem logical, therefore, if the EEC administrative apparatus were
also to focus on environmental policy – with a view at least to harmonising
pollution regulations that might interfere with intra-community trade,
as well as an attempt to cope directly with intra-E.E.C. cases of TFP.

Relatively little progress has been achieved within the E.E.C. thus far
A number of preliminary studies of pollution in the E.E.C. have been
undertaken by the European Commission, including a detailed set of
proposed guidelines and regulations. These were essentially the product of
the Paris Summit Conference of October 1972, which mandated the
Community agencies to establish a detailed environmental action programme by the end of July 1973, including a proposed implementation
schedule. The Commission's proposals include plans for implementing, on
an all-E.E.C. basis, the PPP and the uniform calculations of pollution-
control costs in order to minimise competitive distortions. It remains an
open question how far the E.E.C. Council of Ministers will go in support
of the Commission's proposals, since there are wide differences in environmental policies among the member states (as noted in Chapter 2) and
substantial legal harmonisation would be involved

Nevertheless, it is likely that uniform E.E.C. criteria for pollutants such
as lead, sulphur dioxide, carbon monoxide and particulates, as well as
noise, will be developed in the foreseeable future, including systems and
techniques of measurement. A set of European environmental 'norms' in
the form of targets relating to product and process pollution may well
emerge in the foreseeable future. But progress will be slow, as indicated
by the fact that one of the priority E.E.C. targets – the reduction in
lead content of automotive fuels – is not scheduled to occur until 1978,
over five years after acceptance in principle.

Operating on a broader basis is the United Nations Environmental Programme (UNEP), which grew out of the 1972 United Nations Conference on the Human Environment and was established at Nairobi under the leadership of Maurice Strong. Since the United Nations already has a rather large group of organisations and agencies concerned more or less directly with environmental questions – ranging from the United Nations Industrial Development Organization (UNIDO) to the World Health Organization (WHO) – one of the principal functions of UNEP appears to involve a co-ordinative role. Given the nature of the United Nations Organization, this in itself seems an exceedingly complex task, and has to be undertaken alongside possible initiatives originating within UNEP itself. The funding available during the 1972–7 five-year programme totals 100 million dollars.

It is, of course, far too early to evaluate UNEP's performance as a force shaping environmental policies on a global scale. There are, however, some disturbing signs. In addition to its remote location and poor representation in the major diplomatic and business centres, the staffing and construction demands of the organisation seem to be getting out of hand, with almost one-quarter of UNEP's budget spent on administrative costs alone. This is not surprising, given the poor cost-effectiveness record evidenced by other parts of the United Nations; but to begin life in this manner will almost surely hinder UNEP's ability to mobilise future resources for environmental programmes in anything like the required amounts.

There are more substantive problems as well, and the first meeting of UNEP's Administrative Council indicated a wide divergence of views between the developing countries (a two-thirds Council majority) and the developed countries as to the proper scope and content of a global programme of environmental action. The result was a marked de-emphasis of such issues as industrial pollution control and exchanges of environmental data, and a strong concentration on crop-land erosion, land cultivation, irrigation, public health and sanitation, as well as problems of human settlements – for which purpose alone a special fund of 240 million dollars was requested basically to finance municipal infrastructure and urban housing in developing countries.

That a difference of views would emerge in UNEP between the developed and developing countries as to the proper range of activities for the organisation seemed clear from the outset. That the divisions would appear so soon and be so deep is unfortunate, and promises to impair – perhaps permanently – the effectiveness of that organisation in coming to grips with the problems of pollution and its consequences. As one observer notes: 'If the confrontation in UNEP goes on, the industralized countries will sooner or later have to tackle the problem of pollution urgently through another organization, for it brooks no delay.'[7]

There is, of course, a danger in all of this by making the environment yet another confrontational ground between North and South, between developed and developing nations, and once again *institutionalising* this confrontation. The advanced nations may end up making their decisions in the O.E.C.D. where problems of pollution are of paramount import- ance, and a certain degree of harmonisation and co-ordination may well be achieved in that forum. Such common principles will then have to be adhered to by the developing countries whether they like it or not, and they will have been precluded from having a voice in decisions funda- mentally affecting their interests. This has happened before – for example in the fields of international trade policy and international monetary re- lations – with the developing countries' views counting only at the margin through such confrontational institutions as the United Nations Confer- ence on Trade and Development. This was probably unavoidable in view of the imbalance between the two groups in terms of economic power. But the same inevitability need not carry over to the environmental area, because there are no differences between countries in their claim to envi- ronmental quality or in the nature of environmental problems that must be dealt with. It would indeed be unfortunate if opportunism led to such a fragmentation of international environmental policy.

A special problem relates to the planning for environmental control in the socialist countries of Eastern Europe and Asia (S.C.E.E.A.). The principles underlying economic relationships between centrally planned and market-orientated economies have not been well developed. The theory is the same, but use of that theory to predict the direction, product- composition, volume or terms of East–West or intra-S.C.E.E.A. trade leaves a great deal to be desired. The rules of the game are different and we do not always understand them. The rules also change periodically, so that such behavioural constructs as can be developed tend to be un- reliable. The evidence is that several of the S.C.E.E.A. countries are pur- suing environmental goals as energetically as the more advanced developed market-economy countries and indeed implementation in a centrally planned economy may be considerably easier. But the implications for international economic relations are virtually impossible to determine given the present state of knowledge of the way those relations develop.

INDUSTRY ASSOCIATIONS

Multinational corporations and other firms have developed an active interest in international environmental policy, in part to ward off some of the disruptive economic-policy reactions they fear might develop with- out some common ground-rules. They have, for example, generally supported the PPP as a way of moderating the international competitive effects of environmental management.

One approach taken by industry is closer co-operation between enter-prises and governments through industry associations on questions of environmental standards, enforcement, subsidies and related issues, as well as facilitating the flow of technical and cost data to government agencies concerned with pollution matters. As one study noted :

Associations can pool experiences of firms and evolve industry-wide policies and positions on environmental concerns. They can aggregate confidential data from individual firms prior to furnishing data to government. Additionally, they can perform a variety of legislative monitoring and reporting functions, eliminating duplication of effort among member firms, limiting the number of required contact points for interactions, and obtaining greater credibility for their actions and pronouncements than can individual firms.[8]

A principal rationale for the involvement of industry associations is to serve as a back-up to government negotiators at the international level. This assists in providing representatives with the required technical data and policy views of the enterprises not directly involved, without which any agreements reached would face severe problems in ratification. More-over, international industry associations can often reach agreement on points of substance more rapidly and more efficiently than inter-govern-ment negotiations. At an even broader level, the International Chamber of Commerce (I.C.C.), uniting councils of industries at the national level, has frequently taken constructive positions on international commercial and financial issues which have led the way to international agreements. In the environmental field, for example, the I.C.C. held a World Industry Conference on the Human Environment in Gothenburg, Sweden, one week before the opening of the U.N. Stockholm Conference, although it contributed little of substance to the Stockholm debate.

A good example of co-operation between industry and international organisations is the Industry Co-operation Programme (I.C.P.) sponsored by the U.N. Food and Agriculture Organization. Composed of a number of specific groups, it includes, for example, a pesticides subgroup, which has at its disposal a great deal of data on aerial spraying and its environ-mental consequences.

At the same time, the record of industry associations has hardly been unblemished in the field of environment. They have frequently concen-trated on fighting a rearguard action, holding off as long as possible the passage of environmental legislation, and then attempting to frustrate its implementation at the administrative level and through the courts. More-over, there are conflicts of interest among industry associations as well – for example, between the automotive industry and the petroleum indus-try – and this makes it difficult to develop horizontal collaborative efforts.[9]

To this must be added anti-trust regulations, which at the very best narrow the range of international environmental co-operation among business firms.

ENVIRONMENTAL POLICY AND DEPLETABLE RESOURCE STOCKS

Emphasis on environmental management, as we have repeatedly stated, is a matter of collective decision-making, first and foremost at the national level, in the context of a host of complex and frequently conflicting social objectives. It is hardly surprising, therefore, that public concern with the environment should have its ups and downs, as other priorities recede or take precedence. The latest of these is the apparent shortage of depletable raw materials. This issue is often tied to the environmental question because natural resource recovery itself frequently involves serious environmental disruption, because certain natural resources (climate, water supply, space) are part of the environment as normally defined, and because the same kinds of aggregate forces – such as population expansion and economic growth – have similar long-range implications for both the environment and the adequacy of natural-resource supplies. This issue, and some of the remedies suggested to deal with it, have important implications for the future of the international economy and international environmental policy.

Of greatest intermediate-range importance is the so-called 'energy crisis', with a recent four-fold price increase for international petroleum supplies and an outlook of a continued longer-term rise in global energy costs. In the very long-run, the problem may, of course, ease with the development of energy sources not based on depletable natural resources. Countries that previously had a balanced energy economy, for example the United States and the Soviet Union, shift in the intermediate term to becoming major exporters or importers, or both. Countries that were large importers may become less dependent on foreign supplies as local sources of the same fuel or substitutes are discovered and developed at higher cost. Countries that were large exporters shift their strategy from maximum trade volumes at prevailing prices to restricting development and export, husbanding reserves and exploiting their new-found leverage in the international market-place. International commercial and financial relations are affected in a variety of ways.

First, fuel-producing countries such as the United States previously geared to self-sufficiency, although continuing that policy, become increasingly dependent on imports. Incentives for domestic exploration may be maintained or increased, intended to slow the steady rise of energy imports. Incremental domestic production of fuels will in most cases be insufficient to meet incremental demand but the shortage will be narrowed as prices rise, by coal and shale-oil recovery, secondary petroleum recovery techniques and the development of nuclear, fuel-cell and other advanced sources of power.

Secondly, new fuel exporters will emerge as rising prices and shifting national energy policies stimulate exploration and recovery. The list that already includes the Soviet Union, Nigeria and Indonesia, will doubtless grow in the future. These countries have historically been chronically short of foreign exchange and the present value of export receipts is extremely high, causing them to opt for long-term supply contracts, relatively liberal exploration rights, imported capital equipment including turn-key processing plants, and foreign technical-assistance arrangements. As they become mature energy exporters these policies will change, but not in the immediate future.

Thirdly, the major volume suppliers of fuels to the world markets, including North Africa, Venezuela, Iran and the Middle East have increased their bargaining power considerably. Supplier pressure on prices can be expected to continue, along with increasing caution regarding the volume of production and rates of depletion. There is a real question how a country that has a single principal export commodity can maximise its long-term welfare when the supply elements underlying those exports have a finite life and are non-renewable. One can predict that supplier cartels such as the Organisation of Petroleum Exporting Countries (OPEC) may draw closer together and be come more binding on the participants. Fuel-exporting countries will also continue to press for increasing national participation in ownership, management and control of production and transport facilities, and to press further demands for increased shares of export receipts.

One can also predict that efforts will be made to increase the value-added of exports based on crude oil and natural gas. Hence it will hardly be surprising – particularly in the light of the relatively lax pollution standards likely to exist – to find refineries and petro-chemical plants, as well as gas liquefaction plants, being built at the principal OPEC terminals. The major oil firms may be encouraged to participate, or the plants may be state owned and built with technical assistance from abroad. Again it is not necessarily to be expected that pressures of this type originating at the supply end will be received passively in the major markets, particularly in the major fuel-deficit countries of Western Europe and Japan. Hence there is an expected tendency, already in evidence, for national governments to involve themselves individually and collectively in negotiations directly with the exporters. There is also the tendency to tie the principal energy suppliers to the industrial markets by trade agreements and other devices in the search for security in sources of fossil fuels.

These trends will tend to characterise world energy markets in the foreseeable future, perhaps until the end of the century. Demand growth is fairly predictable and supply estimates for traditional fuels are also reason-

ably good – albeit with greater margins for error. What is highly uncertain is the development of subsititues – immediately in the nuclear
field but later in more exotic energy forms – and hence the uncertainty
regarding the price and income elasticity of demand for oil, coal and
natural gas. Experience with nuclear power sources seems to indicate that
the growth of on-line capacity will be gradual, slower than initial projections – partly for environmental reasons. But this does not preclude
major breakthroughs in the 1980s and 1990s which would signal the
start of a new ball game in the international energy sector.

Countries supplying the international market with non-fuel natural
resources, will tend to be subject to the same kinds of market factors,
but the pattern will be much more diffuse. Each type of mineral will
exhibit a unique scarcity pattern, depending on discoveries of new supplies,
demand growth, availability of viable substitutes, and so on. In most cases,
uncertainty about the direction and magnitude of market trends is much
greater than in the case of fuels. Hence it is difficult to project what
shifts in trade flows or changes in world prices will occur. It is even more
difficult to project what will be the policy responses of the mineral-
exporting countries' governments in their efforts to maximise the contribution of available natural resources to national economic growth. They
will demand increasing national control over mining and other recovery
operations, as well as internal processing to attain higher value-added in
exports. Another point that needs to be mentioned, about which very
little is known as yet, is the exploitation of the sea bed, both for fuels and
other minerals. Undersea resources may drastically alter available supplies
of certain raw materials and introduce an entirely new factor into world
markets, and this needs to be drawn into any projections as a *caveat*. There
is also the question of who 'owns' these resources and how they are to be
extracted. This is predominantly a legal issue with strong economic and
political overtones, with which the United Nations is currently occupying
itself. Hopefully, there will be a definitive and enforceable resolution of
this problem well before technical advances make raw material extraction in volume from the sea bed commercially feasible.

Each of the aforementioned developments is linked to environmental
management. As noted, 'shocks' to the international economy such as
posed by the oil crisis affect environmental priorities. Dirty fuels may be
substituted for clean fuels, for example, or more efficient but environmentally damaging combustion processes may be substituted for cleaner
but more fuel-intensive ones. Entire environmental time-tables may be
'stretched out', as countries attempt to grapple with the more immediate
problem and to minimise its over-all economic impact. Again the resolution of conflicting priorities will be different in each country, and will
determine the implications for the international economy. Generally, however, it would not be wrong to expect environmental priorities to reassert

themselves once a particular 'shock' has worked its way through the system and some kind of equilibrium has been restored.

At the same time, the search for new sources of traditional and substitute materials and fuels will place increased pressure on the environment. Pollution safeguards in the extractive industries may have to be relaxed, and the pressure for raw materials may carry into increasingly risky environmental zones.

DIRECTIONS FOR FUTURE RESEARCH

The issues discussed in this book embody a wide variety of dimensions, none of which has been explored thoroughly as yet. We simply do not know which of the international economic implications of environmental management will be very important, and which may well be trivial. All we can do, as we have done here, is identify each of them, point out the possible cause-and-effect linkages that would appear to exist, and make a preliminary assessment of their potential significance including their likely policy content. A substantial amount of additional research is required with this problem, and it may be useful to end this book by indicating what directions such research might productively take.*

Two critical research areas fall outside the area of expertise of investigators likely to be concerned with the international economics of environment, yet represent very fundamental inputs into defensible economic analyses. One is the need for further basic and applied research into the causes and cures of environmental despoilation. This includes narrowing down the precise sources of damage to the environment and distinguishing the immediate, long-term and interregional effects on the human environment. Reducing these uncertainties through research in the relevant physical and life sciences will make a major contribution to evaluating their economic implications. In the meantime we will have to live with these uncertainties, with the often bitter controverises to which they give rise. Also, the economic researcher needs to bear in mind that the presence of uncertainty may have perverse effects on the system, including irrationality and emotionalism on the one hand and extreme caution on the other.

Second is the need for investigation of political responses to environmental issues. Even if all of the consequences of environmental despoilation were known, and especially if they are not, reactions by political collectivities are likely to differ. The question is how and why they differ, and what kinds of factors affect the collective decisions that must be made and when they are made. The need here is for comparative research in the

* This section draws on Ingo Walter, 'Environmental Management and the International Economic Order', in *The Future of the International Economic Order* ed. C. Fred Bergsten (Lexington, Mass.: D. C. Heath, 1973).

social and behavioural sciences focused on this problem, with a view to providing even preliminary indications about what policies nations are likely to adopt in the area of environment and how soon. Until such research has begun to reveal the social equations underlying environmental management, reliance must be placed on revealed preferences in this field – revealed by actions already taken and policy positions that seem to be evolving.

Perhaps the most critical need is a comprehensive inventory, updated continuously, of current environmental policies and programmes in all countries classified according to type of pollutant and affected industries. Based on this sort of continuous stock-taking, it may be possible to develop a defensible set of estimates of the cost of pollution control, by product and by industry. Such cost estimates should contain capital costs, operating costs, research and development, depreciation and other applicable charges per unit of output and, using input–output analysis, also the pollution-control costs of intermediate and raw-material inputs. As we have seen, preliminary attempts to obtain such data are not as reliable as they should be, and much work needs to be done in this area. Estimates such as these would permit determination of which products bear heavy pollution-control costs and which do not, and hence which products and industries may be affected by international differences in environmental management approaches.

Using appropriate demand and substitution elasticity estimates, further research could also indicate the anticipated environment-induced shifts in trade flows and their impact on national economies. Other research might assess the impact of differences in environmental instruments on international prices and trade flows in individual products or product groups. In the near term, a comprehensive approach of this type may not be possible and it may be fruitful to perform a series of global industry-studies focused on sectors that are highly pollution intensive in the first instance. Environmental-control measures affecting a specific industry could be superimposed on a broad-based study analysing supply economics, major markets, industrial structure and trade. Aggregate econometric approaches promise to be very useful in the future, provided improved pollution-control data become available, particularly for drawing balance-of-payments, foreign-exchange, and long-term competitive implications.

Research is needed on the extent to which pollution-control norms bearing on products are applied in a discriminatory manner as between foreign and domestic goods, and how this may lead to a proliferation of non-tariff distortions of trade. To the extent that such standards affect demand patterns, how does this influence imports and exports of consumer durable and non-durable goods, capital equipment, intermediates, fuels and raw materials? There is also a basic question whether a massive and rapidly growing international market for pollution-control hardware and software is a myth or a reality. How does the demand for pollution-control equipment and technology react to tightening environmental standards? Will the same approaches to specific environmental goals be used everywhere, or will significant differences emerge? What is the research and development content of pollution-control equipment, and does this indeed confer a material international competitive advantage on suppliers located in countries leading in environmental management? To what extent will this result in increased tangible exports, licensing or other transactions that may represent a useful offset to leader countries that otherwise would tend to suffer competitively in international markets?

There remains great uncertainty about the prospects for trade in recycled materials. What materials will be recovered as a result of tightened environmental norms and in what volumes? How much further processing is required to render them saleable on national and international markets? How will they compare in quality and price with virgin materials? Where will the recovered materials originate and where are the main centres of potential demand? Since recycled materials compete with virgin materials, how will this affect raw-materials prices and exports of the major supplier countries? How will trends in raw-materials prices develop and, in turn, how does this affect the incentive to recycle? Empirical analysis in this area, as in the aforementioned case of pollution-control hardware, is difficult because standard trade statistics do not provide sufficient detail to permit differentiation between the products in question and other goods unrelated to environmental control. A basic need, therefore, is a reliable source of data indicating whether recycled materials are involved, and whether individual products or product groups are intended for environment-control purposes.

Perhaps less is known about the locational effects of international differences in environmental standards them almost any other aspect of the subject. Will pollution-control differences between nations be sufficient to force a relocation of production? If so, what industries will be affected and how will they tend to relocate? How will this affect development and employment patterns, trade flows and international payments? What commercial policy reactions might be applied in response to capital flight induced by pollution controls? What are the possible sources of conflict between the firm, the home country and the host country in the case of environment-induced shifts in industrial location? Again, most rapid progress can probably be made through firm and industry studies, because this is the level at which the various factors affecting plant location operate. Since industry seems to have adopted location plans in response to differential environmental policies in the United States, perhaps this example can be used to infer what might happen at the international level in the future. Measures of the sensitivity of industries to environmental policies in their locational decisions are of critical importance. The hypothesis that environmental pressures may lead to a shift in industries from high- to low-income regions and countries needs to be tested. Does the political balance really tend to promote location of pollution-intensive plants in the poorer countries? Is there really a trend toward exporting pollution-intensive industries in some of the more advanced industrial countries?

With respect to transfrontier pollution, a primary need is a clear delineation in specific cases of what the transboundary pollution impact zones are, and an assessment of whether the problem is sufficiently serious to warrant inter-government action. Second, there is the question of how environmental spillovers originating in one national state result in economic damage in other countries, and a need for defensible measures of the extent of this damage that can serve as a basis for the mutual search for acceptable solutions. A third question is what forms these solutions may take, and what their economic implications are, especially for the country that is the source of the problem. Assessments particularly need to be made of the need for relocation of industries and fundamental changes in their operating procedures, including the direct cost of environmental control.

On a broader scale, the question of oceanic and atmospheric pollution remains subject to extensive scientific and political uncertainty. Once the precise, long-term effects of individual contaminants on the biosphere have been identified and evaluated, rational solutions can be identified and the international machinery set up to implement them. Progress will probably be made on a piecemeal basis, considering individual contaminants such as mercury, cyanide and D.D.T. and agreement sought on a relatively narrow base but progressively attacking additional contaminants as their impact becomes measurable and visible. The principal problem will be obtaining general agreement among disparate nations with widely differing social goals and political and economic systems which vary equally widely in their subjective identification with the global ecosystem.

Lastly, there is a need for further research on the 'limits to growth', environmental and otherwise. And growth constraints that are identified will clearly affect international economic transactions, while the latter may distribute more evenly demands made on the global ecosystem and hence promote the avoidance of serious environmental bottlenecks. Historically, it is certainly clear that international trade as well as flows of people, capital and technology has alleviated periodic environmental and other kinds of growth limits. The fundamental question is whether this can continue, and in what sectors it will be particularly effective. On the other hand, international commercial and productive-factor flows have also exacerbated regional growth limits in the past, and this is likely to continue and to intensify. The supply capabilities of the globe are limited, and *redistribution* of these capabilites via the international economy can only partly alleviate the problem. The important issues centre on the extent to which this can occur and what kinds of variable will play a critical role.

A derivative question concerns the application of puroseful growth-limiting economic and social policies, particularly with respect to population. The necessity for such limits is not yet entirely clear, and neither is their timing. Research on this question must go beyond dynamic econometric models, based on questionable assumptions and data inputs of poor quality, within the context of fixed or relatively fixed resources. Forecasting technological change will be a major task, of fundamental importance for the outcome of such studies. This has never been very successful, and the question is whether improvements in its reliability are in prospect. However, it is a prerequisite for identification of future pressure-points and growth-limiting factors and for assessing their implications for the international economy.

FURTHER READING

John H. Cumberland 'The Role of Uniform Standards in International Environmental Management', in *Problems of Environmental Economics* (Paris: O.E.C.D., 1972).

Gerard Eldin, 'The Need for Intergovernmental Cooperation and Coordination Regarding the Environment', *O.E.C.D. Observer* (February 1971).

Christian A. Herter, Jr, 'Preserving the Environment: The International Front', *Business Economics* (January 1971).

James C. Hite *et al.*, *The Economics of Environmental Quality* (Washington, D.C.: American Enterprise Institute, 1972).

International Institute of Environmental Affairs, 'The Human Environment: Science and International Decision-Making', Aspen, Colo. Workshop Report, no. 1 (1972).

National Academy of Sciences, *Institutional Arrangements for International Environmental Cooperation* (Washington, D.C.: National Academy of Sciences, 1972).

O.E.C.D., Environment Committee, 'Environmental Standards: Definitions and the Need for International Harmonization', Paris: O.E.C.D. Document ENV (73)33 (11 October 1973).

Philip W. Quigg, 'Organizing for Global Environmental Management', *Columbia Journal of World Business* (May–June 1972).

Anthony D. Scott, 'Transfrontier Pollution: Are New Institutions Necessary?', O.E.C.D. Environment Committee, Document AEU/ENV/73.10 (August 1973).

Ingo Walter, 'Environmental Management and the International Economic Order', in *The Future of the International Economic Order*, ed. C. Fred Bergsten (Lexington, Mass.: D. C. Heath, 1973).

References

CHAPTER ONE

1. Two examples are P. R. Ehrlich and A. H. Ehrlich, *Population, Resources, Environment: Issues in Human Ecology* (San Francisco: Freeman, 1970); and D. H. Meadows *et al.*, *The Limits to Growth* (London: Earth Island, 1972).
2. See Ingo Walter, 'Environmental Management and the International Economic Order', in *The Future of the International Economic Order*, ed. C. Fred Bergsten (Lexington, Mass.: D. C. Heath, 1973).
3. For a comprehensive discussion of air and water pollution, see W. L. Faith, *Air Pollution Control* (New York: John Wiley, 1959); and Allen V. Kneese and Blair T. Bower, *Managing Water Quality: Economics, Technology, Institutions* (Baltimore: Johns Hopkins Press, 1968).
4. James M. Buchanan, 'Individual Choice in Voting and the Market', *Journal of Political Economy* (August 1954); and Anthony Downs, 'An Economic Theory of Political Action in a Democracy', *Journal of Political Economy* (April 1957).
5. On externalities, see especially: J. M Buchanan and W. C. Stubblebine, 'Externality', *Economica* (November 1962); E. J. Mishan, 'The Postwar Literature on Externalities: An Interpretive Essay', *Journal of Economic Literature* (March 1971); as well as R. U. Ayres and A. V. Kneese, 'Production, Consumption and Externalities', *American Economic Review* (June 1969).
6. Mishan, 'The Postwar Literature on Externalities'.
7. E. J. Mishan, 'Welfare Criteria for External Effects', *American Economic Review* (September 1961).
8. E. J. Mishan, 'The Relationship Between Joint Products, Collective Goods, and External Effects', *Journal of Political Economy* (May 1969).
9. See also W. J. Baumol, 'External Economies and Second-Order Optimality Conditions', *American Economic Review* (June 1964); and T. Scitovsky, 'Two Concepts of External Economies', *Journal of Political Economy* (April, 1964).
10. A comprehensive discussion of the economics of environment, which is beyond the scope of this book, may be found in Horst Siebert, 'Ökonomie und Umwelt: Ein Überblick', *Jahrbuch für Nationalokonomie und Statistik*, Bd. 188, Heft 2 (1974); and Allen V. Kneese, 'Environmental Pollution: Economics and Policy', *American Economic Review*, Papers and Proceedings (May 1974).
11. See Chase Econometric Associates, Inc., 'The General Economy', in *The Economic Impact of Pollution Control: A Summary of Recent Studies*, Council on Environmental Quality, Department of Commerce, and Environmental

Protection Agency (Washington, D.C.: Government Printing Office, March 1972).

12. Deutscher Industrie- und Handelstag, *Kostenfaktor: Reine Luft* (Bonn: D.I.H.T., December 1972).

13. Subcommittee of Economic Experts, Environment Committee, O.E.C.D., 'Survey of Industrial Pollution Control Estimates' (Paris: O.E.C.D. Document AEU/ENV/73.3, 16 April 1973).

14. Committee on Public Works, U.S. Senate, *Hearings Before the Sub-committee on Air and Water Pollution*, 91st Congress, 2nd Session (Washington, D.C.: Government Printing Office, 1971) pp. 390–1.

CHAPTER TWO

1. For a review of standard trade theory, see *inter alia* W. M. Scammell, *International Trade and Payments* (London: Macmillan, 1974); or Ingo Walter, *International Economics* (New York: Ronald Press, 1975).

2. See Robert G. Hawkins and Ingo Walter (eds), *The United States and International Markets: Commercial Policy Options in an Age of Controls* (Lexington, Mass.: D. C. Heath, 1972) especially ch. 2.

3. See R. G. Lipsey and K. Lancaster, 'The General Theory of Second Best', *Review of Economic Studies*, no. 1 (1956–7).

4. See, for example, D. H. Meadows *et al.*, *The Limits of Growth* (London: Earth Island, 1972).

5. Cf. Nazli Choucri and James P. Bennett, 'Population, Resources and Technology: Political Implications of the Environmental Crises', *International Organization* (Spring, 1972).

6. See especially W. Beckerman, 'Economists, Scientists and Environmental Catastrophe', *Oxford Economic Papers* (November 1972).

7. Committee on Public Works, 93rd Congress, 1st Session, *The Effect of Pollution Abatement on International Trade*, The First Report of the Secretary of Commerce to the President and Congress in compliance with Section 6 of the Federal Water Pollution Control Act Amendment of 1972 (Washington, D.C.: Government Printing Office, 1973).

8. O.E.C.D., Environment Committee, *Collection and Analysis of Pollution Control Cost Data* (Paris: O.E.C.D. Document ENV/AEU/72.4, 24 March 1972).

9. Ibid. p. 11.

10. O.E.C.D., *Pollution by the Pulp and Paper Industry* (Paris: O.E.C.D., 1973).

CHAPTER THREE

1. Stephen P. Magee and William F. Ford, 'Environmental Pollution, the Terms of Trade and Balance of Payments of the United States', *Kyklos*, Fasc. 1 (1972).

2. Chase Econometric Associates, 'Macroeconomic Study', in *The Economic Impact of Pollution Control*, Council on Environmental Quality *et al.* (Washington, D.C.: Government Printing Office, 1972).

3. Ibid. p. 14.

4. Ralph C. d'Arge, and Allen V. Kneese, 'Environmental Quality and International Trade', *International Organization* (Spring 1972).

5. O.E.C.D., Environment Committee, *Collection and Analysis of Pollution Control Cost Data* (Paris: O.E.C.D., 24 March 1972).

6. Deutscher Industrie- und Handelstag, *Kostenfaktor: Reine Luft* (Bonn: D.I.H.T., December 1972).

7. O.E.C.D., Environment Committee, *Survey of Industrial Pollution Control Estimates* (Paris: O.E.C.D. Document AEU/ENV/73.3, 6 April 1973).

8. Ibid. p. 39.

9. For alternative calculations, see F. Huynh, 'The Relative Pollution Intensity of U.S. Trade', Department of Economics, Michigan State University, unpublished (1973); also W. Leontief and W. F. Ford, 'Air Pollution and Economic Structure: Empirical Results of Input–Output Computations', in *Input–Output Techniques*, ed. A. Brodey and A. P. Carter (Amsterdam: Elsevier, 1973).

10. Cf. Dennis L. Meadows and Jorgen Randers, 'Adding the Time Dimension to Environmental Policy', *International Organization* (Spring 1972); also J. W. Bishop and H. W. Hubbard, *Let the Seller Beware* (Washington, D.C.: Washington National Press Inc., 1969).

11. David A. Aaker and George S. Day (eds), *Consumerism: Search for the Consumer Interest* (New York: The Free Press, 1971).

12. Cf. Ingo Walter, *Environmental Control and Consumer Protection: Emerging Forces in Multinational Corporate Operations* (Washington, D.C.: Center for Multinational Studies, 1972).

13. Cf. G. A. Jentz, 'Federal Regulation of Advertising', *American Business Law Journal* (January 1968); also D. Cohen, 'The Federal Trade Commission and the Regulation of Advertising', *Journal of Marketing* (January 1969).

CHAPTER FOUR

1. Cf. Sanford Rose, 'The Economics of Environmental Quality', *Fortune* (February 1970).

2. For a review and assessment, see Gary C. Hufbauer, 'The Impact of National Characteristics and Technology on the Commodity Composition and Trade in Manufactured Goods', in *The Technology Factor in International Trade* ed. Raymond Vernon (New York: National Bureau of Economic Research, 1970).

3. Cf. R. E. Caves, *Trade and Economic Structure* (Cambridge: Harvard University Press, 1961), especially with reference to the Rybczynski theorem and the possibility of reversals in factor intensities.

4. See Council on Environmental Quality et al., *The Economic Impact of Pollution Control* (Washington, D.C.: Government Printing Office, March 1972); W. Leontief, 'Environmental Repercussions and Economic Structure: An Input–Output Approach', *Review of Economics and Statistics* (August 1970); and W. Leontief and W. F. Ford, 'Air Pollution and Economics Structure: Empirical Results of Input–Output Computations', Harvard University,

mimeo. (1972). The extent of the shift in the transformation function depends, as indicated earlier, on the shape of the environmental-damage function, i.e. environmental assimilative capacity.

5. A. Y. C. Koo, 'Environmental Repercussions and Trade Theory', *Review of Economics and Statistics* (March 1974)
6. Cf. Ralph C. d'Arge and K. C. Kogiku, 'Economic Growth and the Environment', *Review of Economic Studies* (January 1973).
7. Science and Technology Report, 'Pollution Control Market to Grow Rapidly', *Commerce Today* (18 September 1972).
8. See Raymond Vernon, 'International Investment and International Trade in the Product Cycle', *Quarterly Journal of Economics* (May 1966); and W. Gruber, D. Mehta and R. Vernon, 'The R & D Factor in International Trade and International Investment by United States Industries', *Journal of Political Economy* (February 1967).
9. For derivation of the trade-indifference curves, or welfare levels, see James E. Meade, *A Geometry of International Trade* (London: George Allen & Unwin, 1952).

CHAPTER FIVE

1. See, for example, Orris Hefindahl *et al.*, 'Economic Implications of Materials Policy', in *Man, Materials, and Environment*, National Academy of Sciences (Cambridge, Mass.: M.I.T. Press, 1973).
2. O.E.C.D., Environment Committee, 'Guiding Principles Concerning the International Economic Aspects of Environmental Policies' (Paris: O.E.C.D. Document C(72)128).
3. Ibid. para. 4.
4. O.E.C.D. Environmental Directorate, Document AEU/ENV/71.18 (1971) italics added.
5. See R. G. Lipsey and K. Lancaster, 'The General Theory of Second Best', *Review of Economic Studies*, no. 1 (1956–7).
6. Committee on Public Works, 93rd Congress, 1st Session, *The Effects of Pollution Abatement on International Trade* (Washington, D.C.: Government Printing Office, 1973) p. 1.
7. For a survey of the state of the art in concept and measurement of effective protection, see Herbert G. Grubel and Harry G. Johnson (eds), *Effective Tariff Protection* (Geneva: GATT, 1972), especially J. Clark Leith, 'Tariffs, Indirect Domestic Taxes, and Protection'.
8. Ingo Walter, 'Pollution and Protection: U.S. Environmental Controls as Competitive Distortions', *Weltwirtschaftliches Archiv* (March 1974).
9. Robert E. Baldwin, *Non-tariff Distortions of International Trade* (Washington, D.C.: Brookings Institution, 1970); Ingo Walter, 'Non-tariff Protection Among Industrial Countries: Some Preliminary Evidence', *Economia Internazionale* (May 1972); and Ingo Walter and Jae W. Chung, 'The Pattern of Non-Tariff Obstacles to International Market Access', *Weltwirtschaftliches Archiv*, Bd. 108, Heft 1 (1972). A survey of the issues is contained in Ingo Walter, 'Environmental Control and Patterns of Inter-

national Trade and Investment', *Banca Nazionale del Lavoro Quarterly Review* (March 1972).

10. See Charles Pearson, 'Environmental Control Costs and Border Adjustments', School of Advanced International Studies, The Johns Hopkins University, Baltimore, mimeo. (October 1973).

11. See General Agreement on Tariffs and Trade, *Industrial Pollution Control and International Trade* (Geneva: GATT, 1971).

12. See Robert G. Hawkins and Ingo Walter (eds), *The United States and International Markets* (Lexington, Mass.: D. C. Heath, 1972).

CHAPTER SIX

1. Cf. Ingo Walter, *Environmental Control and Consumer Protection: Emerging Forces in Multinational Corporate Operations* (Washington, D.C.: Center for Multinational Studies, 1972).

2. Some of the best references are: Raymond Vernon, *Sovereignty at Bay* (New York: Basic Books, 1971); John M. Stopford and Louis T. Wells, *Managing the Multinational Enterprise* (New York: Basic Books, 1973); and John H. Dunning (ed.), *Studies in International Investment* (London: George Allen & Unwin, 1969).

3. Robert G. Hawkins, 'The Multinational Corporation: A New Trade Policy Issue in the United States', in *The United States and International Markets: Commercial Policy Options in an Age of Controls*, ed. R. G. Hawkins and I. Walter (Lexington, Mass.: D. C. Heath, 1972).

4. Committee for Economic Development, *Social Responsibilities of Business Corporations* (New York: C.E.D., 1971) p. 15.

5. Ibid. p. 24.

6. See R. Likert, 'The Influence of Social Research on Corporate Responsibility', in *A New Rationale for Corporate Social Policy* (New York: C.E.D., 1970).

7. C.E.D., *Social Responsibility of Business Corporation*, p. 36.

8. Some recent developments are reviewed in 'Fellow Americans, Keep Out!', *Forbes* (15 June 1971).

9. See Philip W. Quigg, 'Organizing for Global Environmental Management', *Columbia Journal of World Business* (May–June 1972).

10. See 'Multinationalization of Japanese Companies: Recent Condition and Future Prospects', *Normura Investment Report*, Tokyo (25 June 1973).

11. Ibid. p. 10.

12. 'The Path for a New Japan: The Remodelling of the Japanese Islands', M.I.T.I. Information Office, Background Information, no. 71 (30 August 1972).

13. John G. Welles, 'Multinationals Need New Environmental Strategies', *Columbia Journal of World Business* (Summer 1973) p. 12.

14. Ibid p. 14.

15. Jacqueline A. de Larderel and Anne-Marie Boutin, 'How Do European (and American) Companies Really Manage Pollution?', *European Business* (Winter 1972) p. 56.

16. Ibid. p. 64.

CHAPTER SEVEN

1. O.E.C.D. Environment Committee, *Outline of Programme on Transfrontier Pollution* (Paris: O.E.C.D. Document AEU/ENV/72.7, March 1972).
2. See Christopher B. Bramsen, 'Transnational Pollution and International Law', in *Problems in Transnational Pollution*, pp. 259–75.
3. Ibid.
4. United Nations Document A/Conf. 48/14 (1972) p. 7.
5. Anthony D. Scott, *Transfrontier Pollution: Are New Institutions Necessary?* (Paris: O.E.C.D. Environment Committee, Document AEU/ENV/73.10, 10 August 1973).
6. Ibid. pp. 12–14.
7. See O.E.C.D. Environment Committee, *Study of Different Cost-Sharing Formulas for Transfrontier Pollution* (Paris: O.E.C.D. Document AEU/ENV (73)1, 19 April 1973).
8. Ibid. p. 35.
9. O.E.C.D., Environment Committee, *The Mutual Compensation Principle: An Economic Instrument for Solving Certain Transfrontier Pollution Problems* (Paris: O.E.C.D. Document AEU/ENV/73.12, 17 September 1973).
10. Anthony Scott and Christopher B. Bramsen, *Draft Guiding Principles Concerning Transfrontier Pollution* (Paris: O.E.C.D. Environment Committee, Document AEU/ENV/72.12, 1972).
11. Larry E. Ruff, *The Economics of Transnational Pollution* (Paris: O.E.C.D. Environment Committee, Document AEU/ENV/72.24, 29 December 1972).
12. Ibid. p. 4.
13. See also O.E.C.D. Environment Committee, *Transfrontier Pollution Cost Sharing* (Paris: O.E.C.D. Document AEU/ENV/72.17, 22 January 1973).
14. O.E.C.D. Environment Committee, *Transfrontier Pollution in the Great Lakes* (Paris: O.E.C.D. Document AEU/ENV/72.5, 22 March 1972).
15. For a fuller discussion, see J. L. MacCallum, 'The International Joint Commission', *Canadian Geographical Journal*, vol. 72, no. 3 (1971).
16. O.E.C.D., *Transfrontier Pollution in the Great Lakes*, pp. 8–9.
17. See Willard A. Hanna, *Nationalizing the Strait of Malacca* (Hanover, N.H.: American Universities Field Service, 1974).
18. O.E.C.D. Environment Committee, *Report of the Sub-Committee of Economic Experts on Transfrontier Pollution* (Paris: O.E.C.D. Document ENV (73) 37, 8 November 1973).
19. O.E.C.D., Environment Committee, *Instruments for Solving Transfrontier Pollution Problems*, pp. 7–8.
20. Ibid. p. 8.
21. O.E.C.D., Environment Directorate, *Revised Action Proposal on Principles on Transfrontier Pollution for Submission to the Environment Committee at the Ministerial Level* (Paris: O.E.C.D. Document ENV/MIN (74)8, 12 July 1974).
22. See, for example, Economic Commission for Europe, 'A Study of Environmental Conditions and Problems in the Sector of Transportation', in *E.C.E. Symposium on Problems Relating to the Environment* (New York: United Nations, 1971).

23. International Maritime Consultative Organisation, *Convention for the Prevention of Pollution from Ships* (Geneva: I.M.C.O., November 1973).

CHAPTER EIGHT

1. Thomas L. Blair, 'The Environmental Crisis in the Third World', *Intereconomics* (February 1972).
2. Cf. Mahbub Ul-Haq, 'International Implications of the Environmental Concern', Paper presented at the United Nations Conference on Development and Environment, Columbia, March 1972.
3. 'Development and Environment: The Founex Report', *International Conciliation* (September 1971).
4. Shigeto Tsuru, 'Aid, Investment and the Environment', Columbia University–United Nations Conference on Development and Environment (15 April 1972).
5. See United Nations Conference on Trade and Development, 'Impact of Environmental Policies on Trade and Development, In Particular of the Developing Countries' (Geneva: UNCTAD Document TD/130, March 1972).
6. Cf. Horst Siebert, 'Trade and Environment', *Beitage zur angewantden Wirtschaftsforschung* (Universität Mannheim, mimeo., no. 40 (1973)).
7. See H. Peter Gray, *International Travel, International Trade* (Lexington, Mass.: D. C. Heath, 1971).
8. A discussion of the environment–materials interconnection is contained in Ralph C. d'Arge, Gary C. Hufbauer and Ingo Walter, 'Environmental Quality, Basic Materials Policy, and the International Economy', in *Man, Materials, and Environment* (Cambridge, Mass.: M.I.T. Press, 1973).
9. See, for example, Ingo Walter, 'Non-Tariff Barriers and the Export Performance of Developing Countries', *American Economic Review*, Papers and Proceedings (May 1971).
10. See also Robert E. Baldwin, *Nontariff Distortions of International Trade* (Washington, D.C.: The Brookings Institution, 1971).
11. See United Nations Document UNEP/GC/10 and Annexes (New York: U.N., 1972) on the trade implications of environmental measures for the developing countries.
12. A more detailed discussion is contained in Ingo Walter, 'Environmental Control and the Patterns of International Trade and Investment: An Emerging Policy Issue', *Banca Nazionale del Lavoro Quarterly Review* (March 1972).
13. For two early studies of this issue, see General Agreement on Tariffs and Trade, *Industrial Pollution Control and International Trade* (Geneva: GATT, July 1971); and UNCTAD, 'The Implications of Environmental Measures for International Trade and Development', Document TD/130 (Santiago, 1972).
14. Marshall I. Goldman, *Ecology and Economics* (Englewood Cliffs, N.J.: Prentice-Hall, 1972).
15. Thomas L. Blair, 'The Environmental Crisis in the Third World', p. 52.
16. Michael L. Hoffman, 'Development Finance and the Environment',

Finance and Development (September 1970).

17. A rigorous connection between growth and environmental costs is developed in Ralph C. d'Arge and K. C. Kogiku, 'Economic Growth and the Environment', *Review of Economic Studies* (January 1973).

18. UNCTAD, 'The Implications of Environmental Measures for International Trade and Development', pp. 17–18.

19. See the Proceedings of the Third United Nations Conference on Trade and Development, Santiago, Chile (April 1972).

CHAPTER 9

1. John H. Cumberland, 'The Role of Uniform Standards in International Environmental Management', in *Problems on Environmental Economics* (Paris: O.E.C.D., 1972) p. 245.

2. See O.E.C.D. Environment Committee, 'Environmental Standards: Definitions and the Need for International Harmonization' (Paris: O.E.C.D. Document ENV (73) 33, 1973).

3. Ibid. pp. 13–14.

4. Cumberland, 'The Role of Uniform Standards in International Environmental Management', p. 249.

5. 'O.E.C.D. and the Environment', *O.E.C.D. Observer*, no. 53 (August 1971).

6. Philip W. Quigg, 'Organizing for Global Environmental Movement', *Columbia Journal of World Business* (May–June 1972).

7. Klaus Kwasniewski, 'Trouble with UNEP', *Intereconomics*, no. 5 (1974) p. 130.

8. John G. Welles, 'Multinationals Need New Environmental Strategies', *Columbia Journal of World Business* (Summer 1973) pp. 16–17.

9. See, for example, Communiqué Announcing the Creation of the 'Comité des Constructeurs du Marché Commun' to Promote Uniform Automotive Pollution Standards within the E.E.C. (Paris, 15 November 1972).

Index